THE FORECAST FOR D-day

And the Weatherman behind Ike's Greatest Gamble

T0356901

JOHN E. ROSS

Essex, Connecticut

An imprint of The Globe Pequot Publishing Group, Inc.
64 South Main St.
Essex, CT 06426
www.GlobePequot.com

Distributed by NATIONAL BOOK NETWORK

British Library Cataloguing in Publication Information Available

Library of Congress Cataloging-in-Publication Data Available

ISBN 9780762786633 (cloth) | ISBN 9781493090440 (paperback) | ISBN
9781493008483 (epub)

♾™ The paper used in this publication meets the minimum requirements of
American National Standard for Information Sciences—Permanence of Paper
for Printed Library Materials, ANSI/NISO Z39.48-1992.

This book is dedicated to the men and women who provided weather services to Allied forces in World War II. If wind and cloud were not reasonably close to predictions, the success of strategic bombing missions, airborne operations, and amphibious landings was threatened and airmen, soldiers, and sailors were placed in mortal jeopardy. Whether a professional weatherman, an officer trained in a military course, or enlisted personnel who observed and plotted weather data or transcribed radio reports from ships, aircraft, or enemy stations, all were deeply committed to practicing the very best of known meteorological science. In this book you'll meet Jean Farren, who plotted weather data on maps at Eisenhower's advanced headquarters. When you read her story, you'll feel the intense pressure under which she and her colleagues worked. Without their commitment, the D-day invasion to liberate northwestern Europe may very well have failed and the fate of the world in the last half of the twentieth century could have been catastrophically different.

Contents

Acknowledgments vii

Preface ix

Prologue: Whether the Weather xv

Chapter One: The Front 1

Chapter Two: Polar Extremes 23

Chapter Three: Bitter Maritimes 49

Chapter Four: Unseen Allies 66

Chapter Five: Fractious Fellowship 83

Chapter Six: From the Sea They Will Come 100

Chapter Seven: Nothing Can Stop the Army Air Corps . . .118

Chapter Eight: Ridge of High Pressure 134

Chapter Nine: Earthquake in the Sky 155

Chapter Ten: The Horns of D-day 176

Chapter Eleven: Worst Blow in Forty Years 192

Epilogue 198

Glossary 202

Sources 211

Index 228

About the Author 236

Contents

Acknowledgments

I cannot begin to express my gratitude to Charles Bates, Bob Bundgaard, and John Crowell. Geologists Charles and John, as Army Air Corps lieutenants, were seconded to the Royal Navy to forecast wave heights on Normandy beaches. Bob, a captain, prepared upper-air forecasts for the Army Air Corps. Charles, in particular, but also Bob and John have provided me with reams of documents and excellent guidance, that I, neither a meteorologist nor a historian, desperately needed to tell this story. Brian Booth, retired from the British Meteorological Office, immeasurably increased my understanding of wartime weather services and personnel in the United Kingdom. I also deeply appreciate that Elizabeth Smith, the widow of SHAEF's chief meteorologist, James Martin Stagg, graciously invited me to her home for an extensive interview, as did her son, Sandy, and his wife Brigit. I am similarly grateful to Harold and Jean Checketts, who plotted weather data in Eisenhower's advanced headquarters during the weeks leading up to D-day, and to Maureen Sweeney, who helped gather weather at Blacksod Point in County Mayo where the storm that would have caused D-day to fail first came ashore.

I received assistance of the highest caliber from staff at the United Kingdom's National Archives, the Eisenhower Library, Margaret Newman at the National Museum of the Royal Navy, Anne Shotton and Mark Beswick of the library and archives of the Meteorological Office, Helen Mavin of the Imperial War Museum, Mairead Treanor of the library of Met Éireann, Sam McCown of the National Climatic Data Center, and Gaston Demaree of Belgium's Royal Meteorological Institute. Mike Garstang, Distinguished Emeritus Research Professor in the Department of Environmental

Sciences at the University of Virginia prepared weather charts for the book. Several friends have read and made helpful comments on the manuscript. Among them are Jack and Meredith Whiting, Craig Smith, Ron Basini, and Tom Crew.

This book never would have gotten off the ground had not Steve Culpepper of Globe Pequot Press taken a personal interest in the concept. My agent Joe Spieler introduced me to Deirdre Mullane, who edited the first draft and made scores of helpful comments. I am also grateful to my project editor at Globe Pequot Press, Lynn Zelem, and copy editor Joshua Rosenberg.

To my late wife, Katie Anders, I owe a debt that can never be fully repaid. She encouraged this project from the very beginning when I should have been adding to the family coffers. An anglophile of the first degree, she allowed me to travel to England without her to start research. Somebody had to stay home and supervise workmen remodeling the kitchen. My new wife, Bett Sanders, is not only a font of perpetual encouragement and a fine editor, but shares my interest in stories like this that focus on the intersection of natural and human history.

PREFACE

Soldiers, Sailors and Airmen of the Allied Expeditionary Force! You are about to embark upon a great crusade, toward which we have striven these many months. The eyes of the world are upon you. The hopes and prayers of liberty loving people everywhere march with you. In company with our brave Allies and brothers in arms on other fronts, you will bring about the destruction of the German war machine, the elimination of Nazi tyranny over the oppressed peoples of Europe, and security for ourselves in a free world.

Your task will not be an easy one. Your enemy is well trained, well equipped and battle hardened, he will fight savagely.

But this is the year 1944! Much has happened since the Nazi triumphs of 1940-41. The United Nations have inflicted upon the Germans great defeats, in open battle, man to man. Our air offensive has seriously reduced their strength in the air and their capacity to wage war on the ground. Our home fronts have given us an overwhelming superiority in weapons and munitions of war, and placed at our disposal great reserves of trained fighting men. The tide has turned! The free men of the world are marching together to victory!

I have full confidence in your courage, devotion to duty and skill in battle. We will accept nothing less than full victory!

Good Luck! And let us all beseech the blessings of Almighty God upon this great and noble undertaking.

With these words early on the morning of June 6, 1944, Gen. Dwight David Eisenhower, Supreme Commander, Allied Expeditionary Force (SHAEF), launched the grand invasion to free Western Europe from Nazi German oppression.

The campaign was code-named Operation Overlord, and it entailed the greatest air and seaborne landings the world had yet to see. Along fifty miles of France's Normandy coast stretching east from Ste. Mère-Église to Caen, 111,315 soldiers would breast the surf on invasion beaches the names of which—Utah, Omaha, Gold, Juno, and Sword—would be written indelibly into history with the blood of 10,377 killed and wounded.

Shortly after midnight, 23,400 paratroopers would begin leaping from wildly swerving C-47 transports as five hundred gliders carrying another four thousand troopers would crash land onto the rolling plain above the beaches.

From the sea, as thousands of shells and rockets launched from an immense armada of 1,213 warships bludgeoned enemy positions, 4,126 landing ships and landing craft ferried soldiers and scores of tanks, pieces of artillery, and hundreds of trucks and jeeps through crashing waves and withering cannon, machine-gun, and rifle fire onto the beaches.

Overhead 11,590 Allied aircraft flew fourteen thousand sorties and only 127 were shot down. More than twenty-five hundred heavy and light bombers dropped 5,315 tons of bombs on German targets as 3,483 fighters strafed roads and bridges seeking targets of opportunity whenever the *Wehrmacht* and its air force, the *Luftwaffe,* dared rear their heads.

Months before the Japanese attacked Pearl Harbor on December 7, 1941, President Franklin Delano Roosevelt and US Army Chief of Staff George C. Marshall had known that the United States would eventually lead the campaign to rid Western Europe of the German plague that swept in during May 1940. Planning for the invasion began immediately after the infamous Japanese raids on US bases in Hawaii, Guam, Wake Island, and the Philippines sent the country to war.

Though an apoplectic American public demanded immediate vengeance against the nation of the Rising Sun, Roosevelt and Great Britain's Prime Minister Winston S. Churchill adopted a "Europe first" strategy. In 1942 the Allies invaded North Africa; 1943 brought victory in Sicily and landings in Italy.

Throughout mobilization, training, invasions, and fighting, American factories churned out the weapons, ammunition, tanks, planes, warships, and landing craft (as well as millions of tons of supplies including rations, clothing, plasma, bandages, refined gas and oil, and even toilet paper) required for the invasion.

By the spring of 1944, the United Kingdom was stockpiled with acre after acre of parked vehicles of war, crates of supplies, and camps of anxious soldiers trained to a razor's edge and eager for the invasion to get underway. All was ready. The generals and admirals and their staffs had done their planning. They'd provided for every contingency, but one: the weather.

Like many boys whose dads served in World War II, I read its history voraciously. I was not yet in high school when I checked out Cornelius Ryan's *The Longest Day* from the local library. And when Darryl F. Zanuck made it into a movie in 1962, I was mesmerized by the grand scale of the invasion. I still am.

As I grew older, I became increasingly fascinated by the intersection of natural history and human events. I knew well that Eisenhower had postponed Operation Overlord for twenty-four hours because of the weather. And about a decade ago, probably after a nor'easter dumped twenty inches of unforecast snow on our Virginia village, I began to ponder this: If today, in the twenty-first century, our meteorologists have such trouble predicting storms, how in the world did Lucky Ike know to hold off the invasion for a day because of bad weather? That led me to the question: Who was Ike's weatherman? The more I poked around, the more curious

I became. It turned out that Ike's chief meteorologist, James Martin Stagg, was actually a geophysicist whose only real hands-on weather forecasting experience had been two years in the deserts of Iraq.

Why Stagg had been chosen intrigued me. From eBay, I bought a copy of his book, *Forecast for Overlord*. In it I learned about an American Air Force meteorologist, Irving P. Krick, who insisted that weather on the night of June 4, 1944, would have been quite suitable for the invasion. That was the night when Ike, based on Stagg's forecast, chose not to go. Had he taken Krick's advice instead, the invasion would have foundered in heavy seas, high wind, and thick cloud.

Stagg, Krick, and their colleagues in the three military weather bureaus, or "centrals," as they were called—the United States Strategic Air Force (USSTAF), the civilian Meteorological Office (Met Office), which provided weather services for the Royal Air Force and the British Army, and the Royal Navy (Admiralty)—all had access to the same weather data. How could they be so opposite in their predictions?

Stagg's job was to hammer out the forecast for D-day based on predictions from all three. Each used somewhat different methods for predicting the weather. There were no satellites, and no LiDAR (light ranging and detection) technology; radar was in its infancy. As a science, atmospheric physics was just cutting its teeth and meteorology was only beginning to emerge as a science based on data.

Complicating matters further, the USSTAF and the Met Office forecasting teams were led by meteorologists who before the war had chaired academic departments at competing American universities and who were bitter rivals, each having scant respect for the work or the methods of the other.

They battled each other just like the two more or less permanent meteorological high-pressure systems (one centered over the Arctic and the other between the warm Azores and Bermuda) that dominate weather in the United States and in Europe. Along the southern boundary of the Polar High, the sinuous jet stream races from west to east bringing with it wind, cloud, and rain. When the jet stream is forced north by the Azores High, mild weather prevails over the English Channel. When the Polar High drives south, storms plague the Channel. Knowing the location of the areas of calm and storm was absolutely essential if the forecast for D-day was to be reliable. To find out, the Allies and the Germans dispatched teams of meteorologists to the east coast of Greenland and Spitsbergen (east of Greenland and north of Scandinavia) where they skirmished with each other. Both sides dispatched weather ships into the North Atlantic from where they sent reports at least once a day and sometimes more often.

The capture of a German weather ship provided the keys to reading the Enigma code, which eventually resulted in the muting of the U-boat menace and allowed supplies for D-day to flow almost freely into England. Allied spies in Belgium and Poland regularly radioed weather data to the British. And thanks to the code-breaking wizards at Bletchley Park, the Met Office was reading French and German weather reports.

The more I read, the more I wondered what would have happened if Ike had taken his American compatriot Krick's advice and launched D-day on the night of June 4 instead of waiting for the following night. Had the invasion failed, as it surely would have, the history of the world after World War II would have been dramatically different.

In the following pages, after a bit of history of the artful science of weather forecasting in America and Britain, a history on which the attitudes of Overlord's generals and admirals toward meteorology were based, I'll make an educated guess about what might have happened if Ike and his meteorologist, James Martin Stagg, had gotten it wrong. So much was at stake. The science of meteorology was entering puberty and was little more trusted by adults—the generals and admirals—than if they'd put their faith in what a teenager had to say. Roundly criticized by meteorologists because he was not, by his own admission, a weatherman at heart; distrusted by Americans on SHAEF's senior staff because he was a civilian; and plagued by conflicting views of three separate weather centrals, the fact that he and his deputy Col. Yates got it right is little short of astounding.

Prologue: Whether the Weather

Whether the weather be fine,
Or whether the weather be not,
Whether the weather be cold,
Or whether the weather be hot,
We'll weather the weather
Whatever the weather,
Whether we like it or not!

—Children's Nursery Rhyme

Earth clasps to its surface two oceans, one of water and the other of air. They behave in a similar manner. Cold air is heavier than warm air, thus it sinks. The rotation of the globe and heat from the sun are the principal factors in the movement of currents in the oceans and in the atmosphere. Their behaviors are inseparably wed. Differences between them are legion. But for our purposes, this is the most important: The great stories of exploration of the earth have made the world's seas and their roles in human history as familiar to us as old shoes. The same cannot be said for the atmosphere. Yet it is the atmosphere that brings us the weather that affects more intimately the day-to-day life of every single person on the globe and often directs as well the course of human destiny.

Two weeks after the sneak attack on Pearl Harbor, President Franklin Roosevelt hosted British Prime Minister Winston Churchill in Washington to plan the grand Allied strategy to defeat Nazi Germany and Japan. For three weeks the leaders and their senior aides met in what came to be known as the Arcadia Conference. When the conference concluded on January 14, 1942, the Allies agreed that liberating Europe was their first priority. That said, Americans would do what they could to stem Japan's tide in the Pacific.

Almost immediately after the conference, American soldiers, supplies, and equipment began to flow, first as a trickle but soon in a steady stream, into the United Kingdom, from which the invasion of Nazi-occupied northern Europe would be launched.

By late May 1944, all the soldiers, supplies, equipment, tanks, airplanes, and ships needed to wrest control of Western Europe from the Nazis had been assembled in England and Scotland. Plans were given code names. Establishing the lodgment on the French coast was the goal of Operation Overlord. Operation Neptune covered the Allied navy's plans for putting soldiers ashore. The invasion would commence on what was termed D-day. Only officers receiving top security clearance—BIGOT—were allowed access to the plans. The security code had nothing to do with prejudice. "TO GIB" had been stenciled on the luggage of personnel sent to Gibraltar in advance of Torch. For Operation Overlord, the letters would be reversed, creating a "backronym" standing for British Invasion of German-Occupied Territory.

May entered its final days. All was ready. Gen. Dwight Eisenhower, Supreme Commander, Allied Expeditionary Force, assembled his army, air force, and navy commanders, their senior aides, and the core staff of the Supreme Headquarters Allied Expeditionary Force (SHAEF) at Southwick House, a few kilometers inland from the massive Royal Navy base at Portsmouth. From this advanced headquarters, Ike would make the final decision on the specific date for D-day.

The question before the Supreme Commander had little to do with the readiness of troops or preparation for the invasion by the Germans. What worried Ike from the beginning was weather. During May, staging areas for the invasion had been blessed with a relatively benign spring. That was about to change in ways that few of Ike's commanders could comprehend. Eisenhower wrote: "Some soldier once said 'the weather is always neutral.' Nothing could be more untrue. Bad weather is obviously the enemy of the side that seeks to launch projects requiring good weather, or of the side possessing great assets, such as strong air forces, which depend upon good weather for effective operations. If really bad weather should endure permanently, the Nazi would need nothing else to defend the Normandy coast!"[1]

Military commanders in the 1940s did not trust weather forecasts. In large part, their mistrust lay in the proven uncertainty and inaccuracy of the predictions. Further, World War II's generals and admirals were deeply schooled in a rigid culture in which the very science of meteorology was suspect.

During its earliest years, the weather service in the United States was unreliable and plagued by scandal. The creation of the Smithsonian Institution in 1846 opened the door for its first director, physicist Joseph Henry, to launch America's first network of trained weather observers in 1849. So confident was he in their work, that if word came in of a snowstorm in Cincinnati on Monday, Henry would cancel any lectures scheduled for the following night in Washington, DC.[2] Henry's weather service operated fitfully until quashed by the outbreak of the Civil War.

Another war, this one in the Crimea, gave impetus to the creation of Great Britain's first weather forecasting service. On November 14, 1854, the British fleet at Balaclava was destroyed by a wave of fierce gales. Later it was discovered that the storms had progressed southeastward across Europe. Had telegraphy been available, the fleet could have been warned and saved.[3] The following month, Capt. Robert FitzRoy was appointed chief of the Meteorological Department of the Marine Department of the Board of

Trade. FitzRoy was eminently practical if more than a bit mentally unstable. He was a seadog of renown, having captained the voyage of the HMS *Beagle,* which carried budding clergyman cum naturalist Charles Darwin on his historic voyage.

Beginning in 1861, FitzRoy issued storm warnings, which were inconsistent in their accuracy, but welcomed by seafarers. He called them *weather forecasts,* coining the term.[4] When his forecasts were spot on, wise skippers who had heeded his warning and refused to sail saved the lives of hundreds of sailors and tons of cargo. When they were wrong and captains refused to sail, ship owners and merchants lost thousands of pounds, about which the Board of Trade received numerous complaints.

FitzRoy's assumption, however, that air masses were influenced by moon and sun in the same manner tides were influenced, was roundly panned by established scientists. When FitzRoy refused to refine his thinking, a furor erupted in the prestigious Royal Society. Assaulted on all fronts, FitzRoy, who suffered bouts of depression, slit his throat on May 1, 1865.[5]

In 1870, President Ulysses Grant ordered the Department of War to establish a national weather service. Meteorological observations were assigned to the Signal Service and army officers chafed that weather duties distracted soldiers from more important tasks. The army was scandalized in 1881, when the chief disbursing officer for the service, Capt. Henry W. Howgate, was convicted of embezzling $60,000 (roughly $1.4 million today) and imprisoned. The civilian Weather Bureau was created in 1890, largely to provide forecasts for farmers, and the formal relationship between meteorology and the military in the United States was severed.

But not entirely.

Victory in the Spanish-American War in 1898 gave the army control of telegraph lines in Cuba. The army refused to permit

Cuban meteorologists, whom officers considered inferior, to transmit hurricane forecasts, though the island's weathermen knew more about these violent tropical storms than anyone else in the world. Army opposition to the use of Cuban weather data robbed Isaac Cline, US Weather Bureau station chief in Galveston, of critical information he needed to forecast wave heights as the deadly hurricane bore down on the Texas island city. More than six thousand were killed, among them Cline's wife and daughter. It wasn't until the advent of aircraft as weapons of war that the military got back in the weather business.

Failure by the US Weather Bureau to forecast the weather led to the tragic loss in 1933 of the *Akron,* a US Navy airship. Caught in wind shears from a violent cold front, it plunged tail first into the Atlantic taking the lives of seventy-three sailors. More routinely, the air force needed to know when pilots of its bombers could see their targets on the ground, or whether their landing fields would be socked-in by cloud or swept with high wind. The navy wanted to know about approaching hurricanes so they could steam out of harm's way or batten down their hatches, turn into the wind, and ride out the storm.

With no radars, satellites, global positioning systems, or World Wide Web, their colleagues today would consider meteorologists of the 1940s all but blind. So complex are the components of weather that a differential of a fraction of a degree of temperature can ultimately determine whether rain falls thousands of miles to the east.

Think of the four major variables of weather: temperature, wind speed and direction, atmospheric pressure, and humidity. Multiply them by changes that occur with every one thousand feet of altitude. Multiply again by each of the 360 degrees of longitude. Factor in effects of solar heating and ocean currents. Compound them with the near infinite variables due to the warming of the earth's surface, dust from recent volcanic eruptions and sandstorms, and smoke from burning forests. Ike's commanders would not have been surprised in the least that Edward Lorenz developed his famed chaos theory while attempting to forecast the weather.

CHAPTER ONE

The Front

Our landings in the Cherbourg-Havre area have failed to gain a satisfactory foothold and I have withdrawn the troops. My decision to attack at this time and place was based on the best information available. The troops, the air and the Navy did all that bravery and devotion to duty could do. If any blame or fault attaches to the attempt it is mine alone.—June 5th
—GEN. DWIGHT DAVID EISENHOWER,
SUPREME COMMANDER, ALLIED EXPEDITIONARY FORCE

Eisenhower penciled this note on a sheet torn from a pad and tucked it into his wallet.[6] For the final decision to launch the greatest amphibious invasion the world would have ever seen, Eisenhower, a constant weather worrier, knew the odds of blowing the forecast were high.

Bad weather had turned back scores of bombing missions over Europe. The landing in North Africa had been disrupted by troublesome waves. Vicious unexpected currents swept landing craft far from their destinations on Sicily's beaches. The weather could be an enemy more potent than any defense the Germans might mount.

Since 1942 more than 1,537,000 men, 137,000 vehicles, 4,217 tanks, thirty-five hundred pieces of artillery, twelve thousand aircraft, and sixteen million tons of supplies[7] had been gathered and stockpiled in the United Kingdom. To put the soldiers and supplies ashore, 2,468 landing ships and an additional 1,636 miscellaneous landing craft, barges, trawlers, and rhino ferries (those ungainly ship-to-shore barges) were ready to be deployed. All were to be protected by 1,213 warships.[8] All the preparations were complete.

On June 1, 1944, in a cool light rain,[9] Eisenhower took up residence in his travel-trailer, nicknamed the "Circus wagon," which he had set up by a stream under the trees at Southwick Park. The park surrounded Southwick House, which sat perched on the crest of a hill a few kilometers inland from the huge British naval base at Portsmouth. This once grand manor had grown more than a bit dowdy since the Royal Navy had relocated its school for navigators there three years earlier. Then, in January 1944, Adm. Bertram Ramsay, supreme commander of the Allied Naval Expeditionary Force (ANCXF), selected the mansion as his headquarters. He chose it for its proximity to Fort Southwick and the labyrinth of tunnels beneath Portsdown Hill, which held a Royal Navy command and communications network.

In early April Ike had picked Southwick House as the advanced headquarters for SHAEF. It was there he would decide whether to launch the invasion or postpone it for as much as a fortnight, when low tides would once again favor Allied strategy for invading Normandy in German-occupied northwestern Europe.

SHAEF's window for launching Overlord was narrow. Only two periods of three days each—June 5, 6, and 7 and, two weeks later, June 19, 20, and 21—contained the ideal combinations of low tide (required to clear Normandy beaches of anti-landing obstacles and mines), moonlight, and dawn. Should the weather not cooperate in either of those windows, Gen. Eisenhower fretted over the prospects of delay. In *Crusade in Europe*, Eisenhower wrote that "consequences would ensue that were almost too terrifying to contemplate." Not only was the secrecy of the time and place of the invasion, among its most important elements, liable to be lost to the Germans who would hastily reinforce the Normandy coast, but the whole grand enterprise would be thrown back upon itself producing unimaginable logistical chaos.

Assault troops would have to disembark from transports and be returned to assembly camps, which would have been filled with new waves of soldiers destined to land and expand the beachhead. The number of days available for vital campaigning in summer weather would be drastically reduced with the prospect that the battle to liberate France might extend into 1945. Worse yet was the prospect that morale among the Allies would plummet, robbing the campaign to invade northwestern Europe of its momentum and reopening debate over whether this was the best strategy after all.[10]

Overlord planners stipulated that winds blowing in from the bay not exceed Force 3 (7 to 10 knots, or 8 to 11 mph) and that those blowing out from land be less than Force 4 (15 knots, or 17 mph), lest seas be too rough for landing craft to put soldiers, tanks, and artillery ashore. The landing craft, which included the work-horse half-wood and half-steel Higgins boats, would ferry invaders ashore, though if surf and swell exceeded six to eight feet, the Higgins boats would broach and swamp, drowning their crews and each boat's full platoon of thirty-six soldiers being delivered to the beaches. The invasion would occur at low tide so that engineers would have thirty minutes to destroy anti–landing-craft obstacles sewn by the enemy.[11] Then at 6:30 a.m. the landings would begin.

If winds exceeded 20 knots, paratroopers and gliders released from indefatigable Douglas DC-3s—those beloved *C-47s* to the Yanks and *Dakotas* to the Brits—would be scattered all over the countryside. Gliders could land if wind blew no stronger than 30 knots, and only if the wind was steady and not variable. At least three miles of visibility were required. Arrival of these glider-borne troops behind the invasion beaches just after midnight was essential to hold bridges and crossroads to halt counterattacking Germans and their formidable Panzers.

Anything more than light cloudiness was the enemy of Allied air supremacy on which the invasion also hinged. The height of unbroken clouds could not be less than eleven thousand feet. Otherwise heavy bombers could not drop their payloads on railroad-marshaling yards, airfields, and known concentrations of enemy armor. If below five thousand feet, clouds could not cover more than half of the sky. If they did, fighter-bombers would not be able to knock out coastal gun emplacements and columns of German reinforcements. And light spotter aircraft would be unable to pinpoint targets for the big guns of the battleships and for cruisers, destroyers, and escorts that steamed along the invasion beaches. For Air Chief Marshal Trafford Leigh-Mallory, commander of SHAEF's air forces, weather was a huge concern, and he fretted about it constantly.

THE WAR IN EUROPE BEFORE D-DAY

Senior army generals claim they factor weather into the calculus for successful operations. In reality, Field Marshal Sir Bernard Montgomery, who commanded all of D-day's ground forces, and his contemporaries took huge pride in their abilities to wage war on the enemy under any conditions. To weather, they gave little thought save avoiding mud where tanks and trucks might get stuck.

Highest in commanders' minds was the speedy defeat of Nazi Germany. Yet the war in the west had bogged down. After the quick victory in Sicily in August 1943, the Allies had invaded Italy. Though Italy's civilian government surrendered in September 1943, the Germans remained and mounted an extremely tough defense, halting the Allied advance at Monte Cassino.

The attempted movement to flank the Germans with an invasion at Anzio in January 1944 had stalled and become a carnage of men who by sheer fortitude alone clung to their beachhead until breaking out in May 1944. The stalemate was broken shortly after Polish troops drove the last German defenders from Monte Cassino.[12] Then Allied forces moved north. Rome finally fell on June 5, the day before D-day.

On the Eastern Front, the Red Army under Joseph Stalin, Marshal of the Soviet Union, was winning that side of the war. Against the Wehrmacht, he threw thousands of conscripts drawn from the provinces east of the Urals. With blood and guts, wave after wave of them pushed back the Germans, acre by bloody acre. When German defense of Stalingrad collapsed in early February 1943, the Soviet Army began its inexorable westward march. Also that February, the Red Army recaptured Kursk. A week later Kharkov fell. In December, the Soviets launched a major campaign in the Ukraine despite bitter winter weather. Shortly after the New Year, the Russians began to occupy Poland. By May 1944, they'd liberated Leningrad, opened a new campaign in Belorussia, recaptured Sevastopol, and forced the Germans to surrender the Crimea.

Among Americans and British serving on the Combined Chiefs of Staff committee that coordinated Allied military operations worldwide, there was no doubt that the Allies would eventually prevail. Secure in that assurance, American President Franklin D. Roosevelt and British Prime Minister Winston S. Churchill were focusing on the shape of post-war Europe. Roosevelt, uniquely visionary and realistic at the same time, felt that the three great powers—the United States, Great Britain, and Russia—would share world leadership through a United Nations, the design of which had yet to be resolved.

Though dedicated to defeating Nazism and all it stood for, Churchill, on the other hand, was fighting for something vastly different—nothing less than the restoration of Great Britain's pre-war global empire. "Let me . . . make this clear, in case there should be any mistake about it in any quarter," he is quoted as firmly stating in November 1942. "We mean to hold our own. I have not become the King's first minister in order to preside over the liquidation of the British Empire."[13] Were England to lose her dominance in the Middle East and governance of India, Singapore, and the colonies in Africa, the nation would be stripped of its power and prestige.

Both Roosevelt and Churchill were kept in the dark about Stalin's plans for territories in Eastern Europe that were to be liberated by the Red Army. Yet the results of battles on the Eastern Front were clear to all. Utterly ruthless, "Uncle Joe," as Roosevelt privately called Stalin, would be highly unlikely to withdraw his armies from captured territories. Stalin argued that it was the right of the people of Russia, of whom twenty-three million would be killed in the war, to emerge as a major world power and to secure for itself an empire with similar economic and political power as Great Britain had enjoyed at the start of the conflict.

The only barrier to Soviet domination of Europe after the fall of the Nazi regime would be strong Allied armies holding the ground in France and western Germany.

IF D-DAY HAD FAILED

Had Eisenhower been forced to broadcast the statement he'd penciled on that sheet of notepaper, the shape of post-war Europe and the course of the last half of the twentieth century might have been vastly different.

Even though the German U-boat menace to transatlantic convoys had been dramatically reduced and nearly total Allied air supremacy established, had the invasion failed at least a year would have been required to build up the strength to attempt it again. By then, the Germans would have perfected their *Vergeltungswaffen,* or "retaliatory" weapons—unguided V-1 flying bombs and supersonic V-2 rockets. More than ten thousand were fired at England after they became operational mid-June 1944, a week after D-day.[14] Bombing of their launching sites was less than effective and their firings only ceased when they were overrun by Allied forces.

Though the Europe-first strategy had been accepted in the weeks after Japan's nefarious attack on Pearl Harbor on December 7, 1941, as late as 1943 polls showed most US citizens felt that victory over Japan, not Germany, should be the country's top priority.[15] Restoring stockpiles in Britain for a new D-day would have reduced America's ability to support the island-hopping war in the Pacific. And as things stood, landing craft were in desperately short supply and those used in Operation Overlord were scheduled to be redeployed to the Pacific as soon as possible after the invasion.

Another factor also hung in the balance. By June 1944, Roosevelt was in the thick of planning another race for the presidency, his fourth term. American victories in North Africa, Europe, and Asia were cornerstones of his campaign. It's hard to say whether a failed Normandy invasion would have allowed his opponent, New York governor Thomas Dewey, to overcome Roosevelt's immense popularity. However, in 1948 when Roosevelt's vice president, Harry Truman, ran against Dewey, the botched headline shouted by the *Chicago Daily Tribune*—DEWEY DEFEATS TRUMAN—may well have proven correct.

A failed invasion might also have affected the 1952 presidential contest. Eisenhower, often maligned because, unlike Patton or Bradley, he had never commanded a unit in combat, would likely have been sacked. It would have been unlikely for him to achieve the presidency, perhaps opening the way for Gen. Douglas MacArthur, whose aspirations to assume the executive office churned never far below his signature crushed hat.

Imagine what might have been had MacArthur become the US president.

During the dark early days of the Korean War, when the United Nations troops MacArthur commanded were in desperate straits, the general planned to create a radioactive dead zone by strewing nuclear waste where the Yalu River could be crossed.[16] (Imagine something similar to the wasteland in and around Chernobyl after its meltdown in 1986.) For incessant insubordination, President Truman relieved MacArthur of command. Yet would the same have happened had Dewey been president?

What if MacArthur, sitting behind the desk in the Oval Office, had been commander-in-chief? Would he have demonstrated Ike's finesse in avoiding use of nuclear weapons as the Chinese Communists began shelling the Republic of China's forward positions on the tiny islands of Quemoy and Matsu in 1954? Had MacArthur been president, might he have triggered a nuclear holocaust? And how might that have affected the ways wars were fought thereafter?

Consider this as well. With supply routes to Russia well protected by Allied air and naval forces, Americans would have continued to provide the Soviets with the trucks, armor, and aircraft they needed to keep hammering the Germans. Though the Germans might have shifted some of their divisions in northwestern Europe to the Eastern Front, would that have been enough to slow the Red Army's advance until the Allies succeeded in obtaining a foothold either in southern France, Norway, or the Balkans?

And what would have been the political shape of Western Europe had the Allies and the Russians met on the Rhine instead of the Elbe? Would the Russians have withdrawn to zones of occupation agreed to at the Yalta Conference in February 1945? Would the Iron Curtain have been drawn down over a divided Berlin or along the border between Germany and France? To bring Germany to its knees, would America have deployed an atomic bomb on Munich or Cologne as historians Harold C. Deutsch and Dennis E. Showalter ask in *If the Allies Had Fallen*?[17]

And what of France? In 1944 the French *Parti communiste français* or PCF had earned a reputation as the most effective unit of the Resistance. Its attacks on occupying Germans were legendary for their cunning, stealth, and violence. Had the Allies failed in the Normandy invasion, the PCF would have quite likely stepped up its campaign against Nazis and their sympathizers. When the Allies eventually achieved victory, the PCF might have been hailed as saviors of France. Thus when France's National Assembly reconvened after the war, Communists might have secured a majority. Had that happened, would France have spurned membership in the North Atlantic Treaty Organization and steered the country toward the Eastern Bloc? Had France become a member of the Soviet sphere, what then would be the shape of Europe today?

By spring of 1944, no member of the Allies doubted Germany's defeat. But just how it would happen and how the world would emerge was, like the invasion, anything but certain.

29 May, 1944: Fire in the Maine Woods

SHAEF's advanced headquarters was moved to Southwick House on Sunday, 28 May. With great confidence in victory, many of the senior commanders and their aides took up residence nearby.

Had they known what was shaping up in the skies over the Great Plains of America and Canada, they might have been a bit less cocky.

The same weather systems that had been so gently caressing the south of England for the month of May had also kissed the feathery tops of spruce and pine in the endless Maine woods three thousand miles to the west. Though the sun had yet to lighten the sky, old Ford and Dodge trucks were growling up the sandy cobbly road to a wood lot near Frye, Maine. Jostling in the backs of the trucks were squads of loggers, men in their forties and fifties, too old to go to war but not too old to fight it on the home front. Already bone weary from swinging an axe or pushing and pulling two-man crosscut saws for days on end, when the trucks halted that morning the loggers tumbled down and turned to work cutting pulp for the insatiable Oxford Paper Company mill five miles away at Rumford.

Some say an army travels on its belly. But, in reality, it's paper, ream after ream after ream of paper, that feeds an army. In Maine a man with a sharp crosscut saw and an axe could cut two to two-and-a-half cords of pulp pine in a day. A woodsman would drop a sixty-foot pine and limb it with deft swings of his axe in less than half an hour. Then he'd either buck it into four-foot lengths for the sled to collect or loop a chain around its trunk, hook it to the whiffletree harnessed to the horse, and with a snap of the reins, guide the horse to the wood yard with the trunk of the tree dragging behind. The cutting was easier when the weather was dry. Footing for the logger and his twitch-horse was more certain. Hands or feet that slipped slowed a logger down and caused accidents.

When their hands weren't otherwise occupied, loggers would light up a smoke just as soldiers would. Maybe they'd pull a Lucky from its just introduced new white pack. Men of the Maine woods, a conservative group to be sure, looked yet for the old familiar green pack with the red bulls-eye in the gold circle. But Lucky Strike green had gone to war. In late 1942, green and gold ink had been removed from Lucky Strike's package. Changing the colors of the inks saved enough copper and tin, it was said, to outfit four hundred light tanks.

More likely, though, a logger rolled his own smoke. He'd have struck a kitchen match with his thumbnail, lit up, blew out the flame with his first exhale, and then pinched the smoldering match-head between callused thumb and forefinger before flipping it into the scrub. That's what worried bosses of the wood yard. Fires were their worst enemy. An act of carelessness, no matter how unintended, sabotaged the war effort just as surely as a fire set by a German agent.

Yard bosses kept an eye on the weather, but publication of weather reports was prohibited. The Germans hungered for meteorological information along the western edge of the North Atlantic. They knew that storms observed along the eastern coasts of the United States and Canada would rumble across Europe a few days later. Advance knowledge of the weather would be very helpful to the Wehrmacht.

Uncommonly dry, this month in the forests of Maine had been. Only one inch of rain had fallen by mid-month. Usually by then, two or three inches would have fallen. Winds, steady out of the west or southwest at 10 to 12 miles per hour, dried the woods as well. After a shower that dropped a tenth of an inch of rain on May 22, the temperatures began to climb, reaching 86°F on the 27th, ten to fifteen degrees warmer than usual. The unseasonably hot weather had baked the lumber as if it had been dried in kiln. About all foremen could do to prevent forest fires was to ban smoking. But when each logger was off on his own, how could such an order be enforced?

Though they did not know it, the source of the foremen's concern was an ocean of warm air centered over the subtropical Atlantic that reached all the way from East Texas into the heartland of

Nazi-occupied France. If viewed from space, this region of high pressure would have resembled a huge amoeba preparing to divide in two. From the western lobe, winds, rotating gently like the hands of a large clock, brought sweltering heat to the East Coast of the United States. The breezes carried millions of tons of water evaporated from the equatorial Atlantic and the Sargasso Sea lying between Bermuda and the string of barrier beaches that runs from Homestead, Florida, to Cape Hatteras, North Carolina. However, there was no adjacent air mass cool enough to cause the suspended vapor to condense. Instead, skies over Maine and the Canadian Maritimes would cloud with the promise of rain and then clear.

Monday, May 29, 1944, dawned almost as fair and warm over troops, vehicles, and supplies massed and ready for D-day in England as it would five hours later in Maine. Early that afternoon, a column of grayish-white smoke bloomed above the hills near Frye where loggers were cording pulpwood to be trucked to the paper mill at Rumford, about fifty miles northwest of Augusta, the state capital. By evening the fire beneath the smoke had spread, urged on by a gentle wind from the southwest. It grew slowly all day Tuesday and Wednesday, consuming five hundred acres of standing timber and an equal number of cords of pulpwood that was stacked and ready to be hauled down to the mill. Squads of men had labored nearly a month to cut the wood, which was only enough to feed the factory's grinding machines for but one day.

The fire burned with building ferocity until its leading edge covered a full mile. In the face of such blazes foresters in the wartime 1940s were relatively helpless. They fought them as best they could. Trucks were few, gasoline was limited, and spare parts for pumps were hard to find. Generally then, as now, it was up to the weather to put out forest fires.

BIRTH OF THE D-DAY FRONTS

On the Sunday before the fire, a ripple in the upper air over Manitoba had begun to organize itself into a low-pressure cell. The Polar High was pushing south, driving cooler air under the warm moist air pumped northward by the Bermuda-Azores High. Between the two highs, the low-pressure cell spun counterclockwise. By Tuesday, it had drifted into upstate New York, and that night its leading edge crossed into Vermont.

The rotating cell drew into it warm air from the south. As the warmer damp air was wedged upward by the advancing cold air, the moisture began to condense. Clouds developed along this small but classic cold front, and they spiraled columns of mist higher and higher into the sky. The mist began to freeze into particles of ice and snow, which rubbed against each other charging the clouds with static electricity. Lightning snapped between the columns. The clouds, now heavy with precipitation that had yet to fall and aligned by the advancing cold front, sailed along eastward over New England.

By Wednesday night, June 1, the cold front dashed across Rumford. Rainfall was short, but thankfully, significant—.15 of an inch in less than an hour between 11:55 p.m. and 12:50 a.m. Official observer Emaline A. Warren found another .03 inch in her official Weather Bureau rain gauge at the local airport when she checked it the next morning.

When a week later the *Rumford Falls Times* carried a story that mentioned how the Frye fire had been extinguished by a "smart electrical storm," editor Everett Martin no doubt thought he was discharging his journalistic responsibilities, despite his breach of strict wartime security. As it was, the storm he reported was a spawn of a rapidly developing series of low-pressure cells. These would produce the front that birthed the high wind and thick cloud that would sweep across western France and up the English Channel on the night of June 4/5, the night Eisenhower and his commanders had set for the Allied invasion of northwestern France.

May had seen an eastern lobe of the Azores High centered over the heart of occupied France. At any other time, such clear blue skies would have been a welcome respite from the usual blustery storms of spring for mademoiselles and messieurs. But in this, the middle months of the fifth year of European world war, and with Allied aircraft raining hundreds of tons of bombs on French rail yards and bridges, only the prospect of landings on the channel coast provided relief from the terror from the sky. The Azores High brought gentle winds to English airfields, lovely weather for flying and for training troops about to invade Normandy. The weather seemed to be doing its part to aid the Allies.

2130 DBST, Friday, 2 June, 1944—
SHAEF Advanced Headquarters, Southwick House, England

Group Capt. James Martin Stagg, SHAEF's chief meteorologist tasked with predicting the weather for the invasion of Normandy, stood by the door to what had been the navigation school's library. With him in the great hall of Southwick House were his deputy, Col. Donald N. Yates of the USSTAF, and Royal Navy colleague, Instructor Commander John Fleming.

A bluish haze of cigarette and pipe smoke shrouded the three waiting weathermen and knots of admirals, brigadiers, and colonels who served as aides to Eisenhower and his subordinate supreme commanders of Allied air, army, and navy forces. Behind the tall closed door, Eisenhower had assembled his most senior commanders. In a few moments Stagg and Yates would be summoned. They would deliver the forecast for the weather that invading forces were likely to encounter Sunday night, June 4, and Monday morning, June 5, the date set for D-day.

With the invasion roughly thirty hours in the offing, soldiers were already tightly packed into troop ships and landing craft that would ferry them about 100 miles south into the Bay of the Seine just over the horizon from the wharves of Portsmouth and a dozen other ports on the English Channel. A massive fleet of battleships, cruisers, destroyers, and escorts was already steaming toward their rendezvous point, code-named Piccadilly Circus, in the center of the English Channel. Never before or ever again would such massive naval might be concentrated in such a small space. The subordinate supreme commanders—Air Chief Marshal Leigh-Mallory, Adm. Ramsay, and Field Marshal Montgomery—were eager to get on with the show. All was ready, everything poised, coiled and ready to strike.

Allied strategists knew pretty well the location and condition of Wehrmacht forces waiting behind Hitler's much propagandized Atlantic Wall. They had utilized aerial photographs, staged commando raids that captured prisoners, and intercepted German messages whose Enigma codes had been broken by the wizards at Bletchley Park. Radio reports poured in from the French resistance and teams of British Secret Intelligence Service and US Office of Strategic Services spies who parachuted into France during the run-up to D-day.

So detailed was the Allies' planning that each platoon in Montgomery's 21st Army Group knew which pillbox, artillery battery, or exit from the beach it was to assault. Leigh-Mallory's bombers had their lists of targets; his troop carriers had their drop zones for airborne assaults. Ramsay's crews were likewise prepared. Officers on fighting ships had their initial firing coordinates, and each landing craft coxswain knew within ten yards where he was to put ashore his cargo of thirty or so soldiers. The combined air and amphibious invasion, of course, contained a trillion vagaries. Most would be overcome by superior air, army, and naval power and by discipline, imagination, and raw courage. The sole exception was the vicissitude of weather.

The door to the room where Eisenhower and his subordinate commanders were gathered opened. Stagg and Yates were beckoned. They were an odd pair. Stagg at 6'2" stood a full head taller than Yates at 5'5". From above deeply set eyes, Stagg's forehead rose like a chalk cliff topped with a mop of coarsely brushed dark auburn hair. His Royal Air Force uniform, which had likely never known a Savile Row tailor, hung from his angular frame. Few service ribbons adorned his chest. Frugal Scot that he was, he'd probably bought the blue-gray uniform off the rack when mobilized into the RAF for a short time in November 1943 to inspect British meteorological operations in Italy. Despite the military uniform, the man inside was still very much a civilian and one not in the least intimidated by the heavy brass arrayed before him.

Following Stagg as they entered the room was the dapper Yates with his Clark Gable mustache. He carried himself with the bearing of the West Point cadet he'd been before graduation and commissioning in 1931. His pilot's wings glowed above campaign ribbons and the Distinguished Service Medal he'd been awarded the year before for establishing the exchange of weather data with meteorologists in the Soviet Union.[18] Accompanying the pair was Fleming, Ramsay's chief meteorologist. Fleming, as the plot officer on the battleship *Duke of York,* earned the Distinguished Service Cross for his "cool and skilled" role in the sinking of the German battle cruiser *Scharnhorst* on December 26, 1943.[19] He too was of ramrod posture.

To their left sat Eisenhower in an easy chair. Next to him was Air Chief Marshal Sir Arthur Tedder and then Lt. Gen. Walter Bedell-Smith, Ike's chief of staff. Off their right shoulders, in three informal rows of overstuffed club chairs and couches, lounged Leigh-Mallory, Montgomery, Ramsay, and their various deputies and chiefs of staff. Were it not for the absence of alcohol and the direness of the hour, this might have been an informal briefing after a long and satisfying evening mess.

In his book, *Forecast for Overlord*, Stagg recalled that Eisenhower fixed him with a gentle smile and opened the meeting with: "Well, Stagg, what do you have for us this time?"

"Broadly, I can only confirm the picture I hope I left with you last evening," Stagg began. "The whole situation from the British Isles to Newfoundland has been transformed in recent days and is now potentially full of menace. In the last 24 hours there has been no clear indication of how it will go, better or worse, but, at the best, weather in the Channel for the next three or four days at least will be very different from what we'd hoped for. Until at least Tuesday or Wednesday there will be much cloud; at times skies will be completely overcast especially in the west of the area and winds will be from a westerly point, often force 4 and up to force 5 at times."

Eisenhower pressed Stagg for more detail about prospects for weather on Tuesday and Wednesday. In 1966, Tedder recounted that Stagg responded after a long pause: "If I answered that, Sir, I would be guessing, not behaving as your meteorological advisor."

According to his book, Stagg doesn't remember replying as Tedder quoted him. Rather, he reports he answered, "With the weather situation as it is, confidence in the outlook for the end of the period is very low; but as I see it now, weather on Tuesday and Wednesday is unlikely to be worse than on Sunday and Monday." Eisenhower asked the group if there were any more questions for the meteorologists. There being none, the three meteorologists were dismissed, but told to wait outside the door in case something came up.

They stood in the hall waiting for several minutes before Gen. Harold Bull, SHAEF's deputy chief of staff, came out of the meeting and informed the meteorologists that D-day was still scheduled for June 5. However, he asked if they would be prepared to give an updated weather briefing for the commanders at 3:30 the following morning. Stagg said they were prepared, but not enough new weather reports would be ready in time so the briefing might not shed any additional light on the forecast.

END OF THE IDYLL OF SPRING

During May, soft spring breezes and sunny days brought into bloom buttercups and daisies in the fields and wild clematis in the woods near Eisenhower's trailer. Green of new leaves frothed the crowns of ancient forests. Mistle thrush and an occasional cuckoo called at dawn and dusk. Showers were few and those that fell were welcomed by homemakers planting victory vegetable gardens. Such consistently lovely weather is not difficult to forecast and the three weather centrals—US Air Force, Royal Navy, and British civilian Met Office whose predictions Stagg was to meld into one—reached agreement with relative ease.

But as beautiful May grew into June, all this would change as if an earthquake had rent the skies. From their weather maps, Stagg and Yates had seen the signs. That's what worried them. A cold front traveling at about 35 mph could swing across the North Atlantic in four days. They knew one or more were on the way. Just when they would arrive and how severe they would be, was almost, but not quite, anyone's guess. Each of the centrals had its own idea of when the weather would change. Dissent among them now brewed darkly like the approaching cold fronts.

2230 DBST, 2 June—Sawyer's Wood, Southwick Park

As soon as they were dismissed from the supreme commanders' meeting, Stagg, Yates, and Fleming made their way through the throng of aides gathered in the hall, pushed through the door, and stepped out onto the south portico supported by heavy Ionic columns. Though the clock said 10:30 p.m. (2230 hours to them), it measured Double British Summer Time (DBST). By the sun or standard Greenwich Mean Time, it was really 8:30 p.m., and the mansion's portico, circular drive, and lawn beyond were bathed in the last of lingering twilight. Hastily they swung left past the columns and strode diagonally across the drive making a bee-line to the door of Fleming's weather office, half of the first Nissen hut next to the manor house. Inside to the right of the door, they heard the endless clatter of the teletype clicking out weather observations from scores of posts in the United Kingdom, from ships tossing in the North Atlantic, and from stations in Greenland, Iceland, and Ireland.

The Republic of Ireland was officially neutral, which saved its cities and people from punishing Luftwaffe raids. But Irish and British meteorologists shared a deep and abiding kinship. After Nazi Germany occupied Czechoslovakia in October 1938, Ireland and England negotiated a secret agreement pledging to share weather data in the event that war broke out. It was signed in August 1939, less than a month before Germany invaded Poland, the official start of World War II.[20]

Stagg and Yates were particularly interested in data from Blacksod Point on the tip of the northern and westernmost coast of Ireland. It was here that any weather that could threaten the invasion would first blow ashore. Blacksod Point lies roughly 520 miles northwest of Normandy's beaches. A fast-moving front could cover the distance in less than twenty-four hours.

Across from the door stood the drafting table where Royal Navy ratings were plotting synoptic data, meaning weather observations taken at the same time at a number of fixed points on the surface of the earth. Empty circles, about the diameter of a pencil eraser, marked the latitude and longitude of the place where observations were taken. If viewed as the face of a clock, the altitude of high and medium cloud would be neatly written at twelve o'clock. At two o'clock, air pressure at mean sea level would be posted; four o'clock, a symbol for past weather; six o'clock, altitude of low cloud; eight o'clock, dew point; nine o'clock, present weather and to the left of that visibility; and at ten o'clock, temperature.

Drawn perpendicular to the circumference of the circle was a thin vane pointing to the direction from which the wind was blowing. Perpendicular to the end of the vane were straight bars representing the force of the wind in knots. A full bar at the end of a vane represented a wind of 8 to 12 knots. Two bars showed winds of 18 to 22 knots.

As does water, wind flows from high to low. Only wind swirls in the northern hemisphere clockwise down and out of a high then turning counterclockwise as it enters the low. Just like mapmakers connect points of equal elevation thus creating the contour lines shown on topographic maps, meteorologists connect points of equal pressure to create isobars. The farther apart the isobars, generally speaking, the gentler the winds and the more stable the weather. Where isobars crowd together winds pick up. Shifts in wind direction, say from southeast to northwest over the North Atlantic, suggest a change in weather. And like cartographers who can discern the lay of the land by reading contour lines, so too can good meteorologists see the pattern of the weather by looking at a map of isobars.

Stagg, Fleming, and Yates paused for a moment, taking a final look at the weather map that hung on the wall to the right of the drafting table where ratings continued to plot fresh data. Having satisfied themselves that the forecast they'd just presented to Eisenhower and his commanders was the best they could offer, Stagg and Yates took leave of Fleming and set off down the cinder lane to their tent beneath the trees in Sawyer's Wood where Eisenhower had parked his trailer, a fifteen-minute walk from the mansion.

They knew that the first ships of the grand Allied armada were putting to sea from the northernmost ports in the United Kingdom. With each hour, more and more warships would weigh anchor and begin steaming toward the rendezvous point in the English Channel. In reality, the invasion had been launched this night on the strength of Stagg's forecast even though the outlook was for weather far below conditions set by D-day planners.

With stone crunching underfoot in the evening's early and nearly silent dark, the two meteorologists talked of the difficulty in recalling the gathering naval forces. They worried about the very real possibility that German reconnaissance might spot the fleet or blunder into it with catastrophic results. That's what happened little more than a month earlier when nine German E- or motor torpedo boats on a training exercise of their own stumbled upon a convoy of LSTs (Landing Ship Tank), transports, and their escorts off the British beaches at Slapton Sands. Two LSTs were sunk, another set afire and run onto the beach, and a third was damaged by friendly fire. A total of 638 lives were lost.[21]

Weighing more heavily on the minds of Stagg, Yates, and their superiors was the likelihood that the armada would be discovered. Then the Germans would know roughly where the Allies planned to invade. Should the element of surprise be lost, Rommel could rush reinforcements to the coast with potentially devastating effect on the landings.

With this in the backs of their minds, Stagg and Yates reached their olive drab wall tent beneath the trees in the woods, hung up their uniforms, settled onto their cots, and sought a few hours' nap. They did not have long to sleep. They were due back at Fleming's weather hut at 0400 DBST to prepare for the 0500 teleconference with the three feuding weather centrals.

CHAPTER TWO

Polar Extremes

Lying on his cot, Stagg fought for sleep as doubts about the weather churned in his mind. His anxieties grasped him in the middle of the night and held him fast.

His assignment as SHAEF's chief meteorologist had been roundly opposed and not just by the American forecasters but by British as well. A weatherman he was not and never had been, really. At heart, he was a geophysicist renowned for his studies of the earth's magnetic fields. And he knew, far better than anyone else, that serving Allied forces in England were a number of meteorologists much more qualified to predict weather than he. These weathermen staffed the three weather centrals whose forecasts Stagg had to weld into one.

The USSTAF maintained its headquarters and weather central southwest of London at Bushy Park. The Met Office held forth a little north of London in Dunstable. The deep underground citadel in the center of London housed the Admiralty's forecasting office. Churchill's war room was nearby. Each central received essentially the same teletypes reporting observations from the same synoptic stations. Each plotted the data in the same format on weather charts. There the similarity and consistency ended.

Each weather central was steeped in the meteorological culture of its own country and service. Americans tended to be empiricists, that is they based their forecasts on what they had observed in the past. Why not? As soon as the telegraph wires were strung across the country in the 1860s, a storm could be tracked from the moment it blew ashore in Seattle. Americans, thus, were fixated more on the *what* and *where* of weather rather than its *why*.

The British were not so fortunate. While the width of the United States spans roughly twenty-six hundred miles, the British Isles including the Republic of Ireland is less than five hundred miles wide with the two divided by 150 miles of Irish Sea. To predict the weather in Birmingham, for instance, the Met Office could not rely, as Americans did, on a string of weather stations stretching thousands of miles to the west, the direction from which weather arrives in the northern hemisphere. Instead they had to be able to understand the why of the weather. They tended to use the murky and then very much emerging science of atmospheric physics to analyze the weather data on which they based their forecasts.

But not entirely. One of the two principal Met Office forecasters was C. K. M. Douglas. An RAF officer who saw action in World War I over France, initially as an observer and later as a pilot, Douglas was among the first to study the weather from airplanes. In 1916 he noticed that when cirrus clouds, which children know as mare's tails, sketched across a clear blue sky, the air temperature above them was often warmer than that below. He hypothesized that a mass of cold air was sinking and flowing under a body of warm air, creating a zone that may contain high wind, rain, thunderstorms, or rarely even tornadoes.

Douglas joined the Met Office in 1919. His memory was prodigious. Mentally, he had catalogued nearly thirty years of daily weather for the British Isles. One glance at a freshly drawn weather map enabled him to describe the weather that had followed a similar situation years earlier. And then he "could, almost blindfolded, pull out of the bulky map files any weather situation that he had in mind," writes Sverre Petterssen, his colleague at Dunstable.[22] "Douglas was a genius, though not a well-organized one. Eloquence was not one of his outstanding talents. . . . Douglas was a Solomon and not a Hammurabi. His wealth consisted more of wisdom than of science. Neither meteorological journals nor analects can record what he knew."[23]

Petterssen, a Norwegian who before the war had chaired the department of meteorology at the Massachusetts Institute of Technology (MIT), was an academic infused with patriotism. After graduating from the University of Oslo, he studied for a time with meteorologists of the Bergen school from which grew the first understanding of how cyclonic storms evolved. Vilhelm Bjerknes devised this school of thought in the seacoast town of Bergen because Norway's economy depended in significant measure on commercial fishing. Boats were wooden and in the early 1900s many carried sails, not motors. Every year, storms off the North Atlantic drowned scores of sailors. Some method had to be found to predict the lethal weather.

With nothing but cold sea to the west, no source of oncoming weather observations lay at hand. Bjerknes, his son Jacob, and a handful of pioneering physicists versed in fluid dynamics (air behaves much like a fluid) discovered how vortexes form in the atmosphere. A disciple of the Bergen school, the academic Petterssen thrived on theoretical discussions of the making of weather. He and Douglas seldom saw eye to eye, though they agreed forecasts more than two days in advance were next to useless and longer-range predictions than that were a waste of time. Not so the principal USSTAF meteorologists.

Dominated by Lt. Col. Irving P. Krick (though he was actually outranked by his colleague Lt. Col. Benjamin Holzman), American forecasters tended to stress that weather behaved in predictable patterns that repeated themselves. To that end, Krick held that if today's weather map matched closely to one from the past that, generally speaking, the weather that occurred on the day following the historic chart would be very much like that which could be expected for tomorrow. This approach to meteorology was called analog forecasting.

During the Great Depression, Works Progress Administration employees manually coded onto punch cards some two million daily weather observations from 1880 to 1933. The data included locations of major areas of high and low pressure.[24] Readings from each day's observations were then punched into cards that were fed into a primitive International Business Machine card sorter. The machine would spit out the days in history that most closely resembled current observations and identify the weather for the days that followed.[25] With analogs and his weather types, Krick claimed he could forecast weather weeks in advance. "With our weather types we can get by without many observations," Krick is reported as telling Gen. "Hap" Arnold, commander of the US Army Air Corps in 1940.[26] The British thought the idea was pure bunkum.

On matters of meteorology, Petterssen and Krick were perpetually at swords point. They'd done extensive battle when the former chaired MIT's department of meteorology and the latter headed up the met program at the California Institute of Technology known as "Caltech." Yet they agreed on one thing: Stagg had no business being appointed SHAEF's chief meteorologist. Douglas, who knew of Stagg as a longtime geophysicist in the Met Office, no doubt would have much preferred a seasoned forecaster.

Stagg, rumor had it, was an aging bureaucrat, a senior administrator in the Met Office to whom the plum position as Eisenhower's chief weatherman had fallen because of long civil service tenure, not skill as a weatherman. That feeling was likely shared, to a lesser degree, by the Royal Navy's meteorologists. How dare that man Stagg usurp a role that rightfully belonged to one who had devoted his entire career to forecasting weather, not trying to read, as Stagg had, fluctuations in the earth's magnetic field.

Their rancor might have been mitigated had Stagg's personality carried a bit of bonhomie. But it did not. Eisenhower called him a "dour Scot." Others were less charitable. Small talk was not Stagg's forte. Before SHAEF's advanced headquarters moved to Southwick House, Stagg's office at Bushy Park had been next to the war room, which Ike visited almost daily for briefings. Often, he dropped in on Stagg, leaned against the doorjamb, and chatted about the weather.[27]

Beneath this informality, Ike was taking steely measure of his chief meteorologist, the man on whose forecast for D-day so much would come to depend. What he found was a man of principle, adept at synthesizing the views of others, and not deterred by rank from expressing his opinions. These were skills that Ike prized in his senior commanders. He also discovered that Stagg was a consummately skeptical scientist and driven for perfection, a millstone most likely hung around his neck by his mother.

The Son of the Seamstress

Stagg was born on June 30, 1900, in a rude two-room stone row house near Edinburgh. Not two hundred yards down the street from the family abode spread a cattle market. Diagonally across from the pens and to the left of the bridge over the North Esk River stood the abattoir with its drying green for hides. A flourmill anchored the bridge's right abutment. One block south, at the end of Mitchell Street, lined with stately houses, stood a school.

Alexander, his father, was a plumber; Ellen, his mother, a seamstress. They earned their keep doing jobs for the lord and lady of Dalkeith House a short walk up Old Edinburgh Road and across the tracks. On her visits to deliver sewing to gentry in great houses, Ellen caught glimpses of libraries. She knew that if she could somehow encourage her son to concentrate on schooling and not on the goings-on at the football ground across from their door, he might, just might, escape the clutches of poverty that grasped the family.

Stagg was born into the age of the great races to the poles. Capt. Robert F. Scott mushed to within 410 miles of the South Pole during his expedition from 1901 to 1904. As third officer, Ernest Shackleton accompanied Scott's party, but scurvy prevented his joining the trek toward the pole. Five years later in 1909, Shackleton led members of the Nimrod Expedition to within 114 miles of the mark, setting a new farthest south record for Great Britain. If only her son, Jim, could become a noted explorer, Ellen must have dreamed, he might one day achieve the social respectability denied children of her and Alexander's station in life.

While other kids of his station chased balls and hoops and each other, Stagg read books. Evening after evening, he bent over his homework at the table in the kitchen. Never known for being softly mothering, Ellen kept Stagg at his tasks. If his personality is any indication, little foolishness brightened the family's cramped abode. All was serious. Money was incessantly scant. Pennies were pinched until they howled. Under her tutelage, Stagg learned how to discipline his mind, which, as ensuing years were to prove, was very, very bright.

After completing the primary grades, Stagg attended Dalkeith High and Broughton Secondary schools. He showed a penchant for mathematics and physical science, and upon graduation in 1917, he matriculated at the University of Edinburgh. In March 1918 while still seventeen, Stagg dropped out of the university and enlisted in the Royal Flying Corps (RFC) as an air mechanic.[28] Expressing an interest in physics, Stagg was posted to the base at Halton in Hampshire to which the RFC had relocated its school for air mechanics.[29] There he took courses in electricity and wireless repair. After completing his training, he was assigned to the Royal Aircraft Factory at Farnborough, location of the Southern Aircraft Repair depot.

Stagg, like other youngsters of his era, may well have been fascinated by radio. The turn of the century had seen the first transatlantic wireless transmissions. Press in the British Isles was aflame when a radio message from England resulted in the arrest of Hawley Crippen just as he stepped off the steamship *Montrose,* on which he had sailed to America in July of 1910 to flee prosecution for murdering his wife in London. The story filled papers for months until he was executed in November. Two years later, the US Navy pioneered radio communication from airplanes.[30] Radio transmissions, however, were severely affected by fluctuations in the magnetic field that surrounds the earth.

Stagg may have been intrigued by stories of how early polar expeditions and the great explorers of his day relied on magnetic navigation. Earth has two North Poles. One is the geographic top of the earth's axis; the other, and the one used for navigation in the era before long-range radio and satellites, is magnetic. This is the one to which the needle of a compass points. The earth's magnetic field emanates from the north and south magnetic poles. Problem is that the magnetic north pole moves slightly from place to place as the earth's molten metallic core shifts in relationship to the crust on which civilization lives.

The ability to precisely pinpoint the location of those poles was as crucial to navigation in Stagg's day as it is in ours. Solar storms that trigger those glorious aurora curtains of green and red and orange that pulse in polar skies play hob with the magnetic field and with geolocation systems, from the needle compass, essentially unchanged over the past thousand years, to the most sophisticated global positioning systems of today.

His work on aircraft radio and electrical repair came to an end with demobilization in January 1919. He returned to Edinburgh and picked up his university studies, bent perhaps on learning more about the effects of magnetic fields on radio transmission and navigation. A diligent student in the extreme, in 1920 he completed his bachelor of science degree with honors in natural philosophy. In July of that year, he learned he had been awarded the Baxter Physical Science Scholarship, a stipend of £126 or about $4,000 in today's dollars,[31] which allowed him to pursue his graduate studies. Twelve months later he completed teacher preparation at Moray House Training College, received the education diploma from the University of Edinburgh, and graduated with a master of arts with first class honors in mathematics and natural philosophy.[32]

As it had in the United States, the end of World War I thrust the United Kingdom into economic depression. The years were marked by steep deflation where the price of goods and services plummeted by nearly 20 percent.[33] With the return to civilian life of so many servicemen, jobs were scarce, especially so for newly minted theoretical geophysicists like Stagg. Yet his reputation as an emerging scholar earned him a position teaching chemistry and physics at George Heriot's School, then as now, one of Edinburgh's most prestigious private academies.

Still living in his parents' house and with two years of teaching under his belt, Stagg yearned to pursue the study of the earth's magnetic fields that he found so fascinating. He learned of an opening in the Met Office and on July 23, 1923, he applied at the Edinburgh branch. After stating his qualifications, in his letter of application, Stagg wrote: "I have no objection to being set to any post for isolated work, to undertake geophysical work; in fact my preference would be such a post, for a period at least." Here he began his professional quest to investigate how geo-magnetics affects communication and navigation, a career that would place him at the head of a polar expedition and get him sacked, if only for a few weeks, as SHAEF's chief weatherman two months before D-day.

Stagg secured an interview with A. Crichton Mitchell, superintendent of the Edinburgh office and evidently impressed him. In his letter to the director of the Met Office, Mitchell wrote that Stagg "is quite as good a man as J.C. Mann who withdrew. In fact he is better because there is more 'stuffing' in him."[34] His old professors at the University of Edinburgh roundly endorsed his application.

"I had a high opinion of him: he was keen and eager and had a marked natural ability both as a mathematician and as an experimental physicist," wrote Professor E. T. Whittaker in September 1923. "He was offered and accepted an appointment as a teacher in one of the chief secondary schools in Edinburgh, but he repeatedly said to me he would prefer some work of a more practical and creative kind in which he could make use of his advanced knowledge of physics and mathematics. I think he would make an excellent recruit for the Meteorological Service. He has ideas and is a hard worker and good with his hands. And I should say that he is a man who could stand a lot of physical hardship. I found him easy to get on with and have no doubt that he would fit well into an organized system."[35]

Three weeks later, the Meteorological Office received a letter from C. S. Barkla, another of his professors. "I should like to say that I consider Mr. Stagg to be a worker of the very best type. He is not only very able, but apparently he has both the strength and inclination for hard systematic work. He had a brilliant career in the university when he was exceptionally young and probably you have the details of that. He is rather slow and deliberate, but he is far-seeing and ambitious. Given the opportunity, I feel sure he will have a very successful career."[36]

Mitchell, Whittaker, and Barkla saw in Stagg the character traits that would define him throughout his career and into his role as SHAEF's chief meteorologist. Ever persevering, Stagg concentrated his efforts on the task before him. He was a scientist, a mathematical physicist, schooled in the ethos of rigorous doubt. It was his nature to accept nothing at face value. He strove mightily to understand the proof of a hypothesis before he could accept its conclusions.

In late October, Stagg was offered an appointment as a junior professional assistant, which paid £175 per year. Upon passage of the requisite medical examination, he was notified that he would be posted to the Observatory in Kew, established by King George III in 1769 in his deer park on the Thames upstream and southwest a bit from London. With a flash of his classic independence, the new recruit added in his letter of acceptance the proviso that as soon as possible he would like to be transferred to Eskdalemuir or Lerwick in Scotland to continue his magnetic studies.

At Kew, he was to serve as an assistant resident observer gathering and recording temperature, pressure, wind speed and direction, cloud cover, and other synoptic data. He was required to take his readings at 7:00 a.m., 6:00 p.m., and 10:00 p.m., hours beyond the normal work day. For this he received free accommodations, which no doubt pleased his parsimonious soul, Scottish to the core. Here he continued measurements of the strength of the earth's magnetic field as best he could, though the passage of electric streetcars made some of Stagg's observations unreliable.

His appointment required six months' probation. At the end of the period, the assistant director at Kew, Charles Chree, reported: "Mr. J. M. Stagg has been given practical experience in all branches of the work here and has shown aptitude in acquiring the knowledge requisite in a good observer. He has shown his interest in geophysics by engaging in reading and in the measurement of magnetic curves outside ordinary office hours." By 1926 Stagg had become the resident weather observer at Kew. Still day-to-day forecasting for him lacked the attraction of earth magnetism, and he was ordered to devote more time to increasing his ability to read weather patterns before he could take charge at the Met Office station in Leuchars, halfway between St. Andrews and Dundee in his native Scotland.

In March of that year, he'd evidently become proficient enough at forecasting to assume management of the Leuchars office and twenty-one months later earned his long-sought posting to Eskdalemuir. Built in 1908 expressly to study earth magnetism free from disturbance by electric streetcars and other trappings of urban life, the observatory rides the crest of a relatively barren moor in southeastern Scotland not far north of the border with England. Stagg must have been delighted with this transfer and only slightly less so with his move a year later to the Lerwick Observatory at the base of the tail of the Shetland mainland. As a young man who'd applied to the Met Office requesting positions in isolated stations, he'd certainly gotten his wish.

After a year and a half, though, he was transferred again, this time back to Kew. By then, his work on geomagnetism had definitely captured the attention of G. C. Simpson, Director of the

Met Office.[37] Stagg returned to Kew in January 1931, on the eve of the Golden Jubilee of the First International Polar Year in 1882–1883. That international collaboration had been the brainstorm of Carl Weyprecht, an Austrian explorer, who believed that much was to be gained by studying magnetism and meteorology in the Arctic that influences to great degree the world's weather.[38] Forty nations would participate in the Second International Polar Year slated for 1932-1933. Because of his work in geophysics and knowledge of meteorology, Stagg was tapped to lead the six-member British expedition.

Not seven years after joining the Met Office as a junior technical assistant, Stagg was on the cusp of attaining national prominence and the accompanying social respectability for which his mother must have prayed as she carried her sewing basket into the homes of Edinburgh's wealthy. True, the British team was not headed for one of the poles, but to Fort Rae, on Marian Lake up a short river from the northern arm of Great Slave Lake in Canada's North-west Territories. For Stagg, the locale was exotic enough. In May of 1931, Stagg sailed for Canada aboard the SS *Athenia*, which, eight years later, on September 2, 1939, the day after Hitler invaded Poland and the day before England declared war, became the first British ship sunk by Nazi Germany.[39] Stagg's trip on the *Athenia* was the first leg of a reconnaissance of Fort Rae.

Rae was hardly a "fort" in any sense of the word. It consisted of a handful of rude huts in various states of disrepair located on a small island one hundred feet off the mainland. Only fifteen hundred feet long by a thousand feet at its widest point, the island was little more than a rounded hummock of granite smoothed by passing glaciers. Swaths of muskeg surrounded the outcrop. Mosquitoes loved muskeg as much as Stagg and his crew would come to despise them.

Fort Rae's saving grace was the presence of a Hudson Bay Company trading post, quarters for a small detachment of Royal Canadian Mounted Police, a Roman Catholic mission, and a settlement of Dog Rib Indians with whom to trade tinned bully beef for meat of fresh moose, caribou, and once in a great while, bear. The trading post would warehouse the expedition's supplies. Though isolated to be sure, gold and uranium-rich pitchblende had been discovered in the region. It was hopping with prospectors, and floatplanes brought mail and some supplies.[40]

On his return from his reconnaissance in the subarctic, Stagg spent a week with John Fleming, acting director of the Department of Research in Terrestrial Magnetism at the Carnegie Institute of Washington. They attended meetings at the magnetic observatory at Cheltenham, Maryland, and visited the Smithsonian's astrophysics laboratory, the US Coast and Geodetic Survey, and the US Weather Bureau.

Fleming introduced Stagg to H. B. Maris, who was to lead the scientific team of the US Polar Expedition to Fort Conger near Qikiqtaaluk on Ellesmere Island, high above the Arctic Circle and much farther north than Fort Rae. For an afternoon, Stagg and Maris discussed operation of delicate scientific instruments in harsh polar climates. At the end of the week, Fleming wrote Met Office Director Simpson that Stagg "is an ideal man for work in geophysics, and we very much hope that he will find it possible to continue in his chosen field."

Stagg's report on his 1932–1933 expedition to Fort Rae is rich with stories of the fire that nearly destroyed their living quarters, of the explosion of the machine that produced hydrogen for weather balloons (the operator emerged unscathed), and of failures of sensitive instruments in severe cold and jerry-rigged repairs that kept them functioning.

"A custom among the Dog Rib Indians of deserting any dwelling place where a member of the family has died conveniently supplied us with a log hut, which, when denuded of a seemingly endless quantity of iron nails used by the former owners for fastening paper over gaps in the walls, formed a very serviceable protective shell for the magnetic variometers," he wrote. From the outside Stagg and his crew chinked the log with mud, which promptly froze solid. Overhead flamed curtains of the aurora borealis.

After his return to England in late 1933, Stagg remained assigned to the Polar Expedition while supervising the unpacking of equipment at Kew and continuing the collating of data from Fort Rae. In early May, Simpson met with him to discuss his future. Stagg had proven himself an able leader on his assignment and his prospects were bright. "I thought it would be best for him ... not to specialize too intently on observatory work but that he should have more experience in forecasting and also probably to some extent in administration," Simpson wrote. In November 1934 Stagg returned to Edinburgh where he took up forecasting duties and continued analyzing the findings from Fort Rae. Two years later his work earned him the doctor of science degree from the university there.

Seeds of the Fascist expansionism that would burst forth as the Second World War took root in the Middle East when Italy invaded Ethiopia in 1935. Palestine, an unwilling British protectorate, broke into revolt in 1936. In response to the Arab uprising, the British Army began ferrying soldiers and supplies in armed motor convoys.[41] When they were attacked, RAF fighters were summoned by radio, one of the first deployments of close air support for ground operations.

In that the Meteorological Office was under the Air Ministry, which was well aware of the build-up of Hitler's Luftwaffe, Stagg's next assignment to the RAF base at Hinaidi outside of Baghdad proved providential. On December 2, 1936, he sailed to Iraq via Port Said and crossed the border on the 15th becoming eligible for Foreign Service pay. His posting carried a promotion to "Acting Senior Technical Officer." During his two years in Iraq, whatever he learned about forecasting *haboobs,* Arabic for violent blasting winds that trigger dust storms in arid regions, stood him little stead in his forthcoming role at SHAEF, but he gained intimate knowledge of the meteorological needs of fighter and bomber commands, which he later found indispensable.

Once back home from Iraq and doctorate complete, Stagg was appointed to the prestigious post of supervising the observatory at Kew in April 1939. For a time he was able to get back to his love of geophysics.[42] His joy was short lived. Five months later on September 1, Hitler invaded Poland. Stagg was called to Met Office headquarters at Kingsway where he helped devise plans to train the hundreds of weather officers needed to support rapidly expanding RAF and British army commands.

A department of the Air Ministry that oversees the RAF, the Met Office was then and still is a civilian organization staffed with superbly trained and academically credentialed scientists, in that way similar to the US Weather Bureau. Though they wore tweeds and herringbones and not uniform woolens of gray-blue or green, they filled the meteorological needs of the British military—with the exception of the Royal Navy, which had its own weather service.

In time, Stagg became responsible for coordinating weather services for the army, a task that entailed tight liaison with the RAF. He did not make forecasts himself however; he facilitated preparation of forecasts for combined British operations overseas. Although Stagg denied that this was suitable training for his eventual role at SHAEF, it is obvious that among the senior officers of the Met Office he was clearly well suited to fill the role of chief meteorologist for the planning of D-day.[43]

ONE FOR THE MONEY, TWO FOR THE SHOW

After World War II, Irving Parkhurst Krick would tell all in earshot that he was the lead forecaster of the USSTAF meteorological team that told Eisenhower when to launch D-day.

A self-promoter par excellence, Krick had attracted the attention of Henry H. "Hap" Arnold in the early 1930s, when the latter was a lieutenant colonel commanding March Field at Riverside, California, and the former was chair of the new department of meteorology at Caltech. Arnold's trajectory in the Army Air Corps was meteoric. When the Army Air Corps evolved to become the Army Air Force in 1942, Arnold was named its first commander. Though occasionally Krick lived in Arnold's doghouse,[44] in a manner of speaking the general was his godfather. Were it not for Arnold, Krick might well have been chained to Caltech and its program of training forecasters for the Air Force for the duration of the war.

Stagg and Krick were in many ways opposites. In stark comparison to Stagg's rise from rags to respectability, Krick was born into wealth and comfort. Krick's father was a San Francisco banker, and his mother was a pianist and the daughter of novelist and *San Francisco Chronicle* editor Henry Clinton Parkhurst. Like Stagg's mother, Krick's also had definite plans for her son. He was to become a prominent musician. Born in 1906, by age thirteen Krick was locally known as something of a prodigy. And, as it had Stagg, radio caught Krick's attention. During his first two years at the University of California, Berkeley, he studied electrical engineering. But to mollify his mother, he changed his major to music and was soon performing with the NBC Symphony Orchestra.

According to Victor Boesen's book, *Storm—Irving Krick vs. the U. S. Weather Bureaucracy,* which is widely assumed by weather historians to be Krick's thinly veiled autobiography, the budding musician realized "he wasn't good enough to make it to the top in music." He completed two years of courses in physics as a senior and graduated with a bachelor's degree in science in 1928. During college, he enrolled in ROTC and the local unit was aligned with Coastal Artillery. At one summer camp, as Boesen tells it, Krick's gun crew fired a dummy shell that hit the boat towing the intended target. It was then that he began to understand the importance of winds and temperatures at high altitudes, which could deflect, at the top of its arc, the flight of a projectile.

Degree in hand, Krick signed on as assistant manager of Oakland's legendary radio station KTAB, playing the piano, spinning records, and scheduling programming. For him, the 20s were roaring. That is until a new station manager came aboard, called him in, and fired him with these parting words: "One day you'll thank me." Krick's uncle arranged for him to become a runner for a brokerage house just before the stock market crashed. Then, for a while afterward, he sold pianos on commission. Still under pressure from his mother to make music his career, he was hired in 1930 to give piano lessons in Hollywood.[45]

Krick found teaching music not at all to his liking. Married by now and with the country deep in the tunnel of the Great Depression, he knew he needed a steady career. His brother-in-law, Horace R. Byers, then a student at MIT and who would go on to become a pioneer in aviation meteorology,[46] convinced Krick to follow the same career because money could be made in forecasting weather for Hollywood movie studios. Enrolling at Caltech, Krick studied under Beno Gutenberg, who had served in the Meteorological Service of the German army in World War I.[47] Gutenberg's course on atmospheric structure intrigued Krick, and before long he became the professor's disciple.

After two years studying meteorology at Caltech, Krick arranged an interview with Jimmy James, chief pilot and operations officer for Western Air Express (WAE). Founded in 1926, those halcyon days when former World War I aviators vied for federal airmail contracts, WAE was a rough and ready outfit. Pilots wore pistols and flew Douglas M-2 biplanes loaded with mail—along with two daring paying passengers who sat on their parachutes on routes that included Las Vegas, Salt Lake City, Dallas, Kansas City, and Seattle.

Krick impressed James with his knowledge of cold and warm fronts and what they meant for pilots. He hired Krick as a baggage clerk in 1932, the same year that Stagg was leading his polar expedition. As was the custom at the airline, Krick strapped on his pistol and "toted luggage for the passengers, loaded and unloaded mailbags, and made out the forms that showed the weight of the cargo," Victor Boesen writes in *Storm*. Since Western's meteorologist Joe George was vacationing when Krick was hired, James allowed him to fill in on weather duties.

Not on the job long, Krick briefed a pilot headed for Salt Lake City to land at Medford, Oregon, to wait out a cold front's turbulent passage. On his return, the pilot was effusively grateful. The weather was rough, and had he not landed the flight could have crashed in the Wasatch Mountains, the pilot told Krick. Thereafter, Krick was given the green light to draw weather maps showing the locations of fronts, not a universal practice in the early 1930s.[48]

On April 4, 1933, the US Navy airship *Akron* blundered into a vicious thunderstorm east of Barnegat Light, New Jersey. Whipsawed by updrafts and downdrafts, it plunged tail first into the ocean with a loss of seventy-three men. The accident marked the beginning of the end of the navy's use of rigid helium-filled dirigibles.[49] In a graduate paper, Krick argued that the tragedy could have been averted if the US Weather Bureau had not failed to forecast the violent collision of a cold air mass from the northeast and a warm, moist mass from the south.[50]

He was right. A subsequent investigation by the Science Advisory Board, created by President Roosevelt, found the Weather Bureau at fault. The board recommended that the cash-strapped bureau increase the number of surface and upper-air observations from two times a day to four, increase the number of weather stations, and incorporate storm forecasting techniques developed by the Bjerkneses and their colleagues of the Bergen school.[51]

An acolyte of Gen. Billy Mitchell, Hap Arnold championed the long-range bomber. In 1934 he'd win the MacKay Trophy for leading a flight of ten Martin B-10 bombers from Washington, DC, to Fairbanks, Alaska, and back, a distance of 8,290 miles. "Weather is the essence of flying," Arnold is quoted as saying.[52]

With Krick at Western Air Express and Arnold at nearby March Air Force Base, it's likely that they knew of each other before the *Akron* disaster; aviation circles in Los Angeles were then pretty small. One day in 1934, Arnold called on Robert A. Millikan, who chaired Caltech's executive council. Millikan, who as vice chairman of the National Research Council had set up the Army Meteorological Service during World War I, introduced Arnold to Krick, and Krick promptly informed Arnold that loss of the *Akron* could have been averted had the navy received an accurate forecast from the Weather Bureau.[53] Both men were visionary and zealous, and the flier and the twenty-eight-year-old musician turned meteorologist hit it off. Krick's self-confidence matched Arnold's and the future commander of America's Army Air Force came away impressed with the apparent accuracy of Krick's predictions.

Impressed as well were Gutenberg, Professor Theodore von Karman, and Millikan. Shortly after his analysis of the *Akron* crash, Caltech established a department of meteorology with Krick, new master's degree in hand, as its chair. Always the pragmatist, he taught the courses in practical forecasting and left the theoretical physics to Gutenberg and von Karman.[54] "Caltech was known for its pretty weather maps," remembers John C. Crowell, who was a weather cadet at the University of California Los Angeles in 1940. Crowell would later be seconded to the Royal Navy with another Air Corps lieutenant, Charles C. Bates, to advise its meteorologists on the surf and swell forecasts for D-day.[55]

Soon after taking the helm of Caltech's meteorology department, Krick toured Europe and visited the staff of the Bergen school. He also spent time in Leipzig with Ludwig F. Weickmann, a German meteorologist who said he'd identified a systematic progression of surface air pressure on which long-range forecasts could be accurately based.[56] Krick immediately saw the potential in this. If he could tell growers of oranges and other produce when to harvest their crops before they were blighted by drought or frost, he'd make millions.

Upon his return to Caltech, he and Western Air Express colleague Joe George began developing the system of analog forecasting that would make Krick famous in the eyes of Arnold and other military commanders, and infamous in the opinions of Petterssen at MIT and other atmospheric physicists then adapting principles from the Bergen school to forecasting. By 1937, Professor Krick was moonlighting and selling private forecasting services to a number of companies. Among his first clients was Warner Brothers, which asked him to predict a clear and windless night to shoot the burning of Atlanta for the film classic *Gone With the Wind*. Krick got it right.[57]

In the Temperate Zone

As it geared up for war, the Army Air Corps realized, just as the RAF had, that hundreds of meteorologists were needed to staff weather offices at bases in the United States and overseas. Krick's program at Caltech received its share of new trainees. Among them in 1938 was a snappily uniformed pilot graduate of the US Military Academy at West Point, First Lt. Donald Norton Yates. His first love was flying. He'd thoroughly enjoyed his three years in Hawaii where he piloted Sikorsky and Douglas seaplanes accompanying flights of bombers over the Molokai Channel. Should a bomber ditch, Yates was alongside to land and pick up the crew.

Next, in 1935 the vagaries of army assignment posted Yates to Brooks Field in Texas as base adjutant. It was not, he said in his 1980 oral history, "a very sexy assignment." Fearing he'd be stuck there as a first lieutenant forever, "I got fed up with it . . .," he reported after three years. Consequently, he applied for advanced schooling as an aeronautical engineer either at MIT or Caltech. Those courses were filled, he was told, but a slot was available in meteorology at the latter institution. "I decided, 'well, heck,' meteorology is interesting and certainly of value to a future career as a pilot."[58]

Yates enrolled in Krick's department at Caltech in 1938 and through the end of the war their careers were intimately inter- twined as soon, too, would be Arnold's. On completing his master's degree in 1940, Yates was promoted to captain and posted to Barks- dale Air Force Base in Louisiana as weather officer and assistant operations officer. He also served as airbase squadron commander. Six months later, he was promoted again, this time to major. The Officers' Club was running in the red, and Yates was on its board. In one meeting Yates piped up with ideas on how to clean up the mess. His suggestions earned him an additional duty—that of club officer. It wouldn't be the last time that opening his mouth would rapidly alter his future.

In November of 1941, Maj. Arthur Merewether, the chief of the Air Corps weather section, arrived at Barksdale to inspect Yates's operation. From Yates, now concluding his first year as a weather officer, Merewether wanted to know what was wrong with the Air Weather Service. "I told him," Yates said. "Oh I had a lot of opinions in those days." A few weeks later, the Japanese attacked Pearl Harbor. Two days afterward, Yates was ordered to join the Weather Service in Washington, DC. He left with some trepidation. At Barksdale, he'd been happy, and he wondered what was in store for him after having "blown off my mouth."

Arriving in the capital on Christmas Eve, Yates phoned Merewether, who welcomed him, told him to find housing for himself and his family, and ordered him to be ready to depart in five days for Goose Bay, Labrador, in an unheated B-18 bomber. During the war, thousands of bombers, transports, and fighters would land at Goose Bay for refueling en route to England. But on New Year's Day of 1942, the base was nothing more than a runway of snow packed on top of land recently cleared of spruce and pine along which clustered a few temporary huts. For a guy who three weeks earlier had been enjoying the balmy winter clime of Louisiana, the cold of Goose Bay must have been bitter indeed.

Yates would weather more of it. As they readied the plane for the return flight, it became apparent that the B-18's engines had not been prepared for operation in sub-zero temperatures. Using blowtorches and whatever heaters they could find, the crew needed twelve hours to warm the engines enough to get them started. Once aloft, they limped their way toward Bolling Field outside Washington, but with engines losing oil pressure, they made an emergency landing at Bangor, where Yates was born. He'd never been so glad to see his hometown.

For the next few months, Yates, a lieutenant colonel by this time, led the project to establish weather stations in northeastern Canada and along the coasts of Greenland. These had to be up and operating before the vast air armada needed to defeat Germany could be ferried to England. That assignment did not last long. In the spring of 1943, Yates was made director of the Air Force's primary weather central in the newly opened Pentagon.

In May, Arnold gave Yates two days to obtain the required passport, visa, and ten mandatory inoculations plus Arctic gear needed for a mission to Russia to set up routes to ferry aircraft from Alaska to Moscow and to arrange for the exchange of weather data. He returned in December and for his performance was awarded the Distinguished Service Medal and promoted to colonel. Still director of the Air Force weather central, he arrived back in Washington just in time to have it out with Arnold over Krick's renegade ways.

A Ripple in the Upper Air

Soon after war was declared, Arnold wangled Krick's transfer from his duty as an ensign in the naval reserve to the Air Force as a major assigned to the Weather Research Center to facilitate long-range weather forecasting. His arrival in Washington, DC, in 1942 opened doors to the nation's top generals that normally were closed to junior field-grade officers. Though Krick successfully wooed powerful friends in high places, most leading military meteorologists had little use for his weather types or for his supercilious attitude toward them and their scientific work.

Never shy about trumpeting his own prowess, Krick conspired with Maj. Gen. George V. Strong, who reported on intelligence to Army Chief of Staff George C. Marshall, to combine army and navy meteorologists in one weather service. Without authorization from his boss Don Zimmerman, Krick telephoned Arnold and urged him to support the concept. Zimmerman was incensed at Krick's end run. This wasn't the first time and wouldn't be the last that Krick leap-frogged his superiors. According to John F. Fuller in *Thor's Legions—Weather Support for the U. S. Air Force and Army 1937–1987,* Krick once tried bringing to President Roosevelt's attention a plan "to shift bombing operations from England to Siberia based on his long-range weather prognoses."[59]

When Arnold asked for a thirty-day forecast, Zimmerman and other meteorologists would say it couldn't be done and begin to explain why. That wasn't what Arnold wanted to hear. Krick would say: "Yes sir! Here it is sir." The accuracy of such forecasts was dubious at best. Given the world's network of meteorological satellites, radars, and remote sensing equipment today, predicting on Monday morning the weather for the coming weekend is reasonably reliable. But imagine a family leaning back after Thanksgiving dinner knowing for sure how much wind, rain, sun, or snow they would have when they reunited again for Christmas. With his weather types, Krick believed he could do just that.

It is difficult not to fault Arnold for his unconditional support of Krick. Arnold demanded certainty and abhorred confusion. Meteorology, even with all of today's technology, is still anything but precise. Krick's forecasts, though often wrong, gave Arnold and his commanders a set of weather conditions on which to plan. Krick, of course, was not content to be Arnold's fair-haired forecaster. He wanted in on the action and soon began bootlegging unauthorized weather forecasts to Maj. Gen. George S. Patton, then commanding the Western Task Force sailing on its way to launch Operation Torch, the invasion of North Africa.

Krick's predictions ran counter to those of the fleet's meteorological team, causing consternation among Torch's senior commanders. In late 1942, Yates was assigned to the Joint Weather Central, which coordinated meteorological and support services for the army and the navy. When told Krick was sending independent forecasts to Patton and upon learning that Krick was sidestepping channels and personally advising Arnold, Yates hit the roof.[60]

Yates laid it out to Arnold. "I was scared to death," he remembers in his oral history, "but I put it on the table, and I said: 'Sir, I am afraid I will have to resign or request a transfer if I can't have complete authority over all the individuals in my organization and have absolutely no reports sent around me or any other way. I believe that is no more than I am entitled to ask for. I realize you think Krick is a God as far as meteorology is concerned. As far as I am concerned, he is part of a military organization and is going to have to act like that, or I don't want to have anything to do with it.'" At Barksdale, Yates had always briefed Arnold on weather en route. They'd gotten to know and like each other.

The relationships paid off that day. Arnold "took it the right way, fortunately for me," Yates continues. "He said, 'You may call in Dr. Krick and give him any instructions you want to and remind him that he is a lieutenant colonel and remind him further that I have assured you that I will not deal directly with him on any matter without going through you.'

"At that time I said, 'I might have to transfer him.' He said, 'whatever you do is alright for this round.'" Krick was ordered back to Caltech to compile forty years of daily weather maps for use by the Air Force and the Weather Bureau. He would not be let out of the doghouse until Arnold sent him to London a year later to help the Eighth Air Force perfect long-range forecasting techniques.[61] Krick returned with a recommendation from Lt. Gen. Carl A.

"Tooey" Spaatz, USSTAF commander, that a special section be created from meteorologists assigned to the 18th and 21st squadrons, which flew weather reconnaissance missions. That and a report from Carl Rossby, a consultant to Stimson, prompted Arnold to order Yates to assemble "any forecasters you want" and get them to England to report to Spaatz "and to do it in two weeks."[62]

Yates would be posted to England as USSTAF's Director of Weather Services. He recruited Krick and Lt. Col. Benjamin Holzman, who had also taken Krick's Caltech meteorology course, as deputy directors, with Holzman senior to Krick.[63] In Krick, Yates had measured confidence: "he was a very good strong, practical operational forecaster. There was no question about that. From that point of view, he was a good and strong briefer." Holzman, he considered "an outstanding forecaster and a poor briefer." Yates thought they would complement each other.

And so it came to be that two of the principal American meteorologists participating in the most critical weather forecast the world had yet to see received their initial training from a man whose interest in weather was motivated, not by the lifelong quest to understand and predict the effects of the earth's forces on daily life, but on harnessing the power of weather forecasting to get rich. Yates, Krick, and Holzman lacked the depth of practical experience displayed by Douglas, Petterssen, and even administrator Stagg. Just as the tension built between the Polar High and its Azores cousin to dominate weather over the North Atlantic, so too did friction escalate between British and American meteorologists over which team would author the winning forecast for D-day. The storm was brewing and the fate of the free world hung in the wind.

CHAPTER THREE

Bitter Maritimes

Big whirls have little whirls that feed on their velocity,
And little whirls have lesser swirls and so on to viscosity.[64]

British meteorologist Lewis Fry Richardson coined this charming jingle in 1920 while describing the circulation of winds, turbulence and kinetic energy around the Arctic high. Aloft at thirty thousand feet, the altitude just below that at which most of today's airliners fly, flows the jet stream, a cataract of air racing from west to east at speeds approaching 300 miles per hour and sometimes faster.

Seldom more than one hundred miles wide and three miles thick, the jet stream weaves like a sinuous snake as it circles the top of the northern hemisphere. Though named by German meteorologist Heinrich Seilkopf as the *Strahlströmung* (jet streaming) in 1939, the term did not gain currency among Allied weathermen until 1944 when its fierce winds interrupted high-altitude precision bomb runs.

Within all that jet stream writhing are pods of whirling air. Within each pod, warmer air rises and colder air sinks through convection. As these pods rub against each other, they create smaller pods that circulate in opposite directions like little cogs between big gears. Some of the pods grow into the high- and low-pressure cells with their attendant fronts that bring us the weather we know today. When the jet stream dips far south, oranges on Florida's trees may freeze. When it rides high to the north, Montana can see January temperatures in the 50s. It is along the southern boundary of the jet stream that cold fronts and storms rage across the North Atlantic. The location of the jet stream in the upper atmosphere and of the storms it spawns was of vital interest to the Allies and Germans alike.

CAPTURE OF THE ENIGMA CODES

Before the war, European meteorologists were only too happy to share weather data. None of the countries was large enough to staff its own weather stations on islands in the North Atlantic. The Danes posted meteorologists on Greenland and Iceland, and the Norwegians on the islands of the Svalbard group and Jan Mayen. After the conquest of those two countries by the Germans in the spring of 1940, weather reports covering the vital stretches of the North Atlantic fell silent. Both the Allies and the Germans eagerly sought to restore synoptic data from territories under the other's control.

The interruption of international weather data was anticipated by both sides. Soon after the German invasion of Poland on September 1, 1939, the *Reichswetterdienst,* Germany's national weather service and branch of the civilian air ministry, developed a new code for transmitting meteorological observations. This code utilized six-figure groups and replaced the pre-war International Copenhagen Code. About the same time, the *Zentral Wetterdienst Gruppe,* the main weather center for the Luftwaffe, was creating its own weather code, the *Zenitschüssel,* to be used by German meteorological reconnaissance flights.

On May 9, 1940, the same day that Denmark capitulated to the Germans, a Luftwaffe Dornier 17, a light and fast bomber known as the "flying pencil" and used extensively for met recce, or meteorological reconnaissance flights, was shot down off Scotland's northeast coast. John A. Kington and Franz Selinger in their book *Wekusta*, a comprehensive portrait of German weather flight operations, posit that the crew of the British air rescue boat that reached the downed but still floating aircraft may have seized Zenitschüssel code books and forwarded them to Bletchley Park, that brick and stone mansion of an amusing agglomeration of Victorian, Gothic, and Tudor styles that was home of Britain's famed cryptologists. By the middle of the year, these wizards were beginning to break the Luftwaffe's weather codes.[65]

Meteorological observations were crucial if British and Americans were to forecast weather along convoy routes to England and to the Russians via Murmansk. The Germans had to know how the weather headed their way would affect Luftwaffe's campaign to subdue the Royal Air Force and pave the way for Operation Sea Lion, the planned invasion of England. Furthermore, when the Germans turned on the Russians and launched Operation Barbarossa on June 22, 1941, accurate weather forecasts proved themselves essential. Both sides relied on grueling weather reconnaissance flights and weather ships steaming in endless circles on station in the North Atlantic. But such observations were not nearly as reliable as readings from permanent stations on shore. The weather war for the North Atlantic was about to begin.

On April 10, 1940, President Roosevelt received Danish Minister Henrik Kauffmann, who pleaded that Greenland be protected by the United States under the Monroe Doctrine. Roosevelt and the US Department of State agreed. The Germans must not be allowed to build airfields or ports on the island. Further, the mine at Ivigtut on Greenland was the only source of cryolite, a mineral essential for the extraction of aluminum from bauxite. Were that lost to the Germans, production of fighters and bombers for the Allies would have been dealt a near lethal blow. Although the Danish government was collaborating to a high degree with the Nazis and had ordered Kauffmann not to agree to the establishment of a US protectorate over Greenland, Kauffmann did so anyway in April of 1941.

By then, though, the Germans had their sights set firmly on taking weather observations along the east coast of Greenland. In mid-1940, the German Navy, the Kriegsmarine, dispatched the *Furenak,* a captured Norwegian whaler, to put ashore a meteorological team of four. They were soon apprehended.[66] In September 1940, the weather ship *Sachsen,* a converted trawler, dodged icebergs for weeks while sending from the Greenland Sea. The following year it would ply the waters north of Iceland seeking an escape route for the German battleship *Tripitz* and then spend three months off the coast of Jan Mayen, about 400 miles northeast of Iceland, sending daily weather observations.[67]

Sachsen was the most successful of the German weather ships. On October 24, 1940, the Germans lost the *Adolf Vinnen* to a British submarine. Then three weeks later a weather ship off Jan Mayen, the *Hinrich Freese,* radioed, "Am being chased by enemy vessels." It was never heard from again.[68] In March 1941, the German trawler *Krebs* was fired upon and set ablaze by one of Britain's new large fast Tribal class destroyers, the *Somali,* during a raid to destroy cod oil processing plants—the source of vitamin A which is vital for the maintenance of good vision for pilots and sailors—on the Lofoten Islands where Norway bends east to cap Scandinavia. Upon boarding the smoldering hulk, sailors swept up papers that might yield secrets, and in the captain's cabin, came upon a locked drawer.

Suspecting that the drawer would not be locked if it did not contain something of high importance, Lt. Sir Marshall George

Clitheroe Warmington, the *Somali*'s signals officer and commander of the boarding party, raised his pistol, turned his head to protect his eyes, and fired a shot at the drawer's lock. (He learned this procedure, apparently, by watching movies.) The drawer held a black box. In the box were two round disks with letters on their rims, what appeared to be electrical connections, and indentations that suggested they might rotate on a shaft. Although he knew nothing of Enigma, the famed German naval code, he suspected the disks might be part of a cipher machine and took the box along with him.[69]

He was right. The wheels, known to cryptologists as "rotors," were used to prepare *Wetterkurzschlüssel,* the short German weather cipher. The cipher reduced weather observations—wind speed and direction, temperature, humidity, barometric pressure, cloud cover, and precipitation and their locations into single letters, reducing transmission time from minutes to seconds. The daily ciphers were listed in twenty-one-page code books printed on pink paper in ink that would vanish if the page got wet.

With its 150-watt transmitter and a smaller 40-watt portable version, plus a number of receivers, the 139-foot converted trawler, the *München,* set out on May 1, 1941, from Trondheim for Area 39 on the German naval grid three hundred miles east and slightly northeast of Iceland. The ship was to circle within the fifty-four-square-mile sector for a month sending weather observations twice a day. The sailing of this weather mission was not as secret as the Kriegsmarine thought. At Bletchley, a young analyst, Henry Hinsley, aware of the captured rotors from the *Krebs,* wondered to himself whether German weather observations from sea were broadcast in Enigma code. He convinced his superiors that this must be true, and they urged the Royal Navy to capture a German weather vessel.

That fate fell to the *München*. Apparently from intercepted radio traffic revealing its location, the Royal Navy dispatched a flotilla of three cruisers and four Tribal class destroyers including the *Somali* from the Home Fleet basin at Scapa Flow on May 5. Their mission was to steam abreast roughly ten miles apart through Area 39 in search of a likely target.

On the afternoon of May 7, with only moderate visibility of seven miles or so, the task force began its sweep. At 5:00 p.m. cruiser *Edinburgh* and then the *Somali* sighted smoke from the *München* which, spotting masts on the horizon, put about to flee. It was never much of a race. Turning 32 knots, the *Somali* soon came within range, and its shells straddled the trawler. Fearing for their lives, its crew abandoned ship but not before a petty office had sealed the Enigma machine and its rotors in a lead-weighted canvas bag and heaved it over the side. Warmington led the boarding party as he had done on the *Krebs*. He immediately headed below to the officers' quarters and returned topside in a few moments with Enigma codes for June.[70]

By July 1941, the Allies had seized code books and an intact Enigma machine from U-110, captured that May, and the *Lauenberg*, a third weather trawler that was taken and sunk in the following month. With the code books and the Enigma and with the installation of more first-generation computers (called *bombes* at Bletchley), Hinsley and his fellow colleagues accelerated their decryption of naval radio traffic. As a result, in 1943, the tide turned against the Germans and their U-boat wolfpacks in the North Atlantic. Thanks to this intelligence, tons of supplies, thousands of vehicles, millions of gallons of gasoline and oil, and hundreds of troop ships full of soldiers were convoyed safely to England in readiness for D-day.

ARCTIC WEATHER WARRIORS

On August 22, 1942, as the Allies were two months from launching their drive to liberate Nazi-occupied Europe with landings in North Africa, the *Sachsen* sailed from Tromso in Norway. Despite gales, high seas, and fog, five days later the weather ship pitched and rolled its way into Hansa Bay south of Shannon Island about midway up Greenland's east coast.

The ship's captain, Lt. zur See Hermann Ritter, had selected the protected bay as the place where the ship's party of seventeen would spend the winter. As soon as the *Sachsen* was frozen fast, Ritter sent half the men ashore with materials to construct a hut. Cables were stretched across the ice to provide telephone service and electricity supplied by the ship. The crew stepped the boat's mast, and with torches, cut down its superstructure. Snow was mounded around the hull for added insulation and so that, when viewed from the air, the ship might resemble a hummock of sea ice. Transmission of weather reports began in late September.[71]

Though he was a former sea captain and had hunted extensively on Spitsbergen, Ritter was a bit of an odd choice for command. He was as at home with books on philosophy and religion as he was helming a trawler through the iceberg-infested East Greenland Current. Deeply Catholic, he opposed any killing that was not absolutely necessary, which was why the Gestapo vigorously had opposed his appointment. They questioned whether he was a dedicated Nazi and thus unfit for command. Whether he was trustworthy in the eyes of the party made no difference to the Kriegsmarine. His knowledge of the Arctic islands and waters made him the best man for the job. After he was found in his cabin reading a book by a Jewish author, rumors doubting his loyalty began to circulate among his crew.

What Ritter did not know was that The Sledge Patrol, a group of fifteen Danes, Norwegians, and Eskimos, was headquartered about seven hundred kilometers, roughly five hundred miles, to the south at Eskimoness. Its mission was to root out German weather stations, while making and reporting weather observations of their own. Two Danes, Ib Poulsen and Marius Jensen, were in command. To patrol the area surrounding their headquarters, they divided up into teams of three or four each with a sledge carrying gear and food. Their armament was rudimentary to say the least. They were not armed with Schmeisser submachine guns like the Germans. Instead they carried only bolt action hunting rifles.[72]

In February 1943, Ritter moved most of his men from the *Sachsen* ashore where a second hut had been constructed. From the ship, they transferred equipment for producing and filling weather balloons with hydrogen. The balloons lifted a battery-powered radiosonde to an altitude pre-determined by the size of the balloon. The radiosonde's barometer monitored air pressure and broadcast its readings back to a receiver on the ground. Barometric readings taken high in the atmosphere are essential to determine the location and potential movement of the high- and low-pressure cells that cause warm and cold fronts. Having holed up either on ship or in the hut across the ice during the long Arctic night from mid-November to mid-January, Ritter's men were plagued with cabin fever. The flanking months were lighted by polar twilight and polar dawn, when the sun appeared above the horizon for a few hours each day. As polar dawn broke over Ritter's camp in 1943, his men, having grown increasingly restive, went hunting. Fresh seal or bear meat would augment their boring rations.

One afternoon in March, Jensen, leading a Sledge Patrol team of two Eskimos, came across footprints in the snow. At first he thought downed aircrew had made them. Later as they approached a cabin used by transient hunters, they were astounded to see two men flee into the hills. Inside, they found a German uniform jacket hanging from a peg in the wall.[73] He thought he'd encountered the leading elements of a large party of Germans, and, rather than pursue the escaping men, decided to return to his base at Eskimoness. The Eskimos thought differently. Their dogs were tired and should not be forced to continue, they argued. Instead, Jensen's team bedded down at another hunter's cabin two miles from where they'd spotted the Germans.

The men who'd retreated into the hills soon reached Ritter's post on Shannon Island and alerted him to the enemy patrol. He immediately launched an attack. About midnight, barking dogs and curses of men awoke Jensen's sledge drivers. Jensen grabbed his hunting rifle and stepped out into the bitter Arctic night without his cold-weather gear or food. He urged the Eskimos of his party to set out for Eskimoness, figuring they'd have a better chance to reach base without him. He covered their retreat. Less than a week later, he himself limped into Eskimoness, frostbitten, starving, and certain a German attack was imminent.

The Germans arrived less than a fortnight later. By then, though, Jensen had headed north with another dog sledge to try to locate the enemy force. Ritter, leading the raiding party, called on the squad from the Sledge Patrol to surrender, and, reluctant to kill, ordered his men to fire shots into the air. The Eskimos fled into the night. So did Poulsen who, like Jensen, departed without winter gear or rations. He trekked from hunter's hut to hut, scrounging what food he could find and arrived at the weather station at Ella Island two hundred miles to the south on the verge of total collapse. Rallying there, he ordered the station crew to retreat with him to Scoresbysund another two hundred miles down the coast.

On his scouting mission to the north, Jensen encountered Eli Knudsen, a hunter. He warned Knudsen of the German patrols and recommended that he never approach a hunter's hut unless he knew who was inside. Knudsen ignored the advice and a few days later was mown down as the Germans sprayed him and his dogs with Schmeisser fire. Ritter, the leader generally opposed to killing, was nearly distraught.[74] The next day, Jensen and Peter Nielsen, another member of the patrol, approached the hut where Knudsen had been murdered, and were taken prisoner. Ritter led them back to his weather station on Shannon Island.

On April 5, the gentle Ritter, naïve in the ways of war and needing Jensen's services as an experienced sledge dog driver, set off to the northwest to find a new location for the German weather station. Wilhelm Dege, leader of the last active German weather station in the Arctic, supposes in his memoir *War North of 80* that on the journey Jensen played on Ritter's pacifist leanings. In any event, the pair arrived at Scoresbysund in early May, where Ritter became an Allied prisoner of war and was free to read philosophy until repatriated at war's end.

On May 25, a pair of American B-24s accompanied by two B-17s bombed the *Sachsen* and the weather station on Shannon Island. Though nobody was killed, the occupants scampered to a fall-back camp high in the hills and re-established radio contact with Tromso. Half of the party was evacuated by a Dornier 26 flying boat on June 6. The remainder scuttled the *Sachsen*, destroyed the weather station, and were rescued by the flying boat on June 17.[75]

Two months later, the Germans were returning. In late August, a four-engine Focke-Wulf 200 long-range bomber took off from Trondheim to reconnoiter sea ice on the way to Shannon Island. Overflying the Allied base at Scoresbysund, the plane flew north to Shannon Island, and the US Coast Guard cutter *Northland* on station in the bay opened fire with its ack-ack guns. The weather flight was not damaged and made it back to its base. Ferrying a new weather mission of eight men to the island, the German trawler *Coburg* with its crew of eighteen reached the edge of the Arctic ice pack on the last day of the month. Trying to pick its way through open leads, the boat became trapped in the ice on September 11. Five days later an FW-200 was dispatched to drop supplies and explosives so the crew could blast the ship free. Unable to locate the trawler, the bomber returned to its base.

A second relief mission was launched on September 18. Of nine canisters dropped, two fell into the sea. With what remained, the crew was able to free the boat and steam a few more miles toward the island until sea ice again gripped its hull. September 28 saw another resupply mission and the parachuting of still more dynamite to free the *Coburg*. A few days later the ship was again trapped, this time eleven kilometers off Kap Sussi on the north tip of Shannon Island.[76] After exploring the ice floe, a site for a winter camp was found three kilometers from the ship. The crew hauled across the ice enough materials to re-establish the weather station. It was back-wrenching work done with temperatures well below freezing. Winds blew at gale force incessantly. More and more they were forced to work in the dark.

Twice in early November huge six-engine Blohm und Voss BV 222 flying boats were sent to rescue the meteorological team. Both times foul weather forced them to turn back. A third attempt failed to find the *Coburg* and the stranded weather party. Disaster struck. Ice pressure ruptured the trawler's hull on November 18. She developed a thirty-degree list and was down by the stern. Pumps struggled to keep the ship afloat. Supplies and equipment piled on the ice vanished into the sea. Only its captain and six crew stayed with the boat. The others made it to the camp where life was, in comparison, quite comfortable. All along the meteorologists continued weather reports. Seeking a better location for their work, the meteorologists discovered a huge snowdrift closer to Kap Sussi's shore. They shoveled out caves large enough for small tents to be erected inside. The meteorologists and two crewmembers moved the weather station to the caves in early January 1944.

About seven miles away, the *Coburg* was still held fast, though that was about to change. During a fierce storm on February 20, 1944, the icepack began to break up. The trawler drifted farther out to sea. It was abandoned and the entire party moved into the snow caves. In late March, afraid the caves would soon collapse as temperatures warmed, the men constructed a small wooden hut in the rocks nearby to house the weather equipment and pitched their tents nearby.

Aware of German weather broadcasts from up the Greenland coast, a team from the Danish Sledge Patrol had found footsteps in the snow. Ten men of the patrol planned to attack in early April as weather turned milder. Lt. Gerhard Zacher, military leader of the German team, chose a pleasant afternoon to hunt ptarmigan, an Arctic grouse delicious when roasted or stewed. The attacking patrol was led by Marius Jensen. As he sneaked toward the German's hut, he was surprised by Lt. Zacher, who was then cut down by Jensen, now armed with a submachine gun. The patrol then fired on the hut. The Germans returned fire and charged the patrol, which fled.[77] On June 3, the day many of the ships of the great D-day armada were leaving their ports for Normandy, a Junkers Ju 290 took off from southern France, flew to Kap Sussi via Trondheim, and evacuated twenty-five of the original twenty-six German crew and weather party of the *Sachsen*.

Eight months earlier in September 1943, bird watching, not bird hunting, cost the life of another German officer on a meteorological mission in the Arctic. Eight hundred miles to the north and east of Greenland lies Spitsbergen, the westernmost island of the Svalbard archipelago. Glaciers had scoured and rounded the low outcrops of gray rock along its coasts. When spring finally arrives in late May, lush carpets of purple saxifrage, moss campion, bell heather, and bilberry begin to spread where the land is gentle. In midsummer, the temperature can reach the mid-60s. Too tempting was one particular late spring day for Kapitänleutnant Otto Köhler, former commander of the U 377. Lulled by an idyllic afternoon, he decided to sunbathe in a secluded vale and photograph birds not far from the weather station at Signehamna. Shirtless, he was surprised by a party of four Norwegians searching for the German weather station. They shot him in the chest. There being no medics anywhere nearby, the Norwegians had little choice but, in an act of mercy, to blow out his brains.[78]

At Sea with Iceberg Smith

Less than two weeks after the fall of Denmark in 1940, the US Coast Guard cutter *Comanche* entered the war by gingerly feeling its way through a field of icebergs to Ivigtut, the village roughly three hundred kilometers up the southwest coast of Greenland from its tip, where the cryolite mine was located. To inspect the mine, the *Comanche* put ashore James K. Penfield and his deputy George L. West, who recently had been appointed consul and deputy consul respectively to Greenland by President Roosevelt. When they had returned to the ship, the *Comanche* carried them another six hundred kilometers up the coast to Godthaab, today called Nuuk. There, Penfield established the first US consulate on the island.

Before leaving Ivigtut, a three-inch gun from the boat was mounted on the shore to cover the bay, and fourteen members of the cutter's crew agreed to be discharged so they could provide an armed force to guard the mine. In addition, much needed supplies were delivered to feed the population, which depended solely on imports from Denmark, now under German control.

The voyage of the *Comanche* brought new distinction to the US Coast Guard, the service known for heroic ocean rescues. The collision of the *Titanic* and an iceberg and the resulting drowning of 1,517 passengers and crew on the night of April 15, 1912, had drawn the Coast Guard, then named the Revenue Cutter Service, into patroling Arctic waters. With long experience plying the Alaska Coast ferreting out smugglers and aiding whaling ships in distress, the service was a more logical choice than the US Navy for duty in the iceberg lanes of the North Atlantic.

Coast Guard Capt. E. P. Bertholf, commandant of the service and deeply experienced in sub-polar navigation, was among the US delegation that attended the seminal conference in London where, in the last days of January 1914, the International Ice Observation, Ice Patrol, and Derelict Destruction Service was formed. All of the great sea powers of the day were signatories. The service would become known as the International Ice Patrol. A year later the Revenue Cutter Service and the Lifesaving Service were merged into the US Coast Guard.[79]

The role of the Coast Guard in the Arctic would expand exponentially under Commander Edward H. "Iceberg" Smith. His moniker came not from a steely demeanor but from long years studying seas surrounding Greenland. If ever there was a job made for a man, command of the Coast Guard's Greenland Patrol was perfectly suited for Smith. Born in 1889 on the coast of Massachusetts, his forbearers chased whales off Martha's Vineyard. Naturally, he entered the Coast Guard Academy, known in 1910 when he was appointed a cadet as the US Revenue Cutter Service School of

Instruction. Courses were taught aboard the *Itasca* docked at Arundel Cove in Maryland on Chesapeake Bay.

World War I found him serving as a navigator on the cutter *Manning*, escorting convoys from England to Gibraltar. In the spring of 1920, he shipped out as navigator on the *Seneca*, a cutter assigned to the International Ice Patrol. He also served as scientific observer. With the enthusiasm of a seal chasing a herring, Smith took to his new duties. The heaving wilds of Arctic seas captured his imagination. When not at sea, he studied oceanography at Harvard, and earned a master of arts degree from the university in 1924.

Next, with funding from the American-Scandinavian Foundation, Smith pursued advanced courses in polar climate and Arctic seas for a year at the Geophysical Institute at Bergen, Norway, which was also responsible for that nation's weather forecasts. Though there's no record of their meeting, it seems quite likely that Smith may have encountered Petterssen in residence there and also one of the two principal British meteorologists who would twenty years later fill a crucial role in preparing the forecast for D-day.

Completing his studies at Bergen in 1925, he moved on to three months at the Met Office at Kew outside of London planning joint cooperation for the Ice Patrol. The same year Stagg, too, was posted at Kew where he'd just been promoted to senior professional assistant. It's possible they encountered each other. When Stagg was in Washington in 1931 preparing for his polar expedition to Fort Rae, Smith was serving as navigator on a six-day, eight-thousand-mile cruise of the *Graf Zeppelin* over the Arctic. The airship's marathon voyage was sponsored by Germany's Central Office of Aeroarctic. Smith was the sole American aboard and in readying for the flight, it would not be surprising if he had met some of the meteorologists who would later man German weather stations on Greenland and Svalbard.[80]

Smith arrived off Greenland in the *Northland,* a cutter with a cutaway bow designed to ride up on and break ice. Built in 1927, the ship was originally equipped with two masts that carried sails but proved extremely difficult to steer when under canvas. Before Smith took command, the masts were removed to make way for radio gear and a boom to launch and retrieve an SOC-4 Seagull, one of the last three amphibian scout biplanes made by Curtis-Wright. Smith boarded the *Northland* when it reached the New York Navy Yard after a voyage via the Panama Canal from Alaskan waters where it had been stationed for several years. In June 1940, the cutter embarked on a survey of the western and eastern coasts of Greenland. Charts of those waters were in short supply, with most held in German-occupied Copenhagen.

A year later the Coast Guard's Greenland Patrol was formed and Smith was placed in command. His *Northland* was assigned to sail the northeast coast and it remained his flagship. It was joined by the *Bear,* a sealing ship laid down in 1875 that had served a lengthy term in the Bering Sea, and the *North Star* with its wooden hull. Aware of intercepted radio signals suggesting that the Germans were broadcasting weather reports, he headed for Scoresbysund and the headquarters of the Sledge Patrol.

In early September 1941, the Sledge Patrol reported that a small group of men, possibly Germans, had been put ashore near the mouth of Franz Joseph Fjord, about three hundred kilometers north of Scoresbysund. On the 12th of September, crew on the *Northland* spotted a Norwegian-flagged trawler in MacKenzie Bay near the entrance to the bay. Smith sent a party to board the trawler where they found an array of radio equipment unusual for a fishing boat. Upon interrogation, the crew admitted landing men and radios, and the ship was seized, the first German vessel to be captured by Americans in World War II.

That night a raiding party of twelve from the *Northland*, under the command of Lt. Leroy McCluskey, surrounded a hunter's hut on the coast. They burst open the door, surprising three Germans. Feinting realization that the game was up, the trio offered to make coffee for the Americans and built a fire. With seconds to spare, McCluskey seized the radio code book before the Germans could use it to fuel the flames.[81] In 1943 Smith was promoted to rear admiral and given command of the US Navy's Task Force 24, which included all cutters working the North Atlantic including weather ships broadcasting data on which D-day forecasters would depend.

CHAPTER FOUR

Unseen Allies

When it rains you never feel like you should be anywhere but home.

—WITH APOLOGIES TO ELISE BROACH,
SHAKESPEARE'S SECRET

When Belgium was overrun by the Germans and its King Leopold abdicated on May 28, 1940, thirty-one-year-old Albert Toussaint fled his homeland in a sailing kayak. Toussaint was a "calculator" employed by the Royal Meteorological Institute at its forecast office at Haren, the national airport north of Brussels. The institute was the equivalent of the US Weather Bureau.

Despite efforts by British Prime Minister Neville Chamberlain and the US ambassador to Great Britain Joseph P. Kennedy to appease Hitler, only the most naïve residents of the Low Countries (Belgium, the Netherlands, and Luxemburg) believed war could be avoided. Their flat terrain offered a virtually broad highway hundreds of miles wide across which the Germans had advanced toward France in July 1914 at the outset of the First World War. Oldsters remembered how soldiers of the Deutsches Heer, as the German Army was then known, had moved across the lowlands on foot or in wagons pulled by horses. Trucks were few and armored cars even rarer. Planes of the *Die Fliegertruppen des deutschen Kaiserreiches* ("Imperial German Flying Corps"), principally unarmed biplanes—Albatros B.IIs and Aviatik B.Is—flew reconnaissance missions at a sedate sixty miles per hour. The infamous "Rape of Belgium," rife with brutalities to civilians, stretched on for two horror-filled months in 1914.

Then the Germans came again, crossing the border on May 10, 1940. Capable of top speeds in excess of four hundred miles per hour, Messerschmitt 109s and Focke-Wulf 190s strafed terrified Belgians fleeing from their homes. Stuka dive bombers screamed blind death out of the skies. Panzer IV tanks rumbled farther in one hour than a World War I soldier could walk in eight. Unlike 1914, the Wehrmacht conquest of Belgium required just eighteen days.

A PACK OF BEAGLES

Imagine how frantic these few weeks of May 1940 must have been for the scholarly scientists of Belgian's Royal Meteorological Institute, which was staffed with civilians like the Met Office. Little more than a week after the Germans blitzed into Poland on September 1, 1939, Jules-M. Ch. Jaumotte, the institute's director, implemented plans made in 1936 to transform his agency into a military meteorological service to provide for the needs of the Belgian army and air force. Baron Albert de Dorlodot, a colleague of Jaumotte's, was placed in charge.

But there was no time. The weathermen were ordered to fall back in front of the onrushing German horde. They were supposed to take with them their equipment or render it useless to the invaders. Five days after the fighting started, the institute abandoned its primary forecasting and communications center near Brussels and moved to a new headquarters at De Panne, eighty miles to the northwest on the coast, roughly fourteen miles northeast of Dunkirk.

Thirteen days later the fighting was over. Heeding orders to escape from De Panne as best he could, Toussaint and another meteorologist, Simon de Backer, launched De Backer's frail craft to sail for England, one hundred miles away across the North Sea. With fair winds, it would be a voyage of a week or less. Their alternatives were not palatable. At best they could hide and wait out the German occupation. Chances were good that they'd be captured and placed behind barbed wire as prisoners of war. Worse case: They'd be conscripted as forced laborers.

With astounding good fortune, or maybe a bit of advance knowledge since the British Admiralty had authorized Operation Dynamo, the withdrawal of Allied forces from Dunkirk, two days earlier, Toussaint steered into the path of the evacuation fleet. He and his mate were rescued by the HMS *Skipjack*, a minesweeper, and ferried to England. (On June 1, as the *Skipjack* left Dunkirk with another load of 275 soldiers, she was attacked by a flight of German Ju 88s and sunk.)[82]

Once on British soil, his colleague joined the Free French and was sent to Africa. Toussaint took up a post in London working for Lt. Col. Louis Wouters, the Belgian military attaché. A few months later, he enrolled in the Brigade Prion, the 1st Belgian Infantry Brigade, composed of soldiers from his country and Luxemburg who'd escaped to England. He trained in artillery where he felt his knowledge of how winds aloft affect the flight of shells might be helpful. Soon, though, he became restive. It was apparent that his unit would not see action for quite some time. He put in for intelligence work, overseen by the super-secret British Special Operations Executive (SOE). The officers who vetted his personality and bona fides thought it might be useful if he, a trained meteorologist, might parachute into Belgium and organize a network to send weather reports back to the RAF's bomber command. Such information could also be useful when the invasion of northwest Europe was launched, as everyone in England was sure it would be. Toussaint jumped at the chance. His operation was code-named *Beagle,* perhaps for the small hunting hound.

He no doubt underwent the standard four-week course at Ringway near Manchester to learn how to parachute from a plane like those flown by 161 Squadron, whose mission it was to drop agents into occupied France and Germany. He was then probably schooled in the use of clandestine radio codes at Thame Park outside of Oxford followed by Tempsford, from which 161 Squadron and its sibling 138 Squadron, known as "The Cloak and Dagger Squadrons" or "The Tempsford Taxis," operated.[83]

Around 10:00 p.m. on August 23, 1942, Toussaint and two radiomen, Pierre Jooris and Augustin Roblain, climbed the short ladder into the tail section of a twin-engine Whitley, which was favored by SOE for parachuting agents into occupied northern France. The aft fuselage of the Whitley is barely four feet wide. Toussaint and the radio operators sat, legs stretched out, with their parachutes padding their backs against the plane's cold steel ribs. Along with radios built into small suitcases, they carried forged identity papers and a stash of Belgian francs. In a few minutes they were settled, and the awkward-looking aircraft with its twin tail trundled down the taxiway, paused at the end of the runway, revved its engines, and vanished into the dusk.

Two hours later, the jumpmaster helped Toussaint hook up his static line and ease his legs over the edge of the hatch in the floor of the Whitley. With a heave, the agent flung his arms upward, straightened his body, and dropped into the night. A sharp jolt told him his chute had opened and he began to swing gently beneath the drifting canopy. Jooris and Roblain followed. The sound from the blacked-out bomber faded away.

They landed safely with all equipment intact. The surroundings, though, confused Toussaint. The landmarks did not match those described in his briefing. The pilot had erred and dropped the clandestine team near "Herdin" (probably Hesdin) in occupied France, which was, according to the pilot's after-action report, about forty miles from the intended drop zone close to Rienne in southwestern Belgium, just across the border from France. The trio buried their chutes, picked up their gear, and began their long stealthy trudge across country.

IN SEARCH OF ZÉRO

Jooris and Roblain had been sent to make contact with Zéro,[84] the Belgian resistance group developed by Frans Kerkhofs en Luc, initially to gather economic and political intelligence. During the war, they would rescue scores of downed Allied aircrew. In early September, members of Zéro arranged for Toussaint to lodge in Rienne near an inn managed by Madame Edmond Brichet, a stern widow whose brother had been killed by the Germans in World War I. Her hatred of the *Boche* (Germans) roiled far below her surface like the boiling ferrous magma at the core of the earth. A few days later Toussaint was put in touch with physicist Max Cosyns, who, with Auguste Piccard, had achieved a world-record–setting balloon ascent into the stratosphere a decade earlier. Cosyns had been instructed by Zéro to assist Toussaint in the creation of a network of meteorologists to provide daily weather observations for the British.

Madame Brichet's husband had been a highly regarded watchmaker; their son, Robert, continued the business from the inn. Toussaint adopted the cover of an apprentice watchmaker, about which he knew nothing. He was known as "Arsene Libott." Every day he went to his workbench at Robert's shop. He sat there for all to see working on a broken clock. But it was not a timepiece he was repairing; he was restoring the network of meteorologists who would become weather spies. Robert, a former weather telegrapher, and his sixteen-year-old sister, Thérèse, were Toussaint's first recruits. Robert became "Roland," and Thérèse became "Zézette." He taught Zézette Morse code and, with instruments provided by Cosyns, how to make basic weather observations. On November 1, 1942, Toussaint sent his first report for the RAF. It would be received by Station X, code name for Bletchley Park, decrypted, and forwarded to the Met Office at Dunstable where its validity would be assessed. If the data were consistent with readings from elsewhere, Toussaint's report would be incorporated into weather charts used by the RAF's Bomber Command.

Toussaint and Roland hid their transmitter in the attic of the inn. At first Toussaint and later Roland and two brothers, Emile and Fernand Montreuil (code-named "Etienne" and "Franz") would tap out their weather broadcasts at 2:00 p.m. every day. Downstairs, Madame Brichet stood guard with a big stick. Should she sense the slightest suspicion, she'd beat the ceiling with her stick and the transmission would cease immediately. It was a dicey business. The Gestapo and their radio direction vans were on constant patrol. But Rienne was then as it is now, a tiny town, and the feared German secret police concentrated on Brussels and Antwerp and apparently paid the hamlet scant attention. Yet every time Beagle went on air with its transmissions, there could come the dreaded crash through the door by agents with pistols drawn, and excruciating interrogation that would end, if they were lucky, with execution in the village square.

Toussaint grew his network. On September 13, 1943, Beagle II went on the air from Berneau, about ten miles south of Maastricht. It was joined on March 1, 1944, by Beagle III in Wigene, just west of Ghent and not far from De Panne, the last headquarters of the Royal Meteorological Institute in 1942. Beagle IV first raised its voice on June 24, 1944, from Neder-over-Hembeek, a suburb of Brussels. All told Beagle trained forty weather observers who broadcast 1,297 weather observations from the fall of 1942 until the country was liberated in late 1944.[85]

Philippe Carrozza, in a sidebar to his 2004 interview with Thérèse in *L'Avenir du Luxembourg*, reports that Beagle's observations were made daily at 1:00 p.m. and transmitted at 2:00 p.m. He wrote that the data were compared to readings intercepted from the Germans and became useful in breaking German codes.[86] For their steadfast heroism, Toussaint received the Distinguished Service Order from the British and Thérèse, the Croix de Guerre with palms from the French and the Medal of Courage from the British. Toussaint's valor is testimony to the mettle of many professional meteorologists—Allied and German—during the war.

Baron de Dorlodot, with Toussaint, had fallen back to De Panne and, before the capitulation, Jaumotte sent him to France to re-establish connections with the French weather service. But the rapidity of the German advance made his mission impossible, and he escaped to England. In early 1944 he prepared a lengthy plan for the re-establishment of Belgian's Royal Meteorological Institute to provide weather information when his country was eventually liberated. His plan was forwarded to Stagg on February 26, 1944, but it provides little clue of Stagg's awareness of Beagle.[87] The existence of Beagle was closely held and little if any mention of it is found in Allied documents. Yet weather observations from Beagle, though not their specific source, were well known to the Met Office. Stagg, no doubt, saw their synoptic data on weather charts and may or may not have wondered about their origin.

VOICES FROM THE EAST

While Belgian meteorologists might have had an inkling of the fate that could befall them when the Germans massed on the border in the spring of 1940, their colleagues in Poland had no warning at all. After dark on August 31, 1939, Nazi Alfred Naujocks led a group of secret agents, dressed in Polish army uniforms, to seize the radio station at Gleiwitz in Upper Selesia, Germany, and broadcast anti-German propaganda in Polish. The following morning Hitler, claiming that this was yet another incident of Polish aggression, launched the *Blitzkrieg,* the first lightning war of coordinated assault by armor, aircraft, and infantry in the world, which would see it again in Hitler's invasion of Belgium eight months later.

By the end of September, Poland had been partitioned into unequal thirds. To the west, the Germans annexed all the territory adjacent to Prussia including East Prussia. In a secret pact signed prior to the outbreak of fighting, the Russians gained control of lands east of the River Bug. Both invaders were ruthless in their persecution of Polish professionals, considered sub-humans by the Reich and the Reds. At best, capture meant internment in a POW camp and forced labor in a German factory. Thousands, though, were sent by the Russians to subarctic Siberia to cut wood. Once there, they had to build their own camps, and until barracks were constructed, they lived in trenches chiseled in the ground frozen solid with permafrost. The risks of capture by the Reds or the Nazis that Polish meteorologists faced made the fate that could await arrested Belgian meteorologists seem almost benign.

Before the war, the *Państwowy Instytut Meteorologiczny* (PIM), the Polish meteorological service, operated thirteen hundred stations. Though subordinate to PIM, the Polish Army's own weather service provided forecasts to the air force and artillery. After the

German and Russian partition, the observation posts in occupied zones fell under Axis control. Yet about 40 percent of the center of the country, cut off from the Baltic and totally landlocked, was managed by a civic administration known as the General Government. Weather stations not in occupied areas were placed under the department responsible for railways and continued to gather daily synoptic data and issue local forecasts.

Within a year of the invasion, various Polish resistance units coalesced into the *Armia Krajowa*, or Home Army known simply as the "AK." Its first task was to establish reliable communications with the Polish government in exile in London. AK devoted its efforts primarily to sabotage and intelligence gathering. At first, liaison with free Polish leaders in England could be maintained through the country's embassies in Budapest and Bucharest. But when Hungary and Romania joined the Axis powers in 1940, those lines of communications closed, and the AK had to rely on airdrops and risky treks across the Carpathian Mountains. Both required accurate weather reports, and it established a meteorological arm led by Capt. Wiktor Dobrzański, a former met officer with a pre-war Polish bomber squadron.

Dobrzański enlisted the help of noted PIM meteorologist Romuald Gumiński and astronomer Jan Gadomski (for whom a crater on the moon is named) to develop the clandestine weather service. From the Warsaw Observatory, Gadomski provided necessary instruments. Weathermen from PIM stations in Cracow and Lwow in the Russian zone took part as did later staff at observatories in Gordno and Wilno (now Vilnius, Lithuania). The network was expanded to include posts in Zakopane, Pozan, Gdynia, and Lubin. Eventually the secret Met arm deployed mobile observatories that gathered reports as needed.

Mainly women served as couriers carrying weather reports to hidden radio transmitters. Z. Bartkowski wrote in "Polish Meteorology in the Second World War: A War without Weapons", that "In Warsaw, for example, the Observatory sent messages to Snaidecki Street some kilometers away, and the radio transmitter was moved around in the suburbs to deceive the monitors."[88] Such work was rife with danger. Capture meant torture and then that fearsome ride in a railway cattle car to a concentration camp and a cruel, brutal, slow death by beating and starvation. Starting in the first months of 1941, seven reports were sent each day. By 1943 AK's communications regiment was regularly intercepting encoded German radio messages including weather reports that were forwarded to Bletchley's cryptanalysts. The data helped the British Met Office piece together weather charts for Nazi-controlled Europe, intelligence crucial for the weather forecast for D-day.

The straight-line distance from RAF bases in southeast England to the AK's operational area in Poland is about one thousand miles. Early in the war, the Allies had few long-range bombers available to parachute in arms, ammo, radios, or agents to aid the Polish Home Army. In addition, electronic navigation beams were not available to guide supply aircraft to fields where AK soldiers were waiting. Drop zones close to rivers and lakes were selected because those landmarks were prominently visible on moonlit nights. Forecasting from Dunstable whether the moon was shining on a farm south of Cracow was nigh impossible.

A few days before a supply mission was scheduled, the BBC would broadcast a prearranged series of songs to alert the AK to what they called "nights of vigilance." The reception committee that usually included a meteorologist and the group's commander had a radio/telephone so they could talk with the aircraft's pilot when the plane came in range. By that time the meteorologist would have measured cloud height, wind speed and direction, and precipitation. From February 1941 through November 1944, when the Soviets had occupied most of the country and AK's need for arms was thought to be over, 858 air supply sorties were launched and 483 accomplished their missions delivering 345 agents and 4,143 containers.[89]

WHISPERS FROM THE NETHER LAND

Along with weather information from Poland and Belgium, Groep (Group) Packard provided synoptic observations from the Netherlands. In November 1942, resistance members Henk Deinum, Marinus Vader, and aviation technician Aad de Roode, with the assistance of Paul Johan van der Stok (reportedly a British agent), attempted to establish communication with England to provide intelligence and weather reports. Their efforts, code-named Groep Packard, were star-crossed from the beginning and were only resolved with the arrival of a man named Louis d'Aulnis de Bourouill.

Commander of an antiaircraft battery in the uneasy days after the German invasion of Poland, d'Aulnis joined the underground following the surrender of the Netherlands on May 15, 1940. When eighteen members of his group were rounded up and executed by the Gestapo, d'Aulnis fled his homeland for England. Taking an established escape route through Antwerp and Toulouse, he crossed the Pyrenees on foot, was picked up by Spanish Police, interned briefly in Barcelona, and then released to the British pending receipt of a visa to leave Spain. Five months passed until he and another refugee escaped to Seville, sailed to Gibraltar, and ultimately reached Glasgow on January 2, 1942.

Escorted by military police to London, d'Aulnis was held in the Royal Victoria Patriotic School until his identity was verified. By May 1943, he'd been commissioned a second lieutenant in the

Army of the Netherlands' Princess Irene Brigade, completed airborne and code training, and was ready to parachute into Holland. He jumped from a Halifax bomber on the night of June 10 and landed near Meppel. Making his way to Amsterdam, he rendezvoused with Vader and other members of Packard, delivered radios, and helped establish a weather reporting network. By May 1944 he was serving with Groep Kees.[90]

READINGS FROM THE RUSSIAN BEAR

Along with observations from Belgium, The Netherlands, and Poland, within eighteen months after Hitler's invasion of Russia in June 1941, the Allies were receiving synoptic reports from the Soviets. Roosevelt and Stalin were eager to establish air routes to ferry fighters to Russia, and the most likely route brought Bell P-39 Airacobras up though Alaska where they were transferred to Russian pilots at Army Air Stations in places like Galena and Nome for the short hop across the Bering Strait to Siberia.

Stalin insisted that a meteorologist accompany the American mission headed by Maj. Gen. Follett Bradley, and Gen. Arnold had tabbed Yates, then a Lt. Col. and in charge of the army section of the Joint Weather Central at the Pentagon, known as the Air Force Weather Central. Arnold summoned Yates to his office late one Friday afternoon in July 1942 and told him that in two days he was headed to Russia to help set up the ferry route and to coordinate the exchange of weather information with the Allies' new partner.

In Moscow, he met Lt. Gen. Yevginiy K. Federov, chief of the Soviet Hydrometeorological Service. Both thirty-four, they hit it off. Federov spoke a little English and a little French. Yates spoke a little French too. On trips to inspect weather stations Soviet minders did not accompany them and Federov spoke freely. "Anything I can do to help you on you let me know," Yates records in his oral history.[91] Along with organizing the joint flow of weather readings—Yates would later reflect that as meteorologists the Russians were highly skilled and had been effective in breaking German codes[92]—he harvested a trove of information that the Soviets might have preferred to keep secret. Upon return to Washington in December after a very hairy flight that carried him over a Japanese airfield in northern China, Yates was awarded the Distinguished Service Medal for the intelligence he gathered.

Was data from the east of importance to the Allies in the campaign to defeat the Germans? That's difficult to say, according to a retired Met Office meteorologist and historian. Were they pivotal in making the forecast for D-day? Probably not. Did they add a tiny but important piece to complete the jigsaw-like puzzle of the weather chart for central Europe? Certainly.

WHEN IRISH EYES ARE SMILING

Within a pair of months after the armistice that ended World War I, tensions flamed between the Irish Volunteers—later to become the Irish Republican Army—and the Royal Irish Constabulary, the British force established to keep peace in what was then the westernmost of the British Isles. Two years of vicious guerilla warfare ended with the Anglo-Irish Treaty of 1922 and established the Irish Free State, which was officially neutral during World War II. However, the treaty stipulated that anchorages, airfields, radio stations, and undersea communications cables remain under British control. The staffs of the new Irish Meteorological Service and the Met Office could not have been closer cousins. The observatory at Cahirciveen had been one of the stations in the first English weather forecasting network established by FitzRoy in 1860.[93]

The British and the Irish collaborated on the exchange of weather information, a collaboration that continued informally after the Irish Free State was replaced by the Irish Republic in 1937. Within a year officials of both countries were negotiating to establish a pact to formalize meteorological collaboration, which was signed in August 1939, just weeks before the outbreak of the Second World War. Ireland provided daily observations to the Met Office from several stations including Foynes, Valentia, Roches Point, Malin Head, and Blacksod Point roughly 500 miles northwest of the beaches at Normandy.

Blacksod Point, so named because of heavy deposits of peat that once covered this rocky spit that pokes south into the Atlantic on the far western coast of Ireland, would become the home of an extremely important source of weather data when Eisenhower was in the throes of deciding to launch or postpone D-day. In 1942, Maureen Flavin answered an advertisement seeking a clerk for the post office there. Single and needing a job, she made the two-day trip from her home in the south of Ireland, was interviewed by the postmistress, found acceptable, and offered the position. She agreed to come and upon taking up her duties, discovered that among them, she was to record weather data.

The dun stuccoed post office was the largest building on Blacksod Point. A fistful of houses and sheds for processing fish surrounded it. To the south sat a square and squat granite lighthouse. The bay provided a sheltered anchorage for transports and the ridge to seaward was dotted with observation posts manned by members of the Irish Defence Forces. Weather observations were taken from instruments housed in a corner of the post office and telegraphed to Dublin where they were forwarded on to Dunstable.

"We had to make our own fun," Maureen Flavin said in a 2011 interview. "We'd have parties and afterwards the readings in the rain gauge were sometimes suspect."[94] It was here that the D-day storms first blew onto European soil.

READING THE GERMANS' MAIL

Without a doubt the best clandestine source of weather data for the Allies came from the Germans themselves. Just weeks before the outbreak of war in September 1939, the Poles presented to astounded British and French cryptologists a pair of Enigma machines. Secreted in diplomatic pouches, the devices were shipped to Paris. There the English retrieved theirs and spirited it across the channel on August 16, the day the commander of German U-boats, Kommodore Karl Dönitz, ordered his submarines to their war stations. Afraid that prying German eyes might spot the cumbersome diplomatic pouch as it passed through customs in Dover, the Britons arranged to have it included in the mountain of baggage accompanying a pair of actors returning from France.[95]

Its final destination was Bletchley Park. There it would be put to use reading the Germans' meteorological mail by a tall, brilliant, mild-mannered, often disheveled, scholar, George C. McVittie, head of the weather section at the Government Code and Cypher School.[96] McVittie was a physicist with a passion for astronomy. In 1923, McVittie entered the University of Edinburgh to study natural philosophy and mathematics under Professor E. T. Whittaker, who that same year warmly recommended Stagg for his employment with the Met Office. In 1930, McVittie earned his doctorate and entered academe. It was a pleasant life of tea, teaching, and research. He wrote and presented papers, and in 1937 authored what he described as a "little book, *Cosmological Theory*."

McVittie became a weatherman by accident. As he told David DeVorkin during an oral history interview in 1978, he registered with the Royal Society "to do whatever one thought one could do, if a war did come on. . . . There was obviously not going to be any astronomy involved in the war—not in 1938—so I put myself down to do meteorological work. Not that I knew any meteorology. Not that I knew anything about it, but it seemed the nearest approach to what I did know about. And so, indeed, it proved to be. Except of course, that what I did eventually get involved in was not mathematical meteorology, but it was reading Hitler's correspondence. . . ." At first, he was the only person at Bletchley trying to break German weather codes, but as 1943 drew to a close his staff would number sixty.[97]

The Kriegsmarine high command had ordered U-boats to broadcast weather reports. A radioman on the sub would translate the report into the Short Weather Cipher, which would be further encrypted by the Enigma machine. Thus doubly encoded, the message was then transmitted. When received by a German radio station on shore, operators there would remove the message's Enigma coding and forward it to meteorologists who could convert the cipher back into weather data. Such messages often contained *Wetter*, the German word for weather. McVittie knew that the Germans had created new ciphers based on the pre-war international weather code and that weather reports were usually transmitted daily at the same time. Since Bletchley possessed captured code books and rotors from Enigma machines, he had a place to start.[98] But no more than that.

Codes changed daily. When McVittie and his crew thought a message might be a weather report, they prepared a *crib*, a guess at some of the plain text like *das Wetter* that the message might include. This was then forwarded to the operators of bombes, mechanical computers that featured banks of spinning disks that correlated with Enigma rotors. The English bombe was developed by Alan Turing and refined by Gordon Welchman from designs the British had seen in Poland.[99] Three or four times a day, couriers on motorbikes sped from Bletchley to Dunstable carrying thin cards bearing intercepted German weather codes stripped of their

Enigma cipher. At Dunstable, a team of cryptanalysts would further decode the German reports and pass the data on to meteorologists who would plot it on charts.[100] While at first it took days to decipher a message, by 1944 only a few hours or less were usually required.

As D-day approached, the bombing of rail lines and communication centers quickened and members of resistance movements in occupied countries severed telephone and telegraph cables. Increasingly, Germans had to rely on radio transmissions to gather and disseminate weather observations. They had no choice. But according to R. P. W. Lewis, writing in *Meteorological Magazine*, "within a year or two (of the invasion of Poland) British Intelligence was able to supply the Central Forecasting Office at Dunstable with information of such good quality, so fast, that surface and upper-air charts could be plotted, covering the whole of Axis-occupied Europe, that for two-thirds of the time were nearly as good as if there had not been a war on at all."[101]

CHAPTER FIVE

Fractious Fellowship

If minds get out of harmony with one another it is like a storm that plays havoc with the garden.

—BUDDHIST SAYING

At the close of the 1930s, two schools of meteorological thought vied for supremacy. Their principles would produce heated dissent among D-day's weather centrals. Furious growth of commercial aviation in the United States following World War I fueled the need for better understanding of the weather. The US Post Office inaugurated airmail between Washington, DC, and New York City on May 15, 1918. The route covered 218 miles with a stop in Philadelphia. A pilot would telephone the next landing field, check weather conditions there, look at the sky as he walked to his plane, climb up on the wing, step into the cockpit, fasten his seatbelt, check the throttle, set the magnetos, and yell to the ground crew to pull the prop. Flying at about sixty miles per hour, the pilot could be reasonably certain that the weather would not change much en route. The first airmail pilots seldom flew higher than three thousand feet so they could see landmarks on the ground and thus be reasonably assured of where they were.

As the power of aircraft engines doubled and doubled again and routes grew longer and planes flew higher, the need for better weather data became apparent. After World War I, a pilot would fly as far toward his destination as he could, but when he encountered a cloud bank, if he were prudent, he'd turn around and land, sometimes at an airport, but frequently in a farmer's field. Commercial aviation was revolutionized in 1926 when Ford introduced its aluminum-skinned Tri-motor airliner. It was capable of five-hundred-mile flights at altitudes up to eighteen thousand feet, though it was usually flown below ten thousand feet for the comfort of its ten passengers and crew. Douglas gave commercial aviation a terrific boost when it brought forth its DC—for Douglas Commercial—series of airliners in 1933. These could cover one thousand miles non-stop.

American meteorology failed to keep pace. According to Charles C. Bates and John F. Fuller in *America's Weather Warriors*, forecasters lacked much in scientific training beyond an aptitude for collecting data and plotting it on maps. Owing to the nation's vast telegraph and increasingly widespread telephone networks, the US Weather Bureau refused to accept theories being pioneered in Norway by Vilhelm and Jacob Bjerknes. The bureau received updates, sometimes as often as hourly, from hundreds of weather stations located at airports scattered across the country. In Washington, meteorologists were continually drawing new maps and making forecasts from observations from these stations. Because weathermen in New York City could pick up the phone and call to find out if it were snowing in the nation's capital or in Nashville or St. Louis, why spend time and money on theoretical atmospheric physics that had yet to be proven accurate?

A REFRESHING BREEZE FROM BERGEN

The Bjerkneses, father and son, were located in Bergen on the coast of Norway and, unlike the Americans, couldn't call anyone to discover the weather to the west. Over the decades, based on observations taken during airplane flights; radiosonde balloon ascents; and weather data such as air temperature, wind speed, atmospheric pressure, precipitation, and cloud cover recorded when ships logged their positions, they came to believe that storms were produced by conflict between large masses of warm moist air and air that was cold and dry. The conflict they envisioned was not one vertical face butting against another. Rather they understood that cold dry air flowed under warm moist air as if it were a wedge pushing the more humid air upward. One felt and could mark the boundary between the two air masses on the ground. If one could plot the angle at which the wedge sloped, its speed, and variations within it, then one would produce a more reliable forecast for the weather for some distance.

The Bjerkneses' view of the weather was three-dimensional, but the United States mainly thought of it in two-dimensional terms based on what its meteorologists could see from the ground. To improve reliability of air travel, the Army Air Service in 1922 installed a string of lighted beacons to guide pilots from Norfolk, Virginia, to New York City and thence west to Dayton, Ohio, where the service tested new aircraft designs. Along the route numerous stations were installed to keep pilots advised of changing weather conditions. The emphasis was on providing pilots with current observations and not forecasts.[102]

That began to change when a twenty-seven-year-old Swiss-born Swede, Carl-Gustav Rossby, turned up at the US Weather Bureau in 1926 courtesy of a grant from The American-Scandinavian Foundation. Rossby was something of a meteorological wunderkind. Having earned the equivalent of a three-year bachelor's degree in mathematics, mechanics, and astronomy from the University of Stockholm in less than a year, he joined the Geophysical Institute in Bergen, Norway, where Bjerknes held forth. In his biography of Rossby, Brigham Narins cites comments by Tor Bergeron, a meteorologist who also worked at Bergen: "the twenty-year-old Rossby had 'amazing persuasive and organizing' abilities; though inexperienced, Rossby presented ideas that Bergeron reported 'took our breath away.'"

Though brought to the Weather Bureau explicitly to study the application of Bergen's polar theory to American weather, under the hide-bound leadership of Charles F. "Mossback" Marvin, chief of the Weather Bureau since 1913, Rossby's ideas were given the shortest shrift. Further upsetting the chief and his colleagues, the Daniel Guggenheim Fund for the Promotion of Aeronautics chose upstart Rossby to work on weather aspects of flight planning. After a fractious and frustrating year, Rossby left the bureau in 1927 for a position with the fund. Piqued to say the least, Marvin declared Rossby *persona non grata* and sent letters to all of its stations ordering them to have nothing to do with him.

The bureau's acute disapproval carried very little weight. Rossby would become one of the most highly regarded among America's meteorologists. His work for the Guggenheim Fund carried him to San Francisco. There he and the local office of the Weather Bureau established a prototype of a service for providing weather information to pilots. The experiment was so successful that the bureau ate its humble pie and extended the reports to all its stations.[103]

His assistant was another bright meteorologist, the twenty-two-year-old Horace Byers, who would in a few years advise his brother-in-law, young Irving Krick, to forget a career in music in favor of forecasting the weather.[104] By 1928, Byers was an associate professor at the Daniel Guggenheim Aeronautical Laboratory at MIT. In the late 1930s, building on the work of Jacob Bjerknes, Rossby developed a mathematical formula for predicting the location of what we know as the jet stream, which brings us our daily weather.

Rossby was not the only one making waves among meteorologists in Washington during the 1920s. Soon after he set foot in the Weather Bureau's headquarters at 24th and M Street, he was no doubt sought out by First Lt. Francis W. Reichelderfer, who headed the navy's aerological desk there. "Reich," as he was known to all, had read Jacob Bjerknes's seminal paper *On the Structure of Moving Cyclones,* which was published in 1918. Schooled on Willis I. Milham's *Meteorology,* first published in 1912, and the confusing and contradictory tome *Weather Forecasting in the United States* written by a quartet of the bureau's most senior forecasters and published by the service in 1916, Reichelderfer must have felt about the arrival of Rossby with his firsthand study under the family Bjerknes the way one feels when a fresh cold front flushes away the oppressive humidity of a stifling summer day. It was Reich who brought Rossby to the attention of the Guggenheims.

Reichelderfer became chief of the bureau in 1938, largely on the recommendation of Robert A. Millikan, chairman of Caltech's governing executive council. Millikan, a German weatherman during World War I, had gotten to know him well when the navy had sent him out to California to assess the new meteorology program that Krick was chairing at the university. Reichelderfer engineered Rossby's return to the bureau in 1939 as assistant chief for research and development. Together they would set to work laying a new foundation based on modern science for the service's forecasts.[105]

Throughout the war, they would clash repeatedly with Krick's unfettered end runs around constituted authority and his unshaken belief that his analog weather types were the *sine qua non* of weather forecasting. Yet in the long run, disciples of the Bergen school were amassed against him. Three of the four university departments training wartime meteorologists in the United States were led by

Bergen adherents. Rossby, in 1941, headed a new department at the University of Chicago. Jacob Bjerknes ran the program at the University of California, Los Angeles. And Norwegian Sverre Petterssen, who'd fled his homeland prior to the German invasion in 1940, held forth at MIT. Among them they'd train hundreds of forecasters for the military. However, Krick, at Caltech, remained a dominant force largely because of his skills as a self-promoter.

MAELSTROM IN WASHINGTON

Italy invaded Ethiopia in 1935, and Germany began flexing its military muscle in the Spanish Civil War in 1936 by aiding Franco's fascists with armor and airpower. Then Japan was ravishing China by 1937 after seizing Manchuria in 1931. The United States public and Congress stood staunch in its desire to remain isolated from any foreign conflict, a position adopted after World War I when President Woodrow Wilson failed to convince Congress to ratify the war-ending Treaty of Versailles and then refused membership in the League of Nations.

Instead of preparing for war as most of Germany's neighbors were desperately trying to do, the American military focused mainly on defending the nation's borders. The Signal Corps provided weather services for the army and its Air Corps. These consisted primarily of a string of posts that made observations and gave information to aviators. But on the first of July 1937, orders were cut separating most of military meteorology from the Signal Corps and placing it under Air Corps command. After all, weren't the army's fliers the primary clients for knowledge about the weather?

The edict further ordered that all Air Corps meteorological officers must be rated pilots or navigators. After the switch, the fledgling air weather service numbered just twenty-two officers and 280 enlisted men, woefully inadequate for events unfolding in Europe and Asia. Yet in classic Washington bureaucratic style, the Army refused to cede development and supply of meteorological equipment and supplies as well as all weather-related communication to the Air Corps. Those stayed in the hands of the Signal Corps.[106]

Just two months before the invasion of Poland, Sverre Petterssen ran into Luftwaffe general Richard Habermehl at a conference of the Maritime Commission of the International Meteorological Organization in Berlin. Habermehl told Petterssen that the German air force employed roughly 2,700 meteorologists, most of them PhDs. In contrast, the British had about one hundred; France, eighty; and Norway, fewer than twenty.[107] Six years earlier in 1933, Hitler had appointed Hermann Goering head of the Reich Air Ministry, the Luftwaffe had been reorganized later that year, and ever since the Nazis had been preparing for unprecedented offensive air war.

Hitler's blitzkrieg across Europe caught America flat-footed. Washington was in near panic. Interventionists who knew the nation would ultimately be drawn into the war were afraid that Britain would fall and that Germany would be victorious before the United States could come to the aid of its longtime allies England and France. In 1939, the Air Corps' Weather Section was commanded by Merewether, then a first lieutenant, with a staff of just two on the third floor of the Munitions Building in downtown Washington, DC. In the building adjacent to the navy building, a staff of four men constituted the headquarters of its weather service.

With Rommel rolling across France in 1940, the Air Corps' Weather Section "became a madhouse of people rushing around, telephones ringing constantly, and everything having to be done immediately," writes Fuller in *Thor's Legions*. Where plain white paper was the medium of correspondence, now these sheets were edged with red to signal the need for immediate action. Soon red cardboard covers appeared demanding that the recipient address the issue instantly. Added to intense tension was the incessant pounding of jackhammers and periodic choking fogs of construction dust as the building was fitted with a fourth story. All that, exacerbated by the capital's brutal summer heat and humidity, felled Merewether's boss with a heart attack.[108] Still, there was nothing else for the Air Corps' skinny staff of meteorologists to do but "keep 'em flying."

By the spring of 1941, the Air Corps Research Center, at Bolling Field in Washington, DC, was providing forty-eight-hour forecasts. Not good enough, thought Hap Arnold, the Air Corps' commanding general. He wanted ten-day forecasts like those provided by Professor Franz Baur, head of the German Institute for Long Range Weather Forecasting. Arnold remembered how Krick had bragged that he could predict the weather a month ahead. He ordered Merewether to phone Krick at Caltech and have him set up a long-range forecasting course for Air Corps personnel.

Though Krick had spent time at Bergen, he had met Baur in Europe in 1934 and had become deeply infatuated with Baur's use of analog forecasting based on weather types. By the time four Air Corps officers could fly to Pasadena to study analog predictions, Krick had developed the course Arnold wanted. A few months later the four were back at Bolling and so was Krick. On October 20, the center issued its first thirty-day forecast for army maneuvers in the Carolinas. The actual weather did not match what had been predicted, but the Air Corps and later the Air Force continued to use Krick's system regardless of its accuracy.[109]

It didn't take long for American military meteorology to leap to its feet after the first Nakijima torpedo bomber began its run on Pearl Harbor's battleship row at 7:48 a.m. Hawaiian time on December 7, 1941. In March 1942, the Weather Section became the Weather Directorate, commanded by Lt. Col. Don Zimmerman.

Zimmerman ran headlong into Krick's coterie of high-ranking brass and was ultimately sacked by Arnold for arguing too stridently that Krick's thirty-day forecasts were not based on any rational science and had been proven inaccurate.

During a heated exchange with Arnold in his office, the crusty general yelled, "Get the hell out of here, Zimmerman." The die was cast. Zimmerman's replacement, Col. Hunt Bassett, was ordered that "no obstacles must be placed in Maj. Krick's way or any other long range forecaster's way in order to get the job done," wrote Arnold's chief of staff, Maj. Gen. George Stratemeyer. According to him, Arnold "was going to have long range forecasting and that he intended to utilize all methods whether they are right or wrong, or at least until they are proven wrong."[110]

Despite occasional stints in Arnold's kennel for his importune approaches to US Chief of Staff Gen. Marshall and for issuing unauthorized forecasts that confused Lt. Gen. Patton and Torch's task force commander, Krick, now a lieutenant colonel in the Weather Directorate, still topped Arnold's list of top-flight Air Corps meteorologists.

At Trident, the third American-British strategy conference, which was held in Washington in May 1943, Roosevelt and Churchill and their combined chiefs of staff set May 1, 1944, as the date for the invasion of northwestern France. With less than a year to go, pressure for improved long-range forecasts grew. Earlier that year, the weather directorate had been consolidated in four rings on the fourth[111] floor of the Pentagon, then the world's largest office building (each floor of the Pentagon is made up of five rings and the weather directorate occupied offices in four of its fourth-floor rings).

Bassett established a program to verify long-range weather forecasts. Six experimental forecasting units were established with one of them, Long Range Forecasting Unit A, using Krick's weather types. One wag on Bassett's staff received permission to organize a seventh unit, the Special North American Forecast Unit, and posted a sign on his door identifying his as the office of SNAFU. When it came to predicting the weather just three days in advance, Krick's techniques fared worse than all others.[112] Yet Arnold and his commander of US Strategic Air Forces in Europe ignored the evidence and, even in the face of disagreement from the Met Office and the Admiralty, backed Krick's forecast for D-day, though it would prove to be very wrong.

ENGLISH EYES ON THE SKIES

Surrounded by crowds moments after returning to England following his infamous meeting with Hitler on September 30, 1938, British Prime Minister Neville Chamberlain waved a document that he and the Reich's Führer had signed pledging to work together to avoid war. That afternoon, on the steps of 10 Downing Street, Chamberlain uttered the sentence that would haunt him forever: "My good friends, for the second time in our history, a British Prime Minister has returned from Germany bringing peace with honor. I believe it is peace for our time. We thank you from the bottom of our hearts. Go home and get a nice quiet sleep."[113] That's just what the Nazis hoped the British would do. For the very day after the pact was signed, Hitler violated its principles and rolled into the Sudetenland, the German-speaking region of Czechoslovakia. Fortunately, Hitler's plundering Germany's neighbor to the south peeled the scales from the eyes of the British Met Office.

As Malcolm Walker puts it in *History of the Meteorological Office*, in the advent of war plans were laid to disperse operations from London "to the provinces." The Forecasting Division was slated to move into new offices at Dunstable, a small town with high ground for excellent radio reception about thirty-five miles north of London. The RAF's main communications center was five miles away and seven miles farther was Bletchley Park. The new quarters were not ready as Germans massed on the Polish border. With just scant three-days' notice, the division was evacuated from London to temporary quarters in Birmingham on August 27, 1939. The forecasters arrived at their new home at Dunstable during a heavy snow in February 1940. From the moment it left London, the Met Office never missed making a forecast.

Code-named ETA, either for the seventh letter of the Greek alphabet or for initials of Evacuation Temporary Accommodations,[114] the low wooden hutments at Dunstable were surrounded by a high chain link fence topped with barbed wire. Tall steel poles supported wire netting festooned with leaves fashioned from lead and sprayed with camouflage paint to hide the buildings from aerial surveillance. RAF pilots knew it well as that phony hill near Downs. Forecasters worked in a room that resembled a classroom with long rows of adjoining slant-top desks. An aura of academe prevailed. Revetments surrounding the building prevented forecasters from seeing much of the weather outside, and they seemed to have little interest in it, so intent were they in analyzing synoptic data that streamed endlessly into the wireless room. The exception was Douglas, the former Royal Flying Corps observer, later pilot, and then aerial meteorological pioneer, who paid it rigorous attention.[115]

Three of the forecasters were Norwegian expatriates. Foremost among them was Petterssen, who would come to lead Dunstable's upper-air unit. Toward the end of August 1941, he received a cable from Adm. Hjalmar Riiser-Larsen, commander of Norwegian air forces in Great Britain, asking him to fly to England and provide weather forecasts to squadrons flying missions over his homeland.

At that time, Petterssen was wrapping up his second year as chair of the Meteorology Department at MIT and was deeply engaged in training fledgling Army Air Corps weathermen. When a second more urgent telegram arrived from the admiral, Petterssen donned the frock of a lieutenant colonel in the Norwegian Air Force and flew to the British Isles. He arrived on November 9, roughly a month before the United States would declare war on Japan and Germany.

Shortly after reaching London, Petterssen sat down with Sir Nelson Johnson, head of the Met Office. Johnson asked him where he felt he could make the largest contribution to the war effort and then proceeded to outline the needs he faced. First was forecasting of winds aloft to limit aircraft and aircrew losses and to increase the success of bombing raids on targets in Germany and occupied Europe. In addition, long-range forecasting was proving a thorny issue. Though a team at Dunstable was evaluating different techniques, none appeared reliable. Finally, Johnson thought that Petterssen might be very helpful as a consultant in the preparation of forecasts for major operations.

After weighing the options, Petterssen decided against accepting responsibility for long-range forecasting, which he felt was a quagmire that showed little promise. He felt the role of roving expert might be fascinating, but just how effective could he be? And he wondered how he'd get along as a Norwegian interloping on British turf. Knowing that weather at high altitude often foretold and could dramatically influence that on the ground, he told Johnson that he would prefer to work on upper-air forecasting.[116]

In January 1942, Petterssen began to build a staff and took over the space in Dunstable's forecast room that had been vacated recently by the team decoding foreign weather reports.[117] That group had been established in April 1940 and was known as IDA, perhaps after Mount Ida, the mountain of Greek mythology mentioned in the *Iliad* and the *Aeneid*. It was the Met Office unit responsible for decoding weather data intercepted from countries occupied by the Germans.

Due to its vastness, the outbreak of war with Finland, and the nonaggression pact signed with Hitler, Russia was one of the few European countries that encoded internal transmission of its weather data before September 1939. IDA set its sights on cracking that code and achieved remarkable success.

After war began, Russia continued to use the same code to broadcast weather data to other stations in the country. The Germans received these reports and rebroadcast them within an hour or so, this time encrypted with Enigma. These messages and IDA's reading of the original Russian messages were telexed to Bletchley, which added immeasurably to deciphering Enigma. Eventually, IDA was reading weather data from Vichy France, Italy, Hungary, Romania, and Bulgaria. The reports fleshed out weather charts for Europe that had gone dark when war began. Weather information from France would become very important when the final forecasts were prepared for D-day.

THE ADMIRALTY UNDERGROUND

Meteorology was an important but not the most crucial concern of the British in May 1940. If Europe were to be liberated from Nazi control, England was the last best place from which the continent could be freed. The Luftwaffe ruled the skies. The growing U-boat fleet would strangle the island of supplies. As French ports along the Channel filled with landing barges, the German's *Oberkommando der Wehrmacht* (OKW), supreme command of German armed forces, raced to complete plans for Operation Sea Lion, the invasion of the United Kingdom.

Unlike in Washington where the fall of France suddenly spurred America's senior military planners to leap with seeming frenzy from one harried decision to the next, their colleagues on Britain's Chiefs of Staff Committee had become keenly aware of the thunder from Germany since 1935 when Hitler abrogated the Treaty of Versailles by instituting a draft. In 1936, the Air Ministry estimated that, should war break out, as many as two hundred thousand could die each week from an onslaught of German bombers. Upon becoming prime minister in May 1940, Churchill implemented a plan initiated by the Committee of Imperial Defence to turn a suite of musty basement storage rooms a short walk from 10 Downing Street into a bombproof subterranean shelter from which the English war effort would be directed.

About a quarter mile to the north, across Horse Guards Parade from the hidden bunker, rose the elegant 1726 Admiralty Office Building, which housed the headquarters of the Royal Navy. Fretful that the Luftwaffe would turn its full attention on London, the Admiralty ordered construction of an underground fortress along the building's western wall. Work began in 1940 and was completed the following year, none too soon. On the night of April 16, 1941, three bombs struck the Admiralty, knocking out its communications with shore bases and ships at sea. Not long thereafter, the Admiralty moved sensitive operations into "an extraordinary object like a mud fort," as Rear Adm. R. K. Dickson, who worked there during the war, described the massive bomb shelter.[118] Roofed with twenty feet of reinforced concrete and with slits in its walls from which guns could fire should German soldiers attempt to capture the city, the Citadel, as it came to be called, was the nerve center of the Royal Navy worldwide during the war. A maze of tunnels linked it to nearby government offices. Air-conditioned and lit by lamps bright as daylight, Dickson remembered it as a "wonderful place inside."

The Royal Naval Meteorological Service set up its central forecasting office in a sub-basement of the Admiralty next door. It was also assigned space in the bowels of the Citadel itself. To reach the center, one entered the Citadel through a conventional-looking door protected by a blast wall, descended two floors to the bottom via a long ramp, passed through what resembled a door to a bank vault designed to protect against bomb blasts and poison gas, and entered a passageway that led to the small room of about twelve feet by sixteen feet. Most of the space was devoted to preparing forecasts for the fleet. The remainder was allocated to a pair of meteorologists who were in on the planning for D-day. All relied on the same synoptic data used by civilians at Dunstable.

The Royal Naval Meteorological Service may have been the smallest of D-Day's three forecasting centrals. At the close of the Great War, four British organizations provided meteorological services: the Air Ministry's Met Office, a branch of the Royal Engineers, a unit of the Royal Navy, and an embryonic department of the RAF. Post-war consolidation brought all four under the umbrella of the Met Office. In 1921, Australian-born Leonard G. Garbett, who had served with distinction during the war on the HMS *Mersey*, was named superintendent of the Met Office's Naval Services Division. Insisting that it must have its own meteorologists to meet the needs of the Fleet Air Arm, the Admiralty took control of weather services for the navy in 1937 and placed Garbett, now a captain, at its head.[119]

The tug of war between the Air Ministry and the Royal Navy for control of the latter's meteorological services was made worse by the fact that most of the navy's weathermen were "schoolies," so called because they served in its Instructor Branch. They tended to have read mathematics or physics in college, useful for teaching navigation to officers and ratings ashore. Often they served aboard ship in a capacity related to navigation like Fleming had as plot officer on the HMS *Duke of York*.

When it came to backgrounds in the science of meteorology, none of the Admiralty's principal weathermen had anywhere near the education or experience of Petterssen, Douglas, or Krick. Neither Fleming, Instructor Commander John Thorpe, Instructor Commander Geoffrey Wolfe, nor Instructor Lt. Lawrence Hogben studied or worked professionally as forecasters before the war. With war raging on the continent, the Admiralty was forced to shorten its meteorology course from six months to three.[120] The British simply lacked the luxury that allowed the Americans to devote nine months to train military meteorologists with intense programs at universities like MIT, Chicago, UCLA, and Caltech.

Fleming, the Admiralty's senior weatherman, graduated with a degree in mathematics and mechanical sciences from St. John's College. He entered the navy as an instructor lieutenant in 1925. Over the next dozen years, he'd serve at sea on the HMS *Frobisher*, *Royal Oak*, and *Leander* and lecture as part of the faculty of the Royal Naval College. Returning to active duty in 1940, he signed up for the Meteorological Forecast Section, received two months training from the Met Office, and was piped aboard the HMS *Duke of York* as fleet meteorological and education officer.[121]

Hogben, a Rhodes Scholar from Auckland, who'd read mathematics to earn his master of arts degree from Auckland University College and in the process won the University of New Zealand's Cook Memorial Prize, was enrolled in New College Oxford when war broke out. As an instructor lieutenant, he served on the HMS *Sheffield* as plot officer and meteorologist and was awarded the Distinguished Service Cross for his role in the sinking of the *Bismarck*.[122] Wolfe joined the Instructor Branch in 1939, trained as a navigator, and completed the Advanced Met course offered by the

Met Office at the Admiralty Compass Observatory. Though Admiralty meteorologists deep in the Citadel lacked the formal education of their Met Office and USSTAF colleagues, their practical experience equipped them to play a pivotal role in the forecast for D-day. Theirs constituted the swing vote.

CHAPTER SIX

From the Sea They Will Come

Roll on, deep and dark blue ocean, roll. Ten thousand fleets sweep over thee in vain. Man marks the earth with ruin, but his control stops with the shore.

—Lord Byron

Since 1837, the three-story Hôtel de la Marine has overlooked the long sweep of sands at Arromanches, a small French fishing and seaside resort village in the westernmost sector of Gold Beach where two British divisions, 50th (Northumberland) and 8th Armored, would come ashore on D-day. Few hamlets on the French shore of the English Channel are more picturesque. In its front, a broad flat beach stretches nearly a thousand yards down to the sea. To the west rises the first of a string of verdant capped bluffs of much fractured shale and flinty chalk with near vertical cliffs that face out to sea. To the east stands a similar scarp. Between the two, a good road climbs up and onto the rolling plateau. On June 9, 1944, the first trucks and tanks would roll across a floating causeway that led from Mulberry B, one of two artificial harbors towed across the channel to Normandy and the only one to survive the ferocious gale on June 19.

Picture a charming pair of hotel patrons sitting on the patio sipping coffee tinged with *calvados* having just finished breakfast of buckwheat crepes, *galettes* stuffed with egg and ham. It's 1938 and the couple is among the hundreds of French bourgeoisie who've been enabled to flee cities torrid in summer heat for the cooling breezes of the mountains or the sea. After working a full year, every French wage or salary worker became entitled to fifteen days of paid vacation, thanks to a national law passed two years earlier.[123]

The couple wear the latest bathing attire, she a cotton bathing dress with broad straps over bare shoulders, full bodice, and pant-like bottom cuffed at mid-thigh, and he, a woven one-piece suit with tight dark blue straps that reveal the full of his tanned back terminating in snug dark red trunks. Wind is light and out of the northeast, and the question on the couple's mind is should they swim on the outgoing tide or when it is coming in. He wants to plunge in right away before the tide reaches low water. She, fearing they could be swept out to sea by an undertow, prefers to wait for a few hours until the tide begins to run ashore. Then they can float in on the gentle waves. In the five hours from ebb to full, the tide will rise about twenty-one feet.[124]

SWELL GUYS OF THE CITADEL

To a far-more-sophisticated degree, a pair of USSTAF geologists seconded to the Admiralty's forecast central in the Citadel, Lieutenants Bates and Crowell, and their British colleagues, Royal Navy lieutenants, Harold Cauthery and J. H. C. Fulford, wrestled with similar questions. How high would the surf be when it broke on Normandy beaches on D-day? And what would be the height of sea swell, the height of waves as they travel over the open Channel? The source of the wind, its strength, and how far it blows—its "fetch" over the water—determine the height of the swell. The slope of the beach and how squarely it faces the wind generally determine, as well, the height of the surf. Breaking waves along

Normandy are usually small, only a foot or two like those of the Gulf of Mexico lapping on the beaches of Florida. But during certain cyclonic storms as fierce as hurricanes they can reach ten feet tall or more.

These four, plus a statistician, Tech. Sgt. Ernest Lachner, a clerk, and two ratings from the Women's Royal Naval Service (WRNS but known as Wrens) made up the Admiralty's Swell Forecast Section. It was so named by Fleming in early 1944 to mislead any German who might get wind of it into thinking that the invasion was being planned for beaches open to waves from the North Atlantic, which Normandy is not. Knowing the state of the channel was just as important to the navy as knowing winds and cloud aloft were to the air force. If conditions were too rough, the Royal Navy, in overall command of Operation Neptune, could not land men, armor and artillery, vehicles, and the hundreds of thousands of tons of ammunition, gasoline, and other supplies needed to achieve a successful foothold and expand the lodgment over the following days and weeks.

By the time of D-day, weather forecasting based on an understanding of the atmospheric physics that creates and moves storm fronts and then allows them to lull was only about a quarter of a century old. In comparison, the application of meteorology to determine swell and surf had been a matter of scientific pursuit for not much more than a decade, and not taken seriously by the American or British military until the start of amphibious operations like the invasion of Guadalcanal in August 1942 or Operation Torch for North Africa the following November.

Operation Torch taught Allied planners a number of lessons critical for the success of D-day, not the least of which was the imperative to better forecast surf and swell. Patton's Western Task Force was to be delivered to the beaches of the Bay of Fedala about fifteen miles north of Casablanca. Though the French had built a breakwater protecting the south half of the bay, its eastern shores were exposed to the full fetch of winds all the way from the Arctic. French plans for the barrier reported that towering swells could arrive without warning causing "hours of violent surf during fair weather," write Bates and Fuller.

The invasion would take place early on the morning of November 8, but on an outgoing tide. Landing craft would need to be handled deftly to avoid grounding by the continuing ebb. Patton, commander of Torch's Western Task Force, and Rear Adm. Henry K. Hewitt, who commanded the naval amphibious force, felt that if they were blessed with three days with swell no higher than eight feet, the invasion would be successful.

Aboard the task force's flagship, the cruiser *Augusta*, Hewitt's meteorologist, Lt. Commander Richard C. Steere, was receiving five-day weather forecasts from the navy weather central in Washington. Using a code he had developed himself, he created surf and swell forecasts for Hewitt. What he did not know was that Krick was sending unauthorized surf and swell forecasts based on theories pioneered by Austrian-born Walter Munk directly to Patton. Eisenhower, in overall command of Operation Torch, worried increasingly about the weather because of conflicting forecasts from the navy, Krick's from the air force, and the Weather Bureau, which chimed in trying to temper his predictions.

Patton wrote to Gen. Marshall of "fair to bad surf conditions" for November 8, the date set for the landings, but added that "the forecasts have been relatively inaccurate." At 11:00 p.m. two days before the invasion, Steere told Hewitt's and Patton's staffs that winds blowing out to sea would calm the surf. Yet an hour later, like a bolt of lightning from a cloudless sky, came a forecast from Washington that sea swell would reach fifteen feet on the 8th.

Hewitt refused to be alarmed, and Torch soldiers rode ashore on waves of two to four feet. Still, poor seamanship and waves pounding a rocky coast damaged 64 percent of the operation's 370 landing craft. Worse was to come. The modest cold front coming in from the west, foreseen by Steere on the 6th, caused the surf to build steadily on the afternoon of the invasion, and in the next two days, many more landing craft were lost.[125]

Weather is a fickle god, as Allied invasion planners were slowly learning. Nine months later, almost to the day, Operation Husky was to put ashore on Sicily 478,000 men who would arrive on transports in an armada of twenty-two hundred ships, the largest joint American and British fleet yet assembled. Landing craft coxswains hoped for seas with a slight chop, just enough to make them harder for enemy gunners on shore to hit, but not so rough that troops became seasick. What a charming dream. In reality, the evening before the invasion found Husky steaming into a cold front bearing winds with gusts to 37 knots and a swell of twelve feet. Steere told Hewitt that wind and wave would abate as the front passed. As Steere had predicted, the wind diminished by dawn. Yet transports heaved mightily in the heavy swell as they hove to and began to disembark thousands of deathly seasick troops and overloaded vehicles into landing craft that bucked wildly along their hulls.

The wind was blowing relatively zephyr-like at 7 knots at Gela in the middle of the American sector where the 1st Infantry Division went ashore on a surf of two to six feet. The height of the waves might not have been too bad had the long shore current not been racing down the beach and causing many landing craft to turn to and broach. It was a different story at Scoglitti, eighteen miles to the southwest. Winds blew at twice the speed and directly onto the beach. Landing craft had to navigate huge offshore breakers.

Thirty-six hours after Husky began, only sixty-six of the 175 LCVPs (landing craft vehicle and personnel) and LCMs (landing craft mechanized) assigned to put the 45th Division ashore had not broached. Three months later, the Allied landing south of Salerno above the buckle on the Italian boot was a cakewalk weather-wise when compared to Torch and Husky.[126]

THE BEACH BOYS

Heavy loss of landing craft during Torch and Husky convinced the Allies that better surf and swell forecasting was an imperative for future amphibious operations. With research by Harald Sverdrup and Walter Munk at Scripps, they had a good start. Before coming to Scripps as director in 1936, Sverdrup had chaired the department of meteorology at the institute in Bergen and was intimately familiar with and appreciative of father and son Bjerknes's theories of cyclonic storms and associated fronts. When he was a teenager, Munk's family had immigrated to northern New York with plans for him to become a banker. He was having none of that. Instead he transferred from Columbia University to Caltech, where he no doubt encountered Krick, and earned a bachelor's degree in physics in 1939.

Deciding to pursue a graduate degree in oceanography, he landed on Sverdrup's doorstep down the coast at Scripps looking for a research assistantship. Trying to dissuade him, Sverdrup told him, "I can't think of any job in oceanography that will open in the next twenty years."[127] Yet he took Munk on, and the latter would win international acclaim for his theories on forecasting ocean surf.

In mid-1942, in preparation for Torch, Munk was asked by the US Navy to develop a surf-and-swell analysis for landing exercises on the North Carolina coast. Though Munk's theories conflicted with those of Krick and others, Scripps was deemed the best place to train military meteorologists in surf-and-swell forecasting, and in May 1943 Crowell and Bates, who held degrees in geology, were ordered to take the ninety-day course there in oceanography. Both had graduated from the Aviation Cadet Meteorology course, which was split between UCLA, where Jacob Bjerknes was teaching, and the University of Chicago, where Rossby held forth.

Sverdrup taught classes at Scripps in the morning with lab exercises every afternoon. The course was rigorous. Sverdrup, along with Scripps colleagues Martin W. Johnson and Richard H. Fleming, had just authored *The Oceans, Their Physics, Chemistry, and General Biology*, a massive tome of four pounds that became the bible for oceanographers during the war years. Essentially Sverdrup and Munk's theories allowed meteorologists to predict the height of swell generated by storms far at sea and to forecast how the swell would translate into waves and currents as they approach shore. Where headlands and bays punctuated the shore, swell would pile waves against headlands, which would break the force and deflect it resulting in gentler waves in the bays. For Crowell, life at Scripps was little short of idyllic. When instruction was finished for the day, students in the class jogged along the beach at La Jolla or played volleyball. Some evenings, they gathered for barbecues. Young unmarried students like Crowell lived in small cabins. Sverdrup, who'd been scientific director of Roald Amundsen's Arctic explorations from 1918 to 1925, was known for his physical prowess, and upon graduation entertained students at a gala party by walking on his hands.[128] Bates avoided most frivolity. Sverdrup had told him that if he could pass a foreign language course he would receive a master's degree in physics and meteorology from UCLA at the end of the oceanography program. Bates stayed up nights studying and barely squeaked through.[129]

After completing the course, Crowell was returned to the Army Air Field in Memphis where he'd served briefly as a weather officer after being commissioned and completing study at the University of Chicago. Bates was ordered to forecasting duty at Stephenville, Newfoundland, a major base for aircraft flying from the United States to the British Isles. In October 1943, Crowell was sent to England, and after a cold flight in a crowded C-54 that missed its waypoint over Iceland, he luckily landed safely in Prestwick, Scotland. He was assigned to the US Army Assault Training Center at Woolacombe Bay in northern Devon, and upon arrival as protocol demanded reported to the commanding colonel in his office, which had been a hotel ballroom. Only one desk furnished the room and behind it was the only chair in the cavernous room. On it sat the colonel.

As Crowell recounts in *Surf Forecasting for Invasions During World War II,* "The colonel stood up as I came in. I popped to and saluted, a salute that he returned very properly.

"'Second Lieutenant Crowell reporting for duty as ordered, sir.'

"'What outfit do you belong to?'

"'The 21st Weather Squadron, sir—I am ordered to join the C.O. of your local weather station, sir . . .'

"'What good do you think you will do the war effort?'

"'Hmmm, ahh,—we will make weather forecasts, especially forecasts of surf heights for the invasion—before and after, sir,— Here at Woolacombe we want to learn how different landing craft behave in surf of different roughness, sir.'

"'Dismissed.'

"As I saluted and spun about and moved toward the door, he muttered, largely to himself. 'You'd probably be a lot more useful behind a rifle shooting Germans.'"[130]

For a month, Crowell served on the staff of the weather station, developing forecasts from synoptic data, but always with an eye on how the weather affected the behavior of landing craft. There were a bunch of them in addition to the ubiquitous LCVPs and LCMs. LCVs (vehicle) were an amphibious version of an open armored personnel carrier. LCPLs (landing craft personnel large) displaced only ten tons. Most often used by the British were LCAs (assault), wooden barge-like boats carrying a single platoon. Variants of these abounded, all with their own slightly different handling characteristics. None, however, was capable of lengthy sea voyages like the LST with its bow doors that swung open, or the smaller LCIs (infantry) which off-loaded two hundred troops with twin ramps that descended from either side of the bow. Except for the LST, all were notorious for broaching in waves not big enough to excite today's moderately skilled surfer dudes.

Among the questions before Crowell and his assistant Lachner were these. How can the height of surf be measured from afar? What's the difference in the height of breakers caused by distant storms compared to those generated by wind waves? Could the time between waves be predicted? How does one predict the decay, if any, of swell caused by a storm off Iceland as it enters the English Channel? Sverdrup and Munk had developed a series of nomograms, charts containing various graphic scales that reflect the values and their relationships required to solve complex equations quickly and with pretty good accuracy. The most useful of Sverdrup's and Munk's nomograms showed how long wind of a certain speed took to raise waves to maximum height given a specific fetch and the rate of decay of swell and resulting waves over distance.

Crowell and Lachner jerry-rigged a system for recording wave height in Woolacombe Bay. Riding in a DUKW, an amphibious version of a two-ton GMC truck, they tied a thin line to a long rod

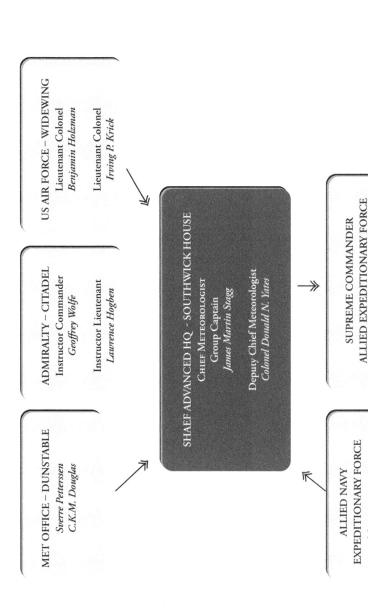

MET OFFICE – DUNSTABLE
Sverre Petterssen
C.K.M. Douglas

ADMIRALTY – CITADEL
Instructor Commander
Geoffrey Wolfe

Instructor Lieutenant
Lawrence Hogben

US AIR FORCE – WIDEWING
Lieutenant Colonel
Benjamin Holzman

Lieutenant Colonel
Irving P. Krick

SHAEF ADVANCED HQ - SOUTHWICK HOUSE
Chief Meteorologist
Group Captain
James Martin Stagg

Deputy Chief Meteorologist
Colonel Donald N. Yates

**SUPREME COMMANDER
ALLIED EXPEDITIONARY FORCE**
General
Dwight David Eisenhower

**ALLIED NAVY
EXPEDITIONARY FORCE**
Meteorologist
Instructor Commander
John Fleming

Organization chart for weather centrals participating in the forecast for D-day

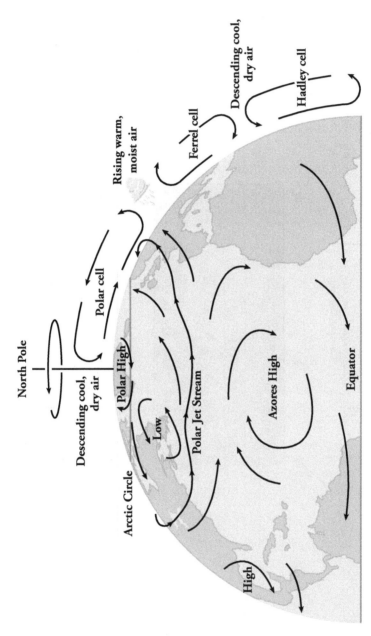

North Pole

Descending cool, dry air

Arctic Circle

Polar High

Low

Polar Jet Stream

Azores High

Equator

High

Polar cell

Rising warm, moist air

Ferrel cell

Descending cool, dry air

Hadley cell

Weather over the North Atlantic is dominated by perpetual conflict between the Polar High and the Azores High. Storms travel from west to east more or less along the jet stream.

COURTESY OF MIKE GARSTANG

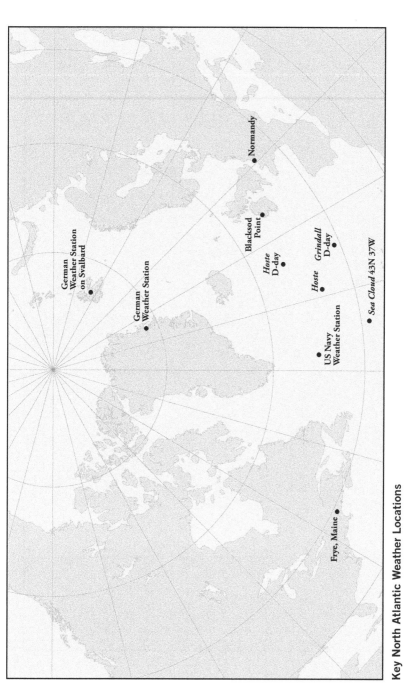

Key North Atlantic Weather Locations

The North Atlantic is about 3,200 miles wide. The fast-moving front that threatened to swamp D-day crossed the ocean in about four days.

Key Weather Stations
The D-day weather front came ashore at Blacksod Point in the Republic of Ireland and rapidly blew across Normandy.

Group Capt. James Martin Stagg, Chief, Meteorological Section, SHAEF
COURTESY OF MET OFFICE, © CROWN COPYRIGHT

Col. Donald Norton Yates, Deputy Chief, Meteorological Section, SHAEF, earned general's stars after the war.
USAF

Lt. Col. Irving P. Krick, Briefer, Weather Section, USSTAF
COURTESY OF THE ARCHIVES, CALIFORNIA INSTITUTE OF TECHNOLOGY

Admiral Bartram Ramsay, commander of D-day's naval forces, leaves the portico of Southwick House with General Dwight D. Eisenhower, Supreme Commander.

Southwick House, SHAEF's Advanced Headquarters for D-day

Veteran Met Office forecaster C. K. M. Douglas (left) and Norwegian Sverre Petterssen (right) surrounded by staff of the weather central at Dunstable
COURTESY OF MET OFFICE, © CROWN COPYRIGHT

A Met Office aide plots weather data on a map of the Northern Hemisphere.
© IMPERIAL WAR MUSEUM (CH 15750)

At Dunstable, German and other foreign weather transmissions were monitored 24 hours a day.

Holzman (front row, 2nd from left), Bundgaard (seated by drink table), and Krick (2nd row from top, far right) of the USSTAF Weather Section

COURTESY OF ROBERT BUNDGAARD

The Royal Navy's forecasting office was located in the Citadel next to the Admiralty in London.

Army Air Corps Lt. Charles Bates was a weather officer in Newfoundland before being seconded to the Admiralty to prepare surf and swell forecasts.

After D-day, Army Air Corps surf and swell forecaster Lt. John C. Crowell led a convoy into Burma.

Coast Guard Captain Edward "Ice Berg" Smith became a rear admiral and commanded Task Force 24, which hunted German weather ships and stations along the coast of Greenland.
USCG HISTORIAN'S OFFICE

RAF Halifax from 517 Squadron being disassembled after its emergency landing in Ireland after an ill-fated met recce flight.
COURTESY OF DENNIS BURKE

The telegraph office and weather station were located in the post office at Blacksod Point.
© MET ÉIREANN

Instruments that Maureen Flavin and Ted Sweeney used to note the passage of the D-day front
© MET ÉIREANN

Ted Sweeney and Maureen Flavin took the weather readings at Blacksod Point that helped convinced Stagg that calmer weather was arriving behind the front that caused Eisenhower to postpone D-day.
COURTESY OF GERARD SWEENEY

Harold Checketts (left) and Jean Farren (right) plotted weather data at SHAEF's advanced HQ, read poetry to each other, and later were married.

For $1 a year, Marjorie Merriweather Post's former yacht was leased to the Navy, renamed *Sea Cloud*, and provided weather data for D-day.

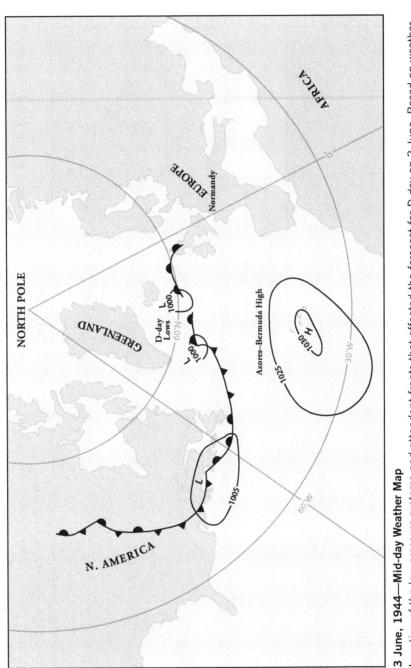

3 June, 1944—Mid-day Weather Map

Location of the low pressure systems and attendant fronts that affected the forecast for D-day on 3 June. Based on weather charts from Stagg's official report and charts provided by the National Climatic Data Center.

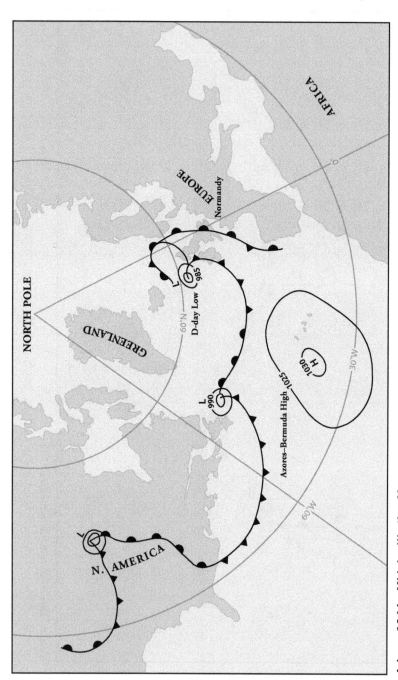

4 June, 1944—Mid-day Weather Map

Location of the low pressure systems and attendant fronts that affected the forecast for D-day on 4 June. Based on weather charts from Stagg's official report and charts provided by the National Climatic Data Center.

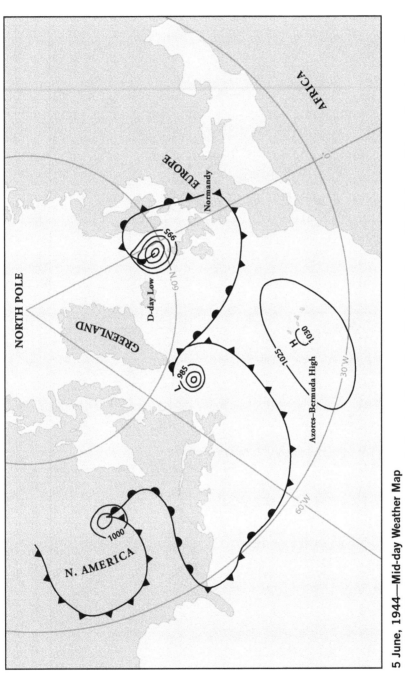

5 June, 1944—Mid-day Weather Map

Location of the low pressure systems and attendant fronts that affected the forecast for D-day on 5 June. Based on weather charts from Stagg's official report and charts provided by the National Climatic Data Center.

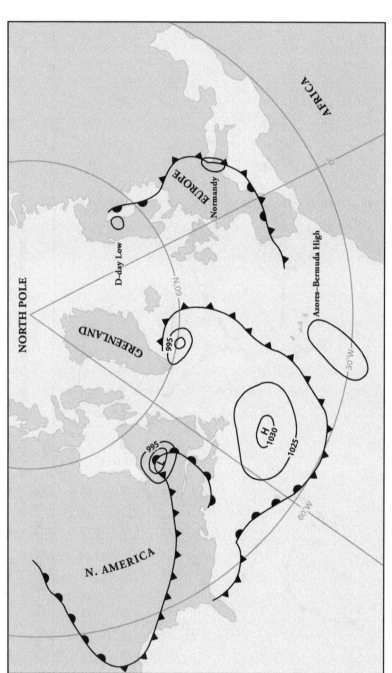

6 June, 1944—Mid-day Weather Map

Location of the low pressure systems and attendant fronts that affected the forecast for D-day on 6 June. Based on weather charts from Stagg's official report and charts provided by the National Climatic Data Center.

resembling a cane fishing pole. A heavy iron weight was attached to the end of the line along which, at intervals of one foot, ribbons of different colors were tied. One man would hold the rod, keep the line tight, and with each passing wave shout out its height to his partner who recorded the data in a notebook. This wasn't the most precise of instruments, but it worked.

To evaluate the validity of Sverdrup and Munk's surf forecasting methods, Crowell and Capt. C. R. Dick Burgess, RN, were ordered in December 1943 to tour beaches in the Azores and North Africa to measure fetches of winter storms produced in the subarctic Atlantic. In Algiers, protected as it is from the Atlantic by the straits of Gibraltar, officers at the air field weather station reported that, for predicting wave height, local winds were far more important than storms way out to sea. A few days later in Casablanca, Crowell found himself dangling in a boson's chair over the side of the *Jean Bart,* the hulk of a large French battleship and pride of the Vichy French navy that had been sunk in port by Allied bombs and shell fire from the *Augusta* on the opening day of Torch. He was painting white stripes on the dreadnaught's hull so he and Burgess could measure the peak of any waves that might roll in to the harbor from storms in the North Atlantic. Alas, the effort was for naught. No big waves came crashing in. A few days later they flew to Terceica in the Azores pursuing their quest to gauge surf and swell from distant storms. As was the case in Casablanca, the distant weather remained tranquil.

Back in London in the end of January 1944, Crowell was "BIG-OTED," meaning that he received top secret clearance and could then be told that the invasion to liberate northwestern Europe would occur in Normandy and not Pas de Calais. Lachner, who was the most capable statistical analyst in the Surf and Swell section, was denied BIGOT clearance because his father was German and he had relatives who still lived there. Should the Nazis ferret out his role in planning for D-day, they could easily threaten to harm or imprison his kin in hopes of forcing him to reveal vital secrets. After the war he earned a doctorate in ichthyology and worked for the Smithsonian Institution for thirty-two years before retiring as curator of fishes.

To adapt Sverdrup and Munk's nomograms to potential invasion sites in France, Crowell, Bates, and Fulford set up fifty-eight wave and swell observation points along the English coast and five provisional landing beaches in Normandy. The Swell Section was instructed to gather data for beaches along Brittany's southwestern shores, which might become a supplemental invasion site, as well as for the Bay of the Seine. Protected by the Quiberon Peninsula from Atlantic swells just as the Cotentin measure shielded Normandy, the beaches between Lorient and St. Nazaier might be particularly suitable. Bates, who in early 1944 joined Crowell in the Citadel, covered observation stations on the English coast while Crowell took those on the west.

Their main concern, though, became how swell coming in from the Atlantic refracted or bent around the Cotentin Peninsula. Also they were concerned about the height of waves and the speed of long shore currents that had caused so many landing craft to broach during Operation Husky in Sicily. They came to believe that sand bars close to shore and the runnels off the beaches affected long shore currents more than did swell refracted by the peninsula.[131] Gathering that intelligence would be left to a separate group of beach boys, the Combined Assault Operations Pilotage Parties.

COPPS ON THE PROWL

Racing along at nearly 400 mph, P-38 Lockheed Lightnings, those twin-engine, single-seat, long-range fighters known as *der*

Gabelschwanz-Teufel or "forked-tailed devils" by the Luftwaffe,[132] with their two .30 caliber, two .50 caliber machine guns, and 20 mm cannon replaced by high resolution cameras, provided Allied D-day planners with thousands of aerial photographs of Normandy. The British converted Supermarine Spitfires and de Havilland Mosquitos into reconnaissance work as well. These aerial photographs revealed that the Germans had infested the beaches with three different types of obstacles by May 1944. At about the line of low tide, ten-foot-high gate-like structures topped with mines were designed to blow up landing craft that floated onto them. Next came several lines of logs of about six feet in height that were driven into the sand about thirty feet apart. These were also capped with mines. But mines of what kind, planners wanted to know. Closest to the high tide line came Czech "hedgehogs," six-pronged steel crosses a little less than five feet high that could withstand sixty tons of force and, when hit from any direction, would pivot and hole the hull of a landing craft and at least stall a tank, making it an easier target for German artillery or armor.[133]

In addition to questions about defenses, planners needed to know more about the beaches. Nautical charts of the era were notoriously out of date and most only provided depth soundings around harbors or known reefs and submerged ridges out to sea. Tide rise and fall were generally known, but how deep was the water beneath the surface? The slope of the beach and the location of sand bars and runnels determined that. Moreover the slope would influence the height of waves arriving as ocean swell or generated by offshore wind. Beyond the strand—average line of high tide—how firm was the beach? Tanks, half-tracks, and trucks, even jeeps, would bog down in powdery windblown sand just as they would in clays and bogs at the back of the beach. There was only one way to gather that intelligence. Commandoes had to go ashore.

That task fell to a band of near-daredevils who had volunteered for Command Operations Assault Pilotage Parties—COPPS in British military slang.

The Dieppe catastrophe burned in the back of the minds of staff planning Overlord. On August 19, 1942, with little other than aerial photographs and intelligence gleaned from picture postcards, the British sent ashore a force of around five thousand Canadians with light armor to probe German defenses at Dieppe across the Channel. The first wave hit the beach at 4:30 a.m., but by mid-morning disaster was apparent. By 11:00 a.m. survivors were evacuated. Lost were 3,367 Canadians killed, missing, or captured and five hundred British commandos. One destroyer was sunk and thirty-three landing craft were either sunk or abandoned. The Royal Navy suffered 550 casualties.[134] Dieppe was a debacle of the first water. Clearly better knowledge of conditions on landing beaches and their defenses was an absolute must if the Allies were to assault German-occupied Europe and North Africa.

The Chief of Combined Royal Navy Operations, Vice Adm. Lord Louis Mountbatten, knew he had the right man for the job when he directed Lt. Commander Nigel Clogstoun-Willmott to begin planning a training regimen for amphibious commandos to gather intelligence for the coming invasions. In preparation for anticipated landings at Rhodes in early 1941, Willmott had studied its beaches through the periscope of a mine-laying submarine. What he saw failed to yield enough detail. Though he'd turned the magnification on the scope to its highest power, he could not make out much beyond the breakers. And he could discern no clues as to what lay underwater in the surf zone. He reported that the only way to truly know the condition of the beach was to visit it.

Back in port, Willmott teamed with army captain Roger Courtney, a can-do engineer with the Special Boat Section, and the pair hatched the scheme to use a collapsible canoe, a two-man kayak really, to paddle out from a submarine on a moonless night to within one hundred meters of the water's edge. Willmott, wearing a clumsy wetsuit, would climb over the side and swim to the beach. He would steal onto the sands, take samples, identify obstacles, return to the kayak, and Courtney would paddle him back to the sub.

It was a good plan. Willmott and Courtney were delivered to the Greek invasion area by the submarine HMS *Triumph*. Once in position, crew of the sub gingerly extracted the collapsed kayak through the torpedo loading hatch onto the forward deck. They assembled it in the dark. The skipper held the sub in the water so that its deck was just awash. Seamen eased the kayak into the gentle chop and held its bow and stern lines. First Courtney then Willmott boarded the craft, taking pains that it did not capsize. Wielding his twin-ended paddle, Courtney pulled toward the faint line of rumbling waves a mile and a half distant. When they were a football field's length off the beach, Willmott began his swim. He crept up on the sand, and crouching to keep a low silhouette, began to explore.

Far down the beach, he spotted a German patrol moving toward him. To hide, he retreated into the surf and froze as the enemy trudged past. Before returning to the extremely frail craft, he scouted three additional landing zones on the beach. He discovered that the beach was studded with outcropping rock and that a bar off shore would halt tank-carrying landing craft far from dry land. On successive nights the pair reconnoitered four more beaches. Though the German reinforcement of Greece nullified the attack on Rhodes, their daring reconnaissance sorties had caught the attention of senior officers of the Royal Navy, and Willmott was recalled from the Mediterranean in the summer of 1942 to develop commando beach recce teams for Torch.[135]

Though the Folbot folding kayak was the watercraft of choice for many COPPS missions in the Mediterranean, it was ruled out for reconnaissance of Normandy's beaches. The difference between high and low tide was far greater in the English Channel and currents were normally fierce. A flimsy collapsible kayak simply would not do. Willmott decided to resort to shallow draft LCN (navigation). Their low profile was unlikely to be detected by German radar. The LCN would drop the recce team a few hundred yards offshore, and they would swim in through the surf vastly reducing the chance that the enemy would discover their mission.

Churchill proposed that the first COPPS visit to D-day's landing zones take advantage of New Year's Eve when the Germans were likely to have let their guard down. On the last day of 1943, Willmott and Maj. Logan Scott-Bowden, along with Sgt. Bruce Ogden-Smith, set off from Gosport near Portsmouth headed for Sword Beach in a pair of motor gunboats each towing a LCN. En route, the wind freshened from Force 3 or about 10 miles per hour, to Force 5, roughly twice that. While seas had been one to two feet, they were now cresting at more than seven feet. Undeterred, Scott-Bowden and Ogden-Smith eased into the waves and began their four-hundred-yard swim. Strong crosscurrents from the incoming tide kept pushing them off course, and they landed about three quarters of a mile east of their destination. The specific location near Ver sur Mer was very important for, during Roman times, the beach had been a kilometer closer to England. Ancient records reported that the Romans had relied on peat bogs behind the beach for fuel. The combination of rising sea levels and a sinking coastline had covered the bogs with sand. Would they now support tanks? That was the urgent concern of D-day planners.

With the raucous sounds of not-too-distant Germans laughing and singing to welcome in 1944, Scott-Bowden and Ogden-Smith pushed their hollow eighteen-inch augers into the soft sand, twisted them, and extracted core samples that they stored in tubes in bandoliers that crossed their chests. With waterproof grease chinagraph pencils they carefully recorded the location of each on white, matte-surfaced tablets.

Laden with their cargo of tubes filled with heavy wet sand, and keenly aware that any gear left behind could tip off the Germans to their mission, they fought their way into the now heavy surf, which tossed them back on shore before they were finally able to swim beyond the breakers. Scott-Bowden was well ahead of Ogden-Smith when he heard him screaming something into the wind. Fearing his colleague was troubled by a cramp, he turned around and began to swim back toward shore only to hear Ogden-Smith wishing him "Happy New Year" at the top of his lungs. "Swim you bastard or we'll be back on the beach," Scott-Bowden yelled, and then returned the season's tiding.

Had Scott-Bowden and Ogden-Smith been captured that night of the New Year, their mission to Sword could well nigh have exposed the ultimate destination of the D-day invasion. As a precaution, other COPPS teams were dispatched to other beaches on the French Channel coast. One of them was, indeed, apprehended off the Pas de Calais, an event no doubt cheered by Overlord Planners because it helped convince the Germans that the Channel's narrow waist was where the Allied forces planned to cross.

To measure beach gradient COPPS deployed thirty-two-foot LCPs (personnel) equipped with drums loaded with nine miles of piano wire. A cast iron weight was attached to the wire that was played over the side with the increasing depth recorded on a rotating paper cylinder similar to that used on a recording barometer.

Between November 1943 and the end of January 1944, three missions were mounted in the waters off Arromanches. They marked the three-fathom contour, and with a line affixed to a weighted wooden pole measured the speed of the tide.

When Americans requested similar reconnaissance of Omaha, Willmott relied on midget submarines, adapted from the fifty-one-foot-long, roughly six-foot-diameter X-craft, which were much less affected by the vagaries of channel weather. Powered on the surface by a diesel engine like that used on British buses and underwater by a battery-powered electric motor, the midget sub carried a crew of five. Through a wet-dry air chamber the pair sent to survey beach sands would exit and return. Condensation wetted everything. Tins of food lost their labels. Life aboard, Willmott cracked, was "like living under a billiard table that leaks."

Between January 17 and 21, 1944, an X-craft carrying Scott-Bowden and Ogden-Smith lay about four hundred yards off Omaha Beach. On three nights, Scott-Bowden and Ogden-Smith struggled into their wetsuits, loaded up their gear, swam ashore, sampling sands that appeared questionable to American planners who had been relying on photo reconnaissance. During the day, the sub crew noted German defenses. One night, as the sub approached a new station, it came across a fleet of French fishing boats. Raising its periscope, Scott-Bowden said in a 2009 interview, "I was a little surprised to find myself staring into the face of a German soldier, perched close by up on the stern of the last fishing boat, thoughtfully puffing away on a pipe. We downed periscope pretty smartly, I can tell you." The sub's skipper piloted the boat under the fleet but above the fleet's suspended underwater nets.

Upon return, Scott-Bowden was immediately summoned to SHAEF's headquarters at Norfolk House in London. Generals Bradley, Bedell-Smith, and Bull questioned him extensively to squeeze from him every ounce of information about exits from the beach for American tanks. Were the tracks wide enough for Sherman tanks? Could draws leading up from the beach be sealed by demolition? Despite having just returned, Scott-Bowden could not provide definitive answers. [136]

CHAPTER SEVEN

Nothing Can Stop the Army Air Corps

OFF we go into the wild blue yonder,
Climbing high into the sun
Here they come zooming to meet our thunder
At 'em boys, Give 'er the gun!
Down we dive, spouting our flame from under
Off with one helluva roar!
We live in fame or go down in flame. Hey!
Nothing can stop the U.S. Army Air Corps!
                          —ARMY AIR CORPS SONG

In December 1943, Gen. Smith, Eisenhower's chief of staff, flew to England under orders to find suitable headquarters for SHAEF, which would become official when its new supreme commander arrived in mid-January. Planning for Normandy had begun in March of that year under Lt. Gen. Sir Frederick Morgan, who was serving as chief of staff to the as-yet unchosen Supreme Allied Commander. Morgan's organization adopted the initials of his title, COSSAC, and it occupied Norfolk House, a seven-story office building on London's St. James Square. By the time Smith arrived, COSSAC was teeming with Allied officers. The Admiralty and the British War Office were no farther away than a quick walk. Air Chief Marshal Leigh-Mallory had let it be known in no uncertain terms that his headquarters and Ike's should be very close together. But Smith didn't get the word, or if he did, he ignored it, as well might have been his wont. After all, he carried Ike's hatchet and used it without qualm.

AWAY FROM THOSE DISTRACTING FLESHPOTS

Instead it was suggested that he take a look at Bushy Park, later code-named Widewing, in Teddington about a dozen miles to the southwest. In 1941, the Ministry of Works, which managed property for the British government, had begun to develop the park as a location for temporary office buildings for companies eager to flee the blitz of the center city. Constructed of block with concrete floors, casement windows, and roofs with just enough peak for rain to run off, each hutment resembled a set of long, low, parallel sheds tied together by a narrow corridor in the center and may have been designed to minimize damage from German bombs. Block "C," where Ike would have his office, and Block "D" were enshrouded in dull brown camouflage netting, the same color as the barren ground. If the purpose had been to hide Widewing from prying German eyes from the air, the attempt was futile. Six additional sets of the sprawling hutments were under construction and would remain uncovered throughout the war.

The park's eleven hundred acres provided ample room to office and house SHAEF's staff, which would swell to 568 officers and 929 enlisted personnel, half again as large as COSSAC's, by January of 1944. Liaison aircraft such as the ubiquitous American J-3 Piper Cub and the British Taylor Craft could land and take off from a dirt strip. And the Eighth Air Force already had its headquarters there. Shared messes and officers' clubs would foster cooperation among Allies. In many ways Bushy Park was an ideal location. Not only were Churchill's War Rooms and the seats of governments of occupied European allies a reasonably close drive away in the center of London, but staff officers were less apt to be distracted by virulent nightlife in the city's West End. When Ike ok'd the site on Smith's recommendation, Leigh-Mallory was livid.[137]

In February 1944, shortly after the Eighth Air Force had moved in, operation of the whole park was placed in the hands of the Americans who promptly designated it as Camp Griffiss, in honor of the first US airman to die while on duty over Europe. The USSTAF weather central was located in the first tier of a set of small, hastily constructed hutments known as "Block F"[138] about two hundred feet to the south of "Block C," where Eisenhower had his office.[139]

Though Stagg had been selected the senior meteorological officer for COSSAC with a full air corps colonel as deputy in November 1943, he was initially assigned no staff.[140] He had no cadre of enlisted personnel trained to plot synoptic data on weather charts, and no staff of junior grade officers trained through the aviation cadet meteorological program to draw weather maps. Instead, he and his deputy relied on weather maps produced by first the Met Office at Dunstable, and then by the USSTAF weather offices after COSSAC became SHAEF and moved to Widewing. Fortunately, Stagg and his deputy worked together almost seamlessly. In March 1944, that relationship would be tested to such a degree that men of lesser mettle might not have persevered.

What if like the Dunstable, the Admiralty, and Widewing, Stagg had had a staff that produced its own maps and, based on them, their own forecasts? Would that have increased the potential accuracy of the final forecast, or would it have merely complicated an already cumbersome process? Was the lack of staff assigned to SHAEF's meteorologists an effort by Americans, the much more powerful partner in the allegiance with England, to minimize the

British impact of a function most crucial to the success of the invasion? Or, on the other hand, did COSSAC planners feel that Stagg and Yates's duty was primarily managerial and not technical like the roles of the three weather centrals?

The planned proximity of his office to Widewing's meteorological operation perhaps obviated, in the minds of Allied senior commanders, the need for Stagg to have his own staff of weather personnel. In addition, George D. Robinson from the Met Office was mobilized in May 1944 as an RAF flight lieutenant to serve as Stagg's aide.[141] He would be the eyes and ears of SHAEF's tiny met team, preserving a slim personal connection with American forecasters when Stagg and Yates moved to Ike's advanced headquarters at Southwick House at the end of that month.

THE UPPER AIR, UNCERTAIN TERRAIN

Similar to the Dunstable, Widewing's weather central contained a unit assigned to prepare surface forecasts and another dedicated to predicting upper-air conditions. Unlike the Met Office where Douglas in charge of surface forecasting and, Petterssen, upper air, held the lead in D-day weather conference calls, at USSTAF briefers Holzman and Krick had no comparable responsibilities. While Krick held forth in Long Range Forecasting A (LRFA), which developed forecasts based on analogs and his weather types, surface forecasts were prepared under the direction of Capt. Rufus G. Bounds; Capt. Robert C. Bundgaard led upper-air forecasting as well as LRFD, which developed long-range forecasts based on statistical analysis of pressure gradients in the upper air.[142]

Before the war American forecasting of upper-air weather was primarily based, according to Bundgaard, on mapping the contours of equal pressure at five thousand feet and ten thousand feet, the altitudes at which pilots of commercial aircraft preferred to fly.[143]

While helpful for letting fliers know where they might encounter storms, this two-dimensional view was not particularly useful for forecasting weather conditions over targets for Allied bombers. Today's bombs are guided to their targets by built-in laser or other homing devices. However the much-vaunted yet mechanical Nordern bombsight used by the Americans in World War II had to be programmed with accurate ballistic information that included wind speed, humidity, and atmospheric pressure before it could compute the range angle which, when matched with the ground speed of the aircraft, delivered bombs with increased accuracy.

Scores of missions flying at eighteen thousand to thirty thousand feet were forced to turn around, unable to aim their bombs, because conditions over targets were not as had been predicted. Hundreds of aircrew and dozens of bombers were lost. Bundgaard and his staff were under intense pressure to prepare more accurate upper-air forecasts. Yates and Bundgaard also believed that accurate knowledge of air pressure at high altitudes could improve the reliability of surface weather maps.

The weather maps we see on the Internet and television and in newspapers reflect conditions at the earth's surface. The locations of highs and lows and the fronts that run between them are based on readings of atmospheric pressure taken at weather stations on the ground. Readings recorded in Denver are taken a mile higher than those in Miami, and to prepare a surface map all are reduced statistically to sea level, as if the countryside were flat as a billiard table. But the atmosphere is not. Thanks to the Coriolis effect, in the Northern Hemisphere air swirls to the right and down out of high pressure cells toward areas of low pressure. Moreover, these meteorological air flows migrate from west to east and ripple north to south and back again in this hemisphere. Thus the atmosphere has its own terrain completely different from that of the ground.

Even though Bundgaard had graduated second out of a class of sixty at UCLA's weather cadet program, he was keenly aware that he had only fourteen months' experience. Soon after arriving in England to take up his new duties in late 1943, he traveled to Dunstable and spent several days discussing upper-air forecasting with Petterssen.[144]

UNSUITED FOR SUCCESS

Stagg divided his time between his office, now staffed with a WAAF corporal, and near Ike's war room and Widewing's upper-air section. That's where the largest share of USSTAF meteorologists had their desks and where extended forecasts were prepared. Stagg had access to the latest maps even as they were being drawn.[145] SHAEF's move to Widewing in March 1944 came during a particularly vexing period for the tall severe Scot. Gen. Harold Bull, SHAEF's assistant chief of staff for operations, to whom Stagg reported, was trying to force him out. When Stagg, a civilian, was posted to COSSAC as chief weatherman on November 30, 1943, he was mobilized as a group captain, the equivalent of a full colonel in the USAAF,[146] bought a uniform, and embarked immediately on a tour of weather forecasting operations in North Africa and Italy.

The purpose of his trip was to observe the needs of army and RAF units on the ground while touring the front with Wing Commander Patrick J. Meade, a former Met Office colleague and now Chief Meteorological Officer for the Eastern Air Command. As they motored through the hills with a flight sergeant from the unit that measured winds for antiaircraft artillery, Meade spied a road twenty-five yards ahead. "I asked the sergeant, 'Where was the front line?'

"He said, 'There isn't one, we don't have one.'

"So I thought that if you want a sensible answer you must ask a sensible question. I therefore tried again and asked, 'Where is the infantry?'

"He replied, 'A couple miles further back—they come forward and go ahead of us in the evening and pull back again in the morning.'

"I was shocked by this information because I had brought to no-man's land the Chief Met Officer for Overlord, and there would be hell to pay if anything happened to him."[147] Stagg wasn't the only high-value officer wandering around well ahead of the front. Another jeep carrying Gen. Montgomery and Alan Brooke, Chief of the British Imperial General Staff, also on an inspection trip, found themselves in similar straits.[148]

Upon return in December, the RAF demobilized Stagg without specific explanation, implying that his wearing of the uniform had provided necessary access to travel in RAF aircraft which he no longer required. He returned to his position as head meteorologist for D-day planners at COSSAC two days before Christmas, but as a civilian in a business suit.

That was unsettling for American officers who were definitely not used to reporting to civilians and who were more than loath to share secrets with them. After all, members of the military wore their ranks on their shoulders and resumes on their chests. At a glance one could tell in which campaigns one had fought and whether he had served with distinction and valor. Gaze at one's uniform and his outfit and one's place in the chain of command was immediately revealed. All you could see by looking at a civilian was whether he preferred herringbones or tweeds and how often he used the clothes press.

Not long after his swing through the Mediterranean, Stagg was assigned an office at SHAEF headquarters in Norfolk House and listed in the phone directory as a group captain. Needing to resolve conflicting reports received from US weather services, a senior American officer telephoned Stagg and asked him to come up to his office to sort things out. Stagg did so, and the officer was utterly nonplussed to find a civilian standing there before him. Deeply confused, the officer stumbled through a series of excuses for postponing the meeting, and Stagg left the man's office. The episode worried Stagg: Did his not being in uniform generate distrust among Americans?

He was right. Gen. Bull continued to let him know in subtle and not so subtle ways that this was a *military* organization. Bull called Sir Nelson, director of the Met Office, expressing concern that Stagg's civilian status limited his effectiveness. Johnson arranged authorization for Stagg again to wear the uniform, but expressly stated to Bull that he had not been re-mobilized. This bit of bureaucratic mumbo jumbo really confounded Bull, a kindly but very straightforward guy.

When Stagg reappeared in the standard RAF uniform of soft grayish-blue, his colleagues smiled knowingly. Yet Bull wasn't finished. He continued to press the Air Ministry about Stagg's "status," as he called it, and finally persuaded his boss, Chief of Staff Gen. Smith, that something had to be done. Smith issued an order on March 29, two months and a handful of days before D-day, placing Yates in command and relegating Stagg to advisory status. As Yates explained the situation, Bull found it intolerable that a civilian should stand between himself and a colonel under his command. As far as Yates was concerned, he and Stagg would continue just as they had. Stagg would brief senior commanders on details of weather forecasts, and Yates would present their military implications for the invasion.

The Air Ministry, however, refused to take Stagg's demotion sitting down. During initial planning for Normandy, the Combined Chiefs of Staff had agreed that the SHAEF's senior meteorologist would be an Englishman, no doubt because they felt a native would have a deeper appreciation of the weather over the Channel and the country from which the invasion would be launched. Alarmed that the Americans were going back on their word, Sir Nelson discussed the situation with Air Chief Marshal Tedder, Ike's deputy. Tedder, no doubt, had a similar conversation with Ike and Smith, which resulted in the latter issuing an order on April 19, a mere six weeks before D-day, reinstating Stagg.[149]

While these strands of red protocol tape swirled around their heads, to their credit Stagg and Yates never missed a beat. They knew the success of the invasion depended on the one element no general or admiral, no matter how great, could control: the weather. And it was their job to provide a forecast that was as close to on the money as humanly possible.

CALM IN THE EYE OF THE STORM

Bull's machinations weren't enough to distract Stagg. He had more on his mind. Betty, his wife, was pregnant with their second child. She and their two-year-old son Peter lived about five miles away across the Thames on Richmond Hill. When his duties permitted, he could go home to her and his toddling son. They'd met when she was a clerk at the Met Office. While Stagg was toweringly tall and often stern, sometimes crossing the line into harshness, Betty was short and elfin with a pixie twinkle in her eyes. She was the perfect antithesis of his mother, who, not cut in the least of warm and loving cloth, had pushed him hard and in the process created a thick shell like that of a conch into which Stagg climbed when pressed.

Only Betty could draw him out. Only with her, and in his diary, dared he express his worries and his deep doubts that he was up to the task at hand. Though he never spoke of it, he must have feared the worst. For him and most Londoners, the terror of the blitz had become a fact of life. Six months before his assignment to COSSAC, a bomb had blown out all the windows in a house just down the street from theirs. When sirens wailed, searchlights probed the sky, antiaircraft batteries hammered away, and deep booms thundered in the distance, Stagg never knew what or whom he would find when he returned in the morning.

With Stagg, Bundgaard had developed a friendship. At first, though, the short-tempered Stagg treated him shoddily. "He and I had some sort of confrontation . . . it had something to do with weather . . . he challenged me on something that I'd done or said. He expected me to knuckle under like a lot of people did. I think he gained a lot of success by being supercilious. I pretty much challenged him, not vulgar or anything. After that he seemed to respect me, it wasn't really confrontational. I just wouldn't accept his point of view. I think in his own mind he sort of agreed that we wouldn't be playing games any more. That nature of him that other people saw, I never experienced it again."[150]

They shared a mutual enjoyment of music. With college degrees in mathematics and music, Bundgaard had directed elementary, junior high, and high school bands in Castle Rock, Colorado, before being drafted into the Army Air Corps in 1942. Sadler's Wells, the famed London dance house founded in 1680 and known for presenting the best of concerts and ballets, had been bombed out of its London theatre and had relocated in Wimbledon a few miles away from Bushy Park. Stagg and Bundgaard would catch the train at Teddington to make the 6:30 p.m. curtain. Performances were early so they would not be interrupted by the blitz. When the Adelphi

Theatre in London put on *The Dream of Gerontius,* a choral work in two parts composed by Edward Elgar and considered to be his finest piece, Stagg and Bundgaard were in the audience.[151]

FATE OF THE FIVE-DAY FORECAST

Never a precise art, in the 1940s weather forecasting beyond the next day or two was hit or miss. Yet Ike's senior commanders demanded accurate predictions of wind direction and speed, surf and swell, and cloud cover for the five days needed to land troops and enlarge the beachhead to ensure that Allied forces would not be driven back into the sea.

Within SHAEF were separate staffs for naval, air, and ground operations. In addition one unit handled intelligence, primarily schemes to mislead the enemy, and another unit carried administrative responsibilities for all. To ascertain the conditions of wind, cloud, and surf and swell that suited the separate staffs, Stagg shuttled back and forth among them, negotiating the optimum requirements for success. All sought a spell of quiet weather, a string of days beginning with the initial invasion and extending long enough to bring ashore reinforcements and supplies. They preferred a full moon that would allow bombers to find their targets; paratroopers, their landing zones. Low tide at first light would be ideal. Engineers would come in first to clear lanes through beach obstacles, and another wave of soldiers could land on the second tide of the day in early evening while it was still daylight. That seemed straightforward enough.

That jibed with Ike's thinking. "We wanted to cross the channel with our convoys at night so that darkness would conceal the strength and direction for our several attacks," he wrote in *Crusade in Europe,* a book of wartime memoirs. "We wanted a moon for our airborne assaults. We needed approximately forty minutes of daylight preceding the ground assault to complete our bombing and preparatory bombardment. We had to attack on a relatively low tide because of beach obstacles that had to be removed while uncovered. These principal factors dictated the general period. The selection of the actual day depended upon weather forecasts."[152]

To refine these factors, Stagg asked SHAEF branch chiefs, "What are the least favorable conditions in which your forces can operate successfully?"[153] The army was less picky. If the navy could put it ashore, if the air force could deliver gliders and paratroops, and if the ground was firm enough for tanks and trucks, soldiers could fight. Airborne forces were worried about wind, cloud, and moonlight. Air force requirements became very complicated. Amounts of cloud that could be tolerated varied with each squadron's mission. High-level bombers like the B-24s and Lancasters couldn't deliver their payloads through cloud below ten thousand feet. Yet sheets of stratus cloud protected the mediums like the B-25, which dropped bombs from lower altitudes, from ground fire. Fog would eliminate the effectiveness of fighter bombers providing tactical support and of reconnaissance planes spotting for naval gunnery. All the aerial operations would be for naught if high surf and swell prevented ground forces from landing on the beach.[154]

By this time, the Allies had an inkling of the vagaries of Channel weather. In Sudland Bay about 30 miles west of Portsmouth, the 7th Brigade of the Canadian 3rd Division was put ashore on October 16, 1943. The rest of the division was to follow during the next three days. The RAF bombers were to support the mock invasion, as was artillery fire from landing craft off shore. But late on the 16th, the weather turned sour. Artillery shells fell short of the beach by hundreds of yards, and RAF flights were cancelled. Bombers could not take off in the fog.[155]

In meeting after meeting, Stagg tried to broker agreement on a set of conditions that were close, at least, to the minimum of each section's requirements. He defined a "quiet day" as one where winds on the Normandy coast blew in from the sea at no more than Force 3 (7 to 10 knots) or out to sea at Force 4 (13 to 18 knots). At Force 4, whitecaps begin to form. The invasion was to take place within one day before to four days following a "new or full" moon. The weather on D-day and three days following was to be "quiet." The amount of cloud was to cover no more than 30 percent of the sky below eight thousand feet and visibility was to be greater than three miles. A broken cloud base generally above three thousand feet with the slight possibility of morning mist or fog was a tolerable alternative.

Stagg reviewed climatological data from years past and concluded, as did a separate study by Americans, that May, June, and July held reasonable prospects, and of them, June was the best, followed by May and July.[156] May 1st had been tentatively set as the date for the invasion, but a shortage of LSTs needed to put five divisions on the beach pushed it back to June. Had the requisite boats been available, the Supreme Commander and his subordinates would have much preferred early May. Not only would that date add an extra month for summer campaigning, but it would have lessened the chances that the Germans would discover that Normandy, and not the Pas de Calais, was the invasion site. The weather over the English Channel in May had been gentle as a spring lamb, but June proved utterly contrary to expectations. "One has to go back to beyond the turn of the century to find a June as bad as that of 1944," Petterssen would later write.[157]

Though the accuracy of forecasts beyond tomorrow deteriorated day by day, Gen. Bull instructed Stagg in early February to generate a five-day forecast for the French coast every Monday morning.

Using Krick's system of analogs and weather types, the weather directorate in the Pentagon was regularly supplying USAAF units in England with long-range weather predictions, and Bull felt that SHAEF's team could do likewise. If the weather were settled, that is no storms were moving toward the Channel, longer-term forecasts covering three or four days might be made with some reliability. But if cold fronts were swinging eastward across the North Atlantic, the day of their arrival and their severity were much more in doubt.

While observations from the northeastern United States, Canada's maritime provinces, Greenland, and Iceland were readily available, only a handful of weather ships stationed in the North Atlantic were providing reports, and aerial weather reconnaissance flights could provide readings no farther than one thousand miles to the west of the British Isles. The Met Office, based on its analysis of schemes for preparing forecasts beyond a day or two, felt these were of extremely limited value. And Douglas, whose knowledge of Channel weather was nothing short of encyclopedic, was utterly against looking forward much beyond twenty-four to thirty-six hours.

Sir Nelson, when recruiting Petterssen, had pressed him to accept responsibility for long-range forecasting at the Met. Despite the fact that Petterssen had prepared successful three- and four-day forecasts for his home country's fishing fleets in the early 1930s, the Norwegian refused. Stagg shared this view. But Bull argued that if the Americans could prepare long-range forecasts, so could the British. Fearing that USSTAF's weather central might be placed in overall charge of meteorological services for D-day, the Met Office with great reluctance agreed to extend their view to three or four days, which Petterssen had done for the invasion at Anzio.[158]

As Bull had ordered, Stagg began preparing five-day forecasts. Secure telephone lines for conference calling would not be available until SHAEF moved from Norfolk House to Widewing. Until then, Stagg arranged for lead Widewing and Dunstable meteorologists to caucus by telephone early on Sunday evening and discuss probable weather for the coming week. Immediately after their conversations, he would call each and learn the salient conditions favored by the separate staffs while reviewing the latest surface weather map freshly arrived by courier from Dunstable. Before retiring for the night, he would draft a forecast for the week. Early Monday morning, Stagg would check with the weather centrals again and incorporate any overnight developments into the weather statement he would then hand to Bull.

On March 6, SHAEF's meteorological operations shifted from Norfolk House in London to Widewing where secure telephone lines permitted the Admiralty, Dunstable, and USSTAF forecasting centrals to be placed in conference. Two meteorologists from each of the weather centrals, the meteorological aides to the supreme commanders of D-day air and naval forces, and Stagg and Yates participated in the calls. The Admiralty was represented by Wolfe and Hogben; the Dunstable, by Petterssen and Douglas; and Widewing, by Holzman and Krick. On Monday, the weathermen were to present a five-day forecast that assumed Thursday was D-day.

At first, the calls went smoothly enough with each side coming to a general agreement with little argument. But then the climate of the calls changed. Krick, in particular, became increasingly adamant that Widewing could predict the amount of cloud and the wind's force and direction for each day of the forecast. Dunstable, deeply steeped in the ways of weather over the Channel, was very reluctant to climb out on that limb.

Widewing was receiving coded weather forecasts from the Pentagon. Krick was using similar techniques in England, and Bundgaard's section was preparing upper-air forecasts based on statistical correlations between highs and lows high in the atmosphere and their effects on surface weather. Writes Stagg: "the U.S. forecasters, Cols. Holzman and Krick, (particularly the latter), sustained by the variety of guidance at their disposal and unhampered by experience of English weather, were usually reluctant to modify their opinions in the course of the conferences."[159]

At Dunstable, scholarly skepticism of the whole three-way forecasting process prevailed like a stalled front with much cloud and drizzle. When Stagg convened a meeting of leaders of the weather centrals to finalize procedures, he heard Douglas remark not quite under his breath: " 'Hook up telephones for conferences, discussions, consultations—you can have as many as you like, they will make no difference: it is just not possible to make regular forecasts five or six days ahead that can have any real value for military operations or any other purpose, at least not in this country.'" His point was that under limited circumstances, it might be possible to make a spot-on forecast for three or four days in advance. To claim to be able to do so on a regular basis was misleading and unfair to commanders whose hands held the fates of thousands of lives.

Douglas's comments worried Stagg. He was afraid they'd get back to Bull who would snort: "If the British center can't forecast their own weather for more than a day or two ahead, Stagg, you must use the only advice available, namely what our people produce from Widewing, and apply your and Yates' judgment to that."[160] The accuracy of the trial five-day forecasts declined as the week progressed. The process was then modified so the predictions could be tweaked every morning, which, in the end, resulted in the evolution of the system that produced the forecast that gave Ike the confidence to postpone the real D-day by twenty-four hours.

CHAPTER EIGHT

Ridge of High Pressure

Three days rain will empty any sky.
Rain long foretold, long last,
Short notice, soon past.

—OLD WEATHER PROVERBS

For nearly the full month of May, zones of high atmospheric pressure dominated the Atlantic almost as far north as Iceland. Occasional weak fronts drifted over Western Europe bringing days of cloud, gentle rain, and hazy sun. As spring moved into summer, trees that had frothed the faintest green gained full leaf and camouflaged depots of tanks, trucks, and those ungainly but efficient amphibious DUKWs, as well as final camps for embarking troops.

Every field that could be plowed and planted was growing crops to feed the island nation. Hedgerows teamed with song thrush whose varied voice Americans from the South no doubt mistook for mockingbirds. GIs, brimming with nostalgia when they heard Vera Lynn croon "There'll be blue birds over the white cliffs of Dover," looked in vain for the spritely orange-breasted, azure-colored field bird that most knew so well. They are not native to England, and American Nat Burton, who wrote the lyrics, had never visited the chalk downs where much of the army was camped.[161]

Since April, the south coast of England had been virtually locked down. All but the most necessary travel by civilians in a ten-mile strip stretching from The Wash in Norfolk in the east to Lands End was prohibited. On April 6, all military leaves were cancelled. In May, mail and telephone services were restricted.[162] Along narrow country lanes leading to the great harbors of Portsmouth, Southampton, Poole, Portland, and points west, endless convoys of ubiquitous GMC "Duce and a Halfs" and snub-nosed Bedford QL three-ton trucks loaded with troops threaded their way toward final marshaling areas. Known as "sausage camps" because their curved oblong shapes resembled links of casing stuffed with ground pork, the camps were surrounded with barbed wire concertina to keep soldiers slated for the invasion out of pubs in neighboring villages. Some of the troopers "likened the sausages to giant livestock pens, 'the kind they kept cows in before sending them off to the slaughter.'"

Some snuck under the wire. Lance Bombardier C. Morris of No. 3 Troop, No. 6 Commando, remembers that on May 28, "The weather was sweltering, and in a nearby park equipped with a swimming pool the local beauties were tripping around in swimsuits in full view and looked very tempting indeed. Three of the camp staff soon tired of this confinement and made a jump for it. They were missed on the evening roll call. A net was immediately thrown over the locality and a search made. The missing men were found in a beer house, which was immediately closed, and the customers, proprietors, and deserters thrown in jail. A similar fate befell a woman talking through the wire to her husband."[163]

Rolling greensward on the downs around Portsmouth held eighteen sausage camps where thirty thousand soldiers were sequestered. They lived there in row after row of six-man pyramid tents, where they were issued new foul-smelling woolen uniforms impregnated with anti-gas chemicals. They packed their waterproof vehicles with supplies, sharpened their bayonets, were briefed on final objectives, played cards and shot craps, and wrote letters home that they prayed would not be their last.[164] Among Allied servicemen enjoying the easy weather on this, the last Sunday in May, was Tech 5 Alphonse Arsenault, a radio operator in the 1st Signal Company, stationed near Bristol, from Mexico, Maine, just east of Rumford where the leading edge of the weather fronts that would threaten the success of D-day had been first observed. Once he'd prepared his radios, Arsenault had little to do so he wrote his sweetheart, Roberta Connors, that he was going somewhere soon and that she might not hear from him for a very long time. He couldn't write about his duties, so he described the lovely English spring and hoped the weather was as fine at home.[165]

Up on Portsdown Hill sprawls Fort Southwick (pronounced SUTH-ik), constructed of red brick in the 1860s to provide coastal artillery defense for Portsmouth Harbor, which lies about a mile to the south and roughly four hundred feet below it. In 1942, Royal engineers chiseled almost a mile of tunnels in the soft chalk one hundred feet below the surface. Thought to be completely protected from any bomb the Germans might drop, the tunnels hid six hundred sailors and Wrens who ran the Royal Navy's communications center. Radar reports would be matched with those of ships plying waters between England and France, providing a complete picture of operations in the Channel. The communications center was linked by underground cable down through a low valley then climbed again to Southwick House, which Adm. Ramsay had chosen as his advanced headquarters for D-day.[166]

Gen. Bull, on March 3, suggested to Gen. Smith that Ike's forward headquarters be located in Southwick Park. Smith was presented with three options: a spur railway line could be laid so that

Ike and his staff could be quartered in a command train, rooms could be made available in Southwick's grand manor house, or he could be set up in a trailer and tents located in Sawyer's wood about a mile down the hill and across a small stream from the estate's mansion. The boy from Abilene, Kansas, chose the woods as being logistically easiest. Through the forest ran graveled track, and about halfway down it a path led south to Ike's encampment. His office tents were adjacent to those for his aides, including Stagg and Yates. About one hundred yards to the south were parked his "circus wagon" and a smaller camping trailer for his driver, Kay Summersby.[167]

THUNDERHEADS OVER THE ATLANTIC

Among all the vehicles heading south in bright sunshine on Sunday, May 28 was a staff car transporting Stagg and Yates over the seventy miles between Bushy Park and Southwick House.[168] Upon arrival they checked into Fleming's Nissen hut, preparing to test its facilities for generating the final forecasts by conference call with the weather centrals. They found it crowded. Fleming would sit in with them on the calls, but his forecaster and Wrens plotting weather fresh off the teleprinter would continue their work, as they must. A desk held the three scrambler phones for conferences with the Admiralty, Dunstable, and Widewing.[169]

"Scrambler" phones were denoted by their aqua green handsets. Each contained a button that when pushed engaged a separate circuit linked to a privacy unit that changed the frequency of the current carrying the conversation so only other scrambler sets could understand it.[170] To initiate a call, Yates called each of the weather centrals and got them all on the line. He then said "scramble," and each punched their buttons and the call was on. That evening the first conference went smoothly enough. The next five days' weather was discussed only in general terms. But in a call later that evening, wide differences among prognosticators revealed themselves.

Petterssen said that Dunstable expected thunderstorms early in the week followed by a period of unsettled weather.

Krick at Widewing predicted calm for all five days.

Speaking for the Admiralty, Wolfe foretold that bouts of disturbed weather and of strong wind would occur through Friday, June 2.

None saw any approaching lows with their fronts that would threaten the invasion now firmly scheduled for Monday morning, June 5.[171]

Stagg, Yates, and Fleming got up from the phones and went over and looked at the latest weather chart hanging on the wall. They agreed that "mainly quiet conditions would continue during the week. Even in the present stable situation, nothing helpful could be said about wind or cloud conditions on D-day, but the risk of conditions changing so much from what they are now as to produce a gale in the Channel seemed rather small.[172]

That was the reassuring message that Stagg passed along to Bull, who passed it up the chain of command where it ultimately reached the Supreme Commander, who, when he heard it, was as relieved as Stagg must have been. About the vicious little front with its thunderstorms approaching Rumford, Maine, they were unaware as they bedded down at midnight in cots in a tent in the woods not far from Fleming's weather hut to the sound of antiaircraft fire rising from Portsdowns.[173]

Shortly after sunup on May 29, Stagg and Yates convened the next teleconference among the weather centrals. The contentiousness of the previous night had faded with the dawn and general agreement prevailed that, despite periods troubled by high wind and cloud on Friday and Saturday, the weather for the coming week would be feasible for operations. Shortly after the end of the call, the pair was summoned into the library in Southwick House to brief Eisenhower and his subordinate commanders. After listening to his report, the commanders wanted to know how long the difficult weekend weather would last. Stagg, unwilling to opine beyond the five-day forecast prepared by the weather centrals, replied that even his vague predictions for the weekend were stretching beyond the capabilities of the centrals. Ike pressed him further, demanding a "possible or not possible" estimate for Monday, June 5, seven days hence.

Stagg replied: "At this time of year continuous spells of more than a few days of really stormy weather are infrequent. If the disturbed weather starts on Friday it is unlikely to last through both Monday and Tuesday; but if it is delayed to Saturday or Sunday the weather on Monday and even Tuesday could well be stormy." Stagg explained that his answer was based on his review of the general climate for late May over the Channel and not on an analysis of current weather data. Though the commanders seemed satisfied, Stagg was not. On the drive back to Bushy Park that afternoon, he worried about the portent to be brought by new synoptic reports coming in from weather ships out in the North Atlantic and from air recce flights headed east from England.[174]

Petterssen bristled to himself that Stagg would venture beyond the five-day maximum outlook agreed upon by the centrals. Neither he nor Douglas had the slightest confidence in predictions beyond a day or two, let alone almost a full week. And as he reviewed his upper-air charts, he could see that the weather over the North Atlantic was about to change with potentially dire consequences for D-day. Huge quantities of frigid air were building up over the Arctic north of Canada. Under normal circumstances it could flow gently south, pushing under warm moist air from the tropics bringing delightfully cooling breezes to East Coast cities like Washington and New York that were sweltering in early summer heat.

But the Azores High over the central Atlantic was much stronger than usual, in effect damming up the cold air along a line running from Labrador through Iceland and over northern Norway. From the Canadian Rockies to Novaya Zemlya, a tiny archipelago north of Russia and the northeastern-most point of Europe, winds rotating clockwise around the Arctic high fed back upon themselves, becoming increasingly bitter with every turn. From his upper-air maps, Petterssen was beginning to see the prospect that a string of storms could begin a dash across England and toward the coast of Normandy.[175]

ABOARD THE SEA CLOUD

The maritime provinces of Canada, Iceland, and the coasts of Greenland were dotted with American weather stations, all gathering synoptic data and feeding it to the Weather Directorate in the Pentagon. As well, eight US weather ships were reporting synoptic data for the North Atlantic. Originally operated by the Coast Guard but under control of the US Navy, Iceberg Smith's Task Force 24 was fully integrated with the navy on April 1, 1944. Members of the US Weather Bureau who had served as civilians gathering meteorological data on Coast Guard cutters were given temporary Chief Aerographer Mate rank in the navy. Weather ships were instructed to steam zigzag courses as rapidly as possible to their stations and then cruise within a hundred-square-mile radius for two to three weeks. From small flat spaces on deck, weather balloons carrying radiosondes were launched. Aerologists aboard ship tracked the balloons with theodolites and recorded surface temperature, pressure, wind speed and direction, cloud cover, humidity, and precipitation. Every three hours, they broadcast their readings and interrupted that schedule only when significant changes in the weather warranted. The work was tedious and dangerous; four weather observers had been killed when the Coast Guard cutter *Muskeget* was sunk by a German torpedo. All hands were lost.

In addition to their meteorological duties, ships of the Atlantic Weather Patrol were on constant alert for aircraft in distress. Among their responsibilities was providing navigation aid for transatlantic flights and rescuing downed aircrew. Even though they were lightly armed, should the opportunity arise they also were to take offensive action against German targets. In fact, a weather patrol frigate, the USS *Forsyth*, participated with the destroyer USS *Sutton* in the seizure of the U-234 bound for Japan on May 15, 1945, a week after the war in Europe had ended.[176]

The first three more or less permanent American naval weather stations in the North Atlantic were located at 39°N, 50°W, about six hundred miles south of the Grand Banks; 54°N, 44.30°W, roughly between Newfoundland and Greenland; and 47°N, 37°W, just about midway between the mouth of the Saint Lawrence and Spain. Ships assigned to these stations were a motley fleet, kind of like a pickup team of players in an unscheduled Saturday basketball game in the park. The USS *Monomoy* was a converted Great Lakes freighter launched in 1918 by Globe Ship Building in Duluth, Minnesota.[177] Also hailing from Duluth, the stubby USS *Conifer*'s keel was laid by the Zenith Dredge Company on July 6 and she slid down the ways three months later on November 3.[178]

Among the first generation of 180-foot buoy tenders, the *Conifer* was designed with a reinforced bow, an ice-belt at the waterline, and rounded bilges for ice breaking. The bow was narrower than earlier tenders, and its draft was deeper, which increased its ability to buck the rough seas of the North Atlantic with less roll and pitch. She was capable of steaming seventeen thousand miles at her nominal cruising speed of 8.3 knots. All of the 180-class tenders were built in Duluth, where, as in most American cities, men were eager to go to war and had enlisted or were drafted. Labor to build the *Conifer* and her sister ships was supplied by women who flocked to the yards and served as welders, machinists, and electricians. They were known as "welderettes." Later, the *Conifer* would be the first ship in the navy to have a fully integrated crew of African Americans and whites.[179]

The era's yachtsmen of great wealth would have thought of the *Conifer* and the *Monomoy* as wallowing tubs. In comparison their pleasure cruisers of choice were positively svelte, often longer by fifty feet or more and always narrower of beam. A long and delicate bowsprit shot forward from their gracefully arched prows, and curving up and out from their low-slung sterns spread broad fantails where swells in white dinner jackets and their elegant evening-gowned ladies sipped cocktails and nibbled canapés as a pianist played the latest tunes from Cole Porter and George Gershwin. Though Hitler's invasion of Poland opened naval war in the North Atlantic, and while no American vessels would be lost until 1941,[180] all but the most pig-headed US isolationists knew that sooner or later their nation would come to England's aid and in so doing would provoke German attack. Many of the yachts of the wealthy would go to war.

Fred J. Fisher, the eldest of seven Detroit brothers who founded the auto coach company—the iconic logo of which, *Body by Fisher,* graced all General Motors cars until the late 1990s—was one who saw thunderheads gathering over the North Atlantic. On December 9, 1940, a year and two days before the United States declared war on Germany, the navy acquired his 235-foot yacht *Nakhodka,* renamed it the USS *Zircon,* outfitted it as a ship to train officer cadets in the art of naval machine gunnery, and sent her on patrols up and down the East Coast. On March 1, 1944, she was assigned to the Atlantic Weather Patrol.[181]

Circling on weather station three, midway between Newfoundland and Spain, the *Zircon* was relieved on June 2 by the USS *Sea Cloud*, an even racier converted yacht. Launched for E. F. Hutton & Company by the Krupp shipworks in Kiel in 1931 as the *Husser II*, her length was 316 feet and her beam, 49 feet. Originally she carried the four masts of a barque but was powered as well by a twin-shaft diesel-electric engine.[182] When Hutton and Marjorie Merriweather Post, heiress to the Postum Cereal fortune and co-founder with him of General Foods, divorced in 1935, she got the *Husser II*. That same year, she married her third husband, Washington lawyer Joseph E. Davies, who two years later became ambassador to Stalin's Soviet Union.[183] The newlyweds renamed the boat *Sea Cloud*.

Shortly after the December 7 sneak attack on Pearl Harbor by the Japanese, Davies offered the barque to the navy. President Roosevelt allegedly refused to accept it because it was "too beautiful," and if its lines are any indication, its interior must have been truly stunning. But on January 7, 1942, the navy reconsidered, chartered it for one dollar per year, and refitted it for the Atlantic Weather Patrol. Her four masts were stripped away, and her hull and superstructure were painted that drab gray common to battleships. She spent a great part of her career on the stations between Newfoundland and Greenland and south of the Grand Banks. On June 2, 1944, she arrived at her mid-ocean station and began broadcasting weather readings just in time for D-day.[184]

She wasn't the only weather ship occupying special stations for D-day. The Royal Navy assigned the HMS *Hoste* to gather weather readings in a block bounded by 52º–59ºN and 20º–25ºW about 470 miles west of Ireland and placed the HMS *Grindall* to cover 42º–49ºN and 20º–25ºW approximately seven hundred miles west of the northwest tip of Spain. Both were destroyer escorts built in the Boston Navy Yard and transferred to the Royal Navy in 1943 under the US Lend Lease Policy. There they were known as frigates, and on April 21, 1944, had been ordered to their stations to provide synoptic observations from a critical area in the eastern North Atlantic where storms approaching final rehearsals for the invasion in Channel waters could be first observed. Returning to port in Londonderry, around May 4, they were sent to sea again on May 25. Once on station they broadcast observations regularly several times a day while doing their best to avoid enemy contact.[185]

The met officer aboard the *Grindall* was Instructor Lt. Henry Curry, formerly a lecturer at the Royal Naval College at Greenwich, which fronted the south bank of the Thames. Having shown an interest in music, he was given seats in a box at Royal Albert Hall by a student and could attend whichever orchestral and choral concerts he desired, and he favored Beethoven concerts held on Friday evenings. He played rugby, squash, and snooker and sang in a production of Handel's *Messiah*. For the good lieutenant, the war was simply "loverly."

Then came the summons to the Admiralty in London in the spring of 1944. Originally to be posted to the HMS *Trouncer*—the former US escort carrier *Perdido* then outfitting in San Diego—Curry's orders were changed and he was assigned to the *Grindall*. His task was to sail into the mid-Atlantic and when on station transmit weather data every three hours. An officer he describes as a "chair-borne prophet of doom" said that the previous weather ship patrolling that sector had been sunk without a trace and that he'd be well served indeed to purchase a Gieves patented life-saving waistcoat of kapok, which was guaranteed to keep one afloat for four days.

His sagacious advisor also recommended that, when the ship was torpedoed and began to capsize, that Curry immediately put on gym shoes so that the soles of his feet were not flayed to ribbons by barnacles as he walked the overturning hull preparing for his swim. Should he fail to heed this advice his bleeding feet would attract rapacious schools of sharks. Curry laughed nervously asking, "Why me? I'm too young to die." He was told, "That's just it lad—you are young and expendable. You don't expect senior officers to risk their necks on jobs like this?" He was sent on his way with a cordial "It's been nice knowing you," as if the foretold future was already assured.

With Curry aboard, the *Grindall* sailed from Londonderry bound for its patrol sector, which came to be known as the Cabbage Patch. It was under orders to avoid contact with Germans and only to defend itself if attacked. Once on station, the ship began its endless routine of zigzagging to the north only to reverse course and zigzag south once again. All the while weather reports were sent by wireless, and the crew was certain German U-boats frequenting the same waters were listening. For entertainment, Curry and his mates tuned radios to pick up propaganda broadcasts of "Lord Haw Haw," the Irish traitor who was hanged after the war.

May, in this section of the Atlantic, was benign. Skies were clear blue and winds were soft. He and his messmates lowered a boat and took a swim in the mirror-smooth sea. But as May matured into June, the seas grew fierce. Mountainous waves tossed the *Grindall* about like a cockleshell. The ship was rolling forty-five degrees to starboard, righting itself, and then dipping forty-five degrees to port. On June 4, the seas subsided and Curry sent word to the Admiralty that a period of calm seemed to be building.[186]

While the *Grindall* patrolled a section of the Atlantic dominated primarily by the main lobe of the Azores High, the high that

Krick believed would protect D-day beaches, the *Hoste*, captained by Royal Navy Lt. Peter James Hill Hoare, was steaming several hundred miles to the west-northwest of Ireland. His ship would feel each of the fronts that threatened Overlord, and reports from the *Hoste* would be pivotal in shaping the forecast.

WEATHERING THE WEATHER ALOFT

With the close of The War to End All Wars, meteorologists representing most if not all the countries resumed collaborating in 1919 through the International Meteorological Organization that had been formed in 1879. Just as in America, the lightning-fast evolution of commercial aviation demanded intense cooperation, this time among countries in Europe. The IMO's old Commission on Wireless Telegraphy formed in 1899 was renamed the Commission on Synoptic Weather Information in 1923. The Commission on Maritime Meteorology suggested the establishment of an International Meteorological Bureau to collect and statistically analyze observations made at sea. A secretariat with that mission started work in 1928. Agreement on the definition of meteorological terms was achieved that same decade. Consistent meteorological codes were approved in 1929 at the IMO meeting in Copenhagen. Meeting in Warsaw in 1931, IMO created the Commission on Aerial Meteorology with members appointed by their governments.

Europe's meteorologists were a tightly knit group. Many had studied with the Bjerkneses in Norway. They were as intrigued by developments for long-range forecasting taking place in Germany as they were with the use of radiosondes, first pioneered in France just at the turn of the century. They read their friends' professional papers, kibitzed at IMO gatherings, and relied on each other's data, broadcast in the new Copenhagen code, to draw their weather maps.

With the German invasion of Poland, the network for exchanging weather data throughout Europe dried up. In response, the British developed a scheme to use twin-engine Blenheim light bombers to conduct weather reconnaissance flights. First based at Bircham Newton in eastern England for flights over the North Sea, by 1941 operations included flights out of St. Eval in Cornwall not far from Lands End over the approaches to the English Channel. In the main, met recce missions departing St. Eval followed a track that took them slightly south of due east at eighteen hundred feet; every fifty nautical miles (roughly fifty-eight miles) the met officer on board collected temperature, humidity, air pressure, cloud, wind speed and direction, and precipitation data. After flying about 575 miles, the aircraft descended to sea level. Another set of readings was taken, then the plane climbed to 18,000 feet with data gathered at every fifty-millibar decrease in air pressure.[187] It was a long, lonely turbulent ride.

Bundgaard, in his presentation at the Fort Ord Symposium commemorating the fortieth anniversary of D-day, asserted: "In many respects, as far as weather was concerned, World War II support was rather agnostic, being carried out and fought according to special game rules. This was especially true in the weather field, because of the past international character of meteorology. For example, almost daily, the Luftwaffe weather reconnaissance out of Brest and the R.A.F. Lancasters out of St. Mawgen, in Lands End, would meet over the water and rendezvous in the Biscay area, saluting each other with wing dips. And those allied planes maintaining weather surveillance over the two German weather subs were carefully instructed, I was told, not to bomb them. Due to an error, however, one did. And the next day or so thereafter, one of the allied weather ships was torpedoed and sunk by the Germans."[188]

As delightfully chivalrous as this sounds, if it ever happened it was only on the rarest of occasions. "During the summer of 1943, two Hampdens of 1404 Met Flight were shot down by long range German fighter planes (Ju88s)," writes Robert J. Gurney, an RCAF Navigator with the 517 Squadron that succeeded the 1404 flight. "It was known that Germans were intercepting the British Met messages and breaking the British codes. Also it was widely believed, correctly as it was later publicized, that the British were intercepting and deciphering the German radio traffic from the Luftwaffe met squadron based on the Brest peninsula. Although no evidence that both sides were purposefully avoiding attacking the opposition aircraft had been found, it was believed that both sides felt that it was in their best interest to allow the enemy aircraft to complete its met reconnaissance mission unmolested and thus benefit from the enemy's information.

"Unfortunately 'The Battle of the Bay' (Biscay) warmed up in the early summer of 1943. Coastal Command brought Beaufighter and, later, Mosquito aircraft into the battle. Not long after, RAF fighters shot down some enemy Met aircraft and, in return, the Luftwaffe obtained revenge by attacking a Hudson of 1404 (code for a meteorological flight) on 22 June 1943 and shooting down a Hampden also of 1404 on 2 August 1943, killing the crew."[189]

Not all losses were due to enemy action. Mechanical failure and depleted fuel brought down several planes at sea. Some landed at emergency fields in Ireland where the plane would be impounded or disassembled and trucked back to the British at the border with Northern Ireland, where the crew had been taken earlier. Such was the fate of a star-crossed RAF Halifax from 517 Squadron (Meteorological). At 0115 DBST on April 21, 1944, the bomber, heavily laden with extra fuel, lifted off from its base at Brawdy in Wales. Immediately, it was found that the ground crew had not removed the cover on the pitot tube, essential for measuring air speed.

The fix was easy. An axe was used to chop a hole in the Perspex nose window in the bottom of the fuselage under met observer John A. Barthram's desk. Barthram tried to reach the cover, but his arms were too short. Another crewman did the job. While he was up from his seat, he headed for the rear of the plane to help pump up the landing gear because the Halifax's hydraulic system was out. The flight droned along and was just finishing its climb to eighteen thousand feet, when the radio died. Not only could Barthram's readings no longer be transmitted, but the plane drifted west of its track and was about out of gas when the emergency landing field at Skibbereen, the southernmost town in Ireland, came into view. The plane made the field, bounced twice on landing, and with no hydraulics and thus no brakes rolled through a fence and collided with a grazing heifer, the only casualty of the flight.[190]

Though the US Air Force had been flying air reconnaissance missions with B-17s and B-24s out of the RAF base at St. Eval, the units involved went through a rapid series of evolutions in the period leading up to D-day when it would be operating at the 8th Weather Reconnaissance Squadron flying out of RAF Watton on the other side of England.[191] The squadron mounted missions, sometimes as many as three a day along "Epicure," seven hundred miles past the Bay of Biscay, and "Allah," which took them six hundred miles beyond southern Ireland. In addition to usual crew, flights carried a meteorologist who took readings at the required fifty-mile interval.

As long as visibility was good enough, and with a ceiling of about one thousand feet and the end of the runway in sight, pilots would take off. While they'd been briefed on the weather en route, they were never exactly sure what they'd encounter. Often the sea was shrouded in fog and rain and the real horizon was invisible. Keeping a B-17 straight and level, just fifty feet above sometimes towering seas when crosswinds were gusting at 40 knots and the slightest down draft would cause disaster and certain death of all crew, required supreme flying skill. Pilots and co-pilots stared, scarcely daring to blink, at the artificial horizon, bank and turn, rate of climb, altimeter, and airspeed instruments as the plane bucked up and down in the choppy air. Imagine their relief when their orders allowed them to climb to 30,000 feet.

Along with the heavies, Americans also flew twin-engined de Havilland Mosquitos on met missions, code-named "Bluestocking," across German-occupied Europe. The crew consisted of a pilot and a navigator, who was also trained in meteorology. Observations were useful to all weather centrals to help verify intercepted German weather reports.[192] Fast, facile, built of plywood with few metal parts save engines and brass screws to secure key parts, Mosquitoes were all but impossible for German radar to detect.[193]

WEKUSTA FROM THE WEST

With the declaration of war by Great Britain, and Allies overrun by the Nazis in 1939 and 1940, weather data previously broadcast by them in the clear using the Copenhagen code disappeared, which prompted the Luftwaffe to mount an aggressive series of weather reconnaissance sorties by meteorological units officially called *Wetterkundungsstaffel* or *Wekusta* for short. Not unlike the British organization, German military met flights had reported to a civilian agency, the state ministry for transportation, and served civilian and military aviation.[194] Weather reporting was moved under control of the Luftwaffe in 1939 with the creation of the Zentrale Wetterdienst Gruppe, which was housed at Luftwaffe headquarters at Wildpark-Werder near Potsdam. ZWG provided the Luftwaffe with strategic weather forecasts, much like the US Weather Directorate in the Pentagon.

Its first leader was Dr. Kurt Diesing, and upon his death, Dr. Werner Schwerdtfeger, who would later head the department of meteorology at the University of Wisconsin at Madison, became its chief. Initial Wekusta flights probed skies over the North Sea, Holland, Belgium, and later France. When France fell, Germany sent its Heinkel 111s, Dornier 17s, and Messerschmitt 110s to overfly England to gather information to support the Blitz. When France capitulated, a number of that country's meteorologists at the airport Le Bourget outside Paris were forced into service of the Nazis.[195] Just as the RAF later did, the Luftwaffe established specific tracks over approaches to the English Channel, and out into the North Sea, and the Norwegian Sea. Civilian weathermen like Schwerdtfeger had before heading ZWG flown daily missions with Luftwaffe crews in weather that often grounded other aircraft.[196]

The Germans, too, felt that, with the loss of Wekusta aircraft above the North Sea and seizure of papers from weather stations on Svalbard in 1941, the geniuses at Bletchley Park may well have penetrated the Luftwaffe's weather code Zenitschüssel. According to Kington and Selinger, "For several months RAF fighters did not attack when German weather aircraft were encountered as their decoded met reports made a useful contribution to the collective received by the British Met Office."[197] Allowing Wekusta flights to proceed unattacked was not standing operating procedure. British fighters shot down scores.

Still, Wekusta 51 flying out of Lew Buc, a small non-commercial airport outside Paris in Toussus–le Nobel, ran tracks over the Western approaches to the Channel, and Westa OKL 1 hooked northwest, then north-northwest to cover the Northern Atlantic west of Ireland. At the same time Wekusta ran daily flights over the North Sea and over sea lanes long favored by convoys loaded with American aid bound for Murmansk.[198] The flow of meteorological data from Wekusta units faded with increasing Allied dominance of skies over western Europe.

SOUTHWICK, CHINESE POETRY, AND LOVE

In early May, a lorry pulled into Lee-on-Solent to collect a small party of Royal Navy officers, ratings, and Wrens, among them Jean Farren and Harold Checketts, an able-bodied seaman. Also in the party was a pair of instructor lieutenants, Leading Seaman Taffy Thomas, and a second Wren, Pamela Pinks. They'd been instructed to bring their personal kits, but weren't told where they were going, how long they'd stay, or what they would be doing. After loading the truck with reams of teleprinter paper, boxes of blank weather charts, barometers, and other equipment, they were wished well by Capt. Garbett, chief of the Royal Navy's met service, climbed aboard, and headed off.

After a drive of no more than a dozen miles, the lorry pulled up behind Southwick House. They disembarked and hauled the supplies into Commander Fleming's weather office in his half of the Nissen hut behind the manor house. On arriving in Lee-on-Solent, Checketts had been assigned to Farren to improve his skills in plotting synoptic data. At Southwick, he found himself teamed with her, under the supervision of one of the lieutenants, to translate weather data (a series of numbers based on the Copenhagen code) from the teleprinter to symbols on the weather chart. The lieutenant would then draw the fronts. A second team was made up of Leading Seaman Thomas, met Wren Pinks, and the other lieutenant.

The team prepared new charts every three hours. Two hours were needed to plot the chart. Once it was finished, Checketts would seek out his lieutenant so he could come in to draw isobars and fronts. Often during the night, Checketts would have to take a flashlight and go find the officer in his tent, roust him from his cot, and bring him to the weather hut. When the lieutenant had finished, Fleming was summoned. He reviewed the chart, made recommendations, and when they'd been incorporated, he rolled up the chart, tucked it under his arm, and made a bee-line for Adm. Ramsay's office.

The two teams alternated every twenty-four hours. Each weekday was broken into six four-hour watches. When off-watch, the ratings and Wrens could return to their bunks and take a nap. Farren and Pinks were quartered in half a Nissen hut with the wife and daughter of a captain assigned to Ramsay's headquarters. Checketts bunked in servants' quarters in the back of the manor house. On weekends, where three watches stretched for eight hours, Farren found it difficult to stay awake.[199]

On their days off, Checketts and Farren began to take long walks. Among their favorite destinations was the top of Portsdown where they could view endless ships of the invasion fleet at anchor. Other treks took them along country lanes past fields and forests thronged with soldiers in their sausage concentration camps and acre after acre of parked jeeps, trucks, and tanks. It was, as historian Chester Wilmot described it, weather for poets. Farren was a fan of Chinese verse and prose, especially Chaing Lee's *The Silent Traveler in Oxford*; Checketts grew enamored of Louis MacNeice's latest poems. Checketts "was a great humorist," Farren remembers, "He made me laugh." They began to hold hands as they strolled. Toward the end of her watches, he would sometimes bring her a mug of cocoa and corned beef sandwiches from the mess. They fell in love and would marry.

In early June, when Stagg and Yates moved to Southwick, they almost hovered over the Wrens' ratings and their officers' shoulders as they drew the charts. When not plotting synoptic information, Thomas and Checketts were responsible for scrubbing the floor in the Nissen hut and took great pride in keeping a spotless deck. One morning, there was a knock at the hut's door. Checketts sprang to his feet, opened the door, and there stood Ike wanting to look at the most recent chart. Alone in the hut, Checketts immediately let him in and dashed off in search of one of the officers to answer any of the Supreme Commander's questions. Immediately he realized he'd "left the bucket, scrubber, and a large bar of Pusser's soap on that half-scrubbed well-soaped slippery floor. . . . (Ike) was nimble enough to slip in but not over. But hanging about not far away I really did wonder how the fortunes of the Allies, and myself particularly, would have fared had he come a cropper on my half-scrubbed floor."[200]

CHAPTER NINE

Earthquake in the Sky

There was a little girl,
Who had a little curl,
Right in the middle of her forehead.
When she was good,
She was very good indeed,
But when she was bad she was horrid.
—HENRY WADSWORTH LONGFELLOW

In room 4D260 of the Pentagon, the USAAF weather directorate, using the analog forecasting method developed for Eastern Airlines by Joseph J. George, who'd been on leave as chief meteorologist for Western Air Express when Krick wedged his foot in that door, churned out an eight-day forecast on May 28 predicting that a lobe of the Azores High would grow toward Ireland by June 5. Consequently, any low-pressure cells with their attendant warm and cold front would migrate, curling northeastward along the northern boundary of the high.

That forecast claimed the origins of these lows would be over the Great Lakes. Analysis of air patterns suggested that currents in the upper atmosphere would bend from the south to the east and eventually peter out over Scandinavia. Because of the building presence of the Azores High, the question for USSTAF forecasters was not just how fast the lows would move or their strength, or how far south, but how far north they would travel. This assessment was quite important for Allies ferrying combat aircraft and flying supplies from Newfoundland to Great Britain by way of Greenland and Iceland. Deterioration of weather over the Channel was out of the question. It would remain reasonably good throughout the period during which the invasion would be launched.[201] With this, Holzman and Krick at Widewing laid the foundation for the string of mostly favorable forecasts that, had Eisenhower accepted them at face value, would have led Operation Overlord into disaster.

However, whatever gods there be of weather failed to adhere to the Pentagon's forecast. Petterssen at Dunstable foresaw the shift in upper-air currents but wasn't so certain that they'd stay well to the north of the Channel. He foretold of a potential deterioration in the stable weather on Thursday, June 1, and Friday, June 2, as well. From the Admiralty, Wolfe concurred.[202]

Monday, 29 May—Morning Forecast—
Meteorological Office, Air Ministry

General Inference: *A ridge over Scotland and North England is moving slightly north and a trough in the South of the country is extending north and northeast. A weak trough across central Scotland is moving little. It will be cloudy in North Scotland with local rain or drizzle. Elsewhere it will be fine but with some risk of thunderstorms in the South later this afternoon and evening. There will be some fog about dawn in England. It will be hot or very hot in the South; rather warm in the extreme North.*

Further Outlook: *Little change but increased risk of thunderstorms in the South.*

1000 DBST—SHAEF Advanced Headquarters, Southwick House, Portsmouth

On Monday morning Stagg and Yates appeared before Eisenhower and reported that, until Friday, June 2, winds would remain fairly quiet, seldom more than Force 4. Stagg explained, though, that by Thursday and into Friday, winds would rise to Force 5 and roughen the western reaches of the Channel. Cloud cover would be somewhere between 5/10th and 7/10th except in thunderstorms. What this meant, Yates explained, was that half the bombers would be able to see their targets and half would not. As cloud cover thickened, only three out of ten aircraft would be able to use optical bombing sights.

Eisenhower pressed him. "How long would the bad weather last, and, in particular, might it extend into Monday and Tuesday (5 June and 6 June)," Stagg wrote in *Forecast for Overlord.* Given the growing "uncertainties" about the weather at the end of the five-day period, "we were already straining our forecasting techniques and experience farther than we should," Stagg told Eisenhower. He added that he'd only made a projection for the weekend because the Supreme Commander wanted a "provisional possible or not-possible" prediction for Monday 5 June, and concluded that his confidence in a forecast for so many days ahead was "low."[203]

The discussion continued. "'What,' one of General Eisenhower's staff (perhaps General Bedell Smith) flung at me, 'What is your own personal view?'"

Speaking from his study of the Channel's climate, Stagg replied, "At this time of year continuous spells of more than five days of really stormy weather are infrequent. If the disturbed weather starts on Friday, it is unlikely to last through both Monday and Tuesday

(June 5 and 6); but if it is delayed to Saturday or Sunday, the weather on Monday and even Tuesday could well be stormy."

After this briefing, Stagg and Yates returned to Widewing. Reports from weather ships in the Atlantic began to trouble Stagg. That's why he was so astounded to hear all three weather centrals express during this evening's conference call that deterioration of the weather over the weekend now seemed unlikely. Though Krick had pushed for a fair weather forecast the previous night, the others had disagreed. Now they changed their minds. After listening to their arguments, Stagg found no substance on which to base their more sanguine view for the weather leading up to 5 June, the date set for the invasion.

No supreme commanders' meetings were scheduled until Friday 2 June back at Southwick House, and Stagg was grateful that he and his staff would not confront Eisenhower tonight. Had Stagg been required to present a briefing, he'd have had to report the rosy consensus of the weather centrals but to condition it with his own more guarded view.[204] In the back of his mind, perhaps, was Douglas's continuing insistence that forecasting for the Channel for more than twenty-four to thirty-six hours in advance was risky at best, and predictions beyond three days were scarcely worth the paper they were printed on. During the evening conference, the centers had mostly concurred that deterioration was in the offing due to building high pressure over Iceland. This could push lows southeastward across the British Isles. Just when in the next few days that bouts of low cloud and stormy wind would reach the Channel was beyond agreement.

Wednesday—31 May—Morning Forecast—
Meteorological Office, Air Ministry

General Inference: *An anticyclone centered near East Iceland is almost stationary and a ridge to the Eastern North Sea is moving slowly East. A weak trough over our Southwest districts is moving slowly northeast. It will be mainly fair in the North and East but with considerable cloud in East Scotland. Local thundery rain or thunderstorms will occur in western districts of England and in Wales. It will be very warm in the South, rather cool in the North.*

Further Outlook: *Thundery conditions spreading slowly east; otherwise little change.*

0830 DBST—Widewing, Bushy Park

Though the Met Office predicted it would be "very warm," Adm. Ramsay reported in his diary that the weather at Southwick was "slightly cooler." He also noted that Fleming, reading the skies for the coming days, was troubled about cloud cover.[205] Ramsay was right to be worried. In that morning's conference call, the centrals agreed that the reasonably favorable weather forecast earlier for the weekend now seemed to be giving way to a less optimistic view. Conditions for Sunday onward seemed to be eroding, but as yet, no specific details appeared certain. All that could be told was that the Azores High appeared to be fading. Yet the forecasters agreed that the Azores High could be strengthened if it were joined by another high-pressure cell. This Stagg reported to Gen. Bull.[206]

That evening Stagg was unavailable to participate in the scheduled call, and Yates took his place. He told Stagg afterward that Dunstable and the Admiralty were "forecasting a rather black weekend." Widewing clung to an opposite, more positive view. Rather than a slow moving front bringing low clouds, Krick and Holzman held that the front would instead transit the Channel rapidly with a ridge of high pressure filling in behind and offering good weather for a Monday morning invasion. Stagg tried to sort out why Widewing's predictions varied so dramatically from those made by the English and could not. In the end, he sided with his countrymen, not necessarily because of fraternity, but rather due to the odds of one for better weather and two against its chances. He hoped desperately that tomorrow morning's conference call would unscramble their differences.

Thursday, 1 June—Morning Forecast—
Meteorological Office, Air Ministry

General Inference: *A complex trough of low pressure from West Scotland to Southeast England is moving east to cover the British Isles tomorrow; weather will be mainly cloudy, there will be occasional rain or drizzle at first in Ireland, Wales & Southwest England; elsewhere in England, there will be outbreaks of thundery rain today, with local thunderstorms, more especially in the East; there will be occasional rain in Scotland; rather cool generally.*

Further Outlook: *Fair in most districts, but rains reaching western districts from the Atlantic late in the period.*

0845 DBST—Widewing, Bushy Park

Stagg's wish for agreement among the divergent centrals during the morning's call was not to be. Dunstable insisted that a sinuous front would be passing through or hanging just north of the invasion beaches. The Admiralty foresaw a series of fronts moving over the region. In either case, skies would be cloudy but wind would not blow stronger than Force 4, the upper limit of acceptable conditions. Widewing felt that a front would cross Friday or Saturday. Weather over the beaches would contain little cloud and limited wind.

In his book, Stagg reports that he told Bull that "prospects for Sunday and Monday, and probably Tuesday, were poor. There will probably be a good deal of cloud throughout those days but the weather centrals are not yet confident enough to say anything helpful about the strength of the wind. The situation is complex and difficult. In accepting this Bull's only comment was, 'For heaven's sake Stagg, get it sorted out by tomorrow morning before you come to the Supreme Commander's conference. General Eisenhower is a very worried man.'"

Stagg had expected Bull to ask whether the centrals were in agreement. When he did not, he suspected that Bull already knew the answer. Perhaps Yates had told him of Widewing's sanguine feeling that the weather would be suitable. Stagg and Yates had been working closely for the last few months, and he felt he was beginning to understand his American deputy's persona. Normally of sunny disposition, the more deeply he became concerned, the more his demeanor clouded.

On their afternoon drive back down to Southwick through a bit of drizzle, Stagg pondered just what lay behind his colleague's concern. It could be that Yates was caught on the horns of a dilemma. The Widewing central reported to him. They were his men and it was his duty to support them, the way a good commanding officer is supposed to do. But he was not a professional meteorologist as seasoned as those at Dunstable. Was he torn between their differing views? Stagg's worry was just the opposite. He felt Widewing was relying too heavily on analog forecasting yet they seemed to be buttressed by other methods of forecasting such as Bundgaard's upper-air analyses. Was his advice to Eisenhower too colored by Douglas's and Petterssen's predictions of thickening cloud and growing wind?

The centrals conferenced again in the afternoon and once more that evening at 2100. Neither was particularly illuminating.

Dunstable maintained its pessimistic view, and Widewing argued that the weather would not affect the landings because a finger of the Azores High was creeping to the northeast. The Admiralty, as always, held the middle ground. Stagg drew some solace from the fact that the first phase of Operation Neptune would not launch until the next morning, when battleships and cruisers sailed from ports in Scotland and Northern Ireland. If the weather actually degenerated the way it appeared, there was time to postpone the invasion, perhaps, long enough until it cleared.

What if, Stagg and Yates worried, Dunstable and Widewing were still diametrically opposed in the morning? Should they then bring the centrals' radically different views to the attention of Eisenhower and his subordinate commanders? Yates thought so, but Stagg was against it, at least for now. They'd been ordered to present a single forecast that met the needs of all services engaged in Overlord. No doubt the air forces and the navies each listened to their own meteorologists, but they did not know the views of the others.[207] Further, when Krick bootlegged those unauthorized forecasts to Gen. Patton that conflicted with those from Adm. Hewitt's weatherman, both commanders had become confused. One set of predictions, even if wrong, was better than two that were at odds with each other. As Stagg and Yates settled into their tent near Eisenhower's headquarters and his circus wagon in Sawyer's Wood, their minds were as occluded as a stalled front rife with low cloud spitting a fitful rain.

Friday—2 June—The Forecast—
Meteorological Office, Air Ministry

General Inference: *A small depression centered over the North Sea is moving away southeast and an associated trough will persist over North Scotland; pressure is high to the Southwest and a low to the Northwest of the British Isles, and a weak trough of low pressure will move southwest across the country. Weather will be partly cloudy in the East and South with some clear periods, while in the West and North it will be cloudy with occasional rain or drizzle.*

Further Outlook: *Occasional rain in the West and more particularly in the North; fair to the Southeast.*

Early in the morning, the pair of meteorologists hustled from their tent and up the cindered lane to Fleming's weather hut. They were eager to see his charts, prepared overnight. Dashing their hopes, the maps showed no clear developments. Scant was any indication of Widewing's assertion that the Azores High was strengthening. Yet the speed, strength, and probable path of the string of lows over the North Atlantic were equally plagued with uncertainties. Wrote Stagg in *Forecast*, "In all the charts for the 40 or 50 years I had examined I could not recall one which at this time of year remotely resembled this chart in the number and intensity of depressions it portrayed at one time."

Yet on the call several minutes later, Widewing not only held fast to its view that high pressure was building but was adamant that it would buffer the Channel from the approaching lows and their fronts. The American meteorologists discounted the drop in barometric pressure reported from Blacksod Point as inconsequential. To the contrary, Dunstable argued forcefully. Over the past three hours, the pressure at Blacksod had continued to fall and this, along with their reading of weather aloft, convinced them that Force 5 (17–21 knots) or stronger winds and abundant low cloud would stream over the invasion beaches. The Admiralty called conditions borderline.

The root of disagreements lay not in synoptic reports or in significant variations of the charts that lay before each central. Maps of the weather had been constructed from essentially the same data. Stagg attributed divergent opinion to "use of misleading techniques or faulty chains of reasoning in which the wrong step lay unwittingly concealed, (and the centrals) arrived, in all sincerity, at quite different answers." He doubted further that, even in an unhurried research environment given endless time, the conclusions of the centrals would have been in complete agreement. He, an academic scientist down to his shoelaces, knew this as did former university department chairs Krick and Petterssen. After much wrangling, Stagg forged a tacit consensus that the weather over the Channel was not going to be as favorable as previously forecast but not nearly as foul as Dunstable predicted and not nearly as good as Widewing would have Eisenhower and his commanders believe.[208]

None of the thousands of soldiers on their final march to embarkation points, pilots having coffee in briefing rooms, drivers steering their vehicles toward waiting maws of landing ships, or sailors reading the invasion fleet had any inkling of the knife edge on which the decision to launch Operation Overlord was balanced. They would go or not only on Eisenhower's order.

1000 DBST—Supreme Commanders meeting—Southwick House

If all went according to plan, in little more than sixty hours airborne troops would be landing near bridges and key crossroads behind the beaches of Normandy. Though it could not be predicted with a high degree of reliability, Stagg's forecast reported that cool winds of Force 5 (17–21 knots) would be pushing under warm moist air from the southwest in the western reaches of the Channel and would bring almost complete overcast to Overlord's operational area. Patches of fog might shroud parts of the coast on Monday morning.[209] Propitious weather for the invasion this was not.

After the commanders' meeting, Stagg set off down the hill and began a lonely stroll through the woods below Southwick House. Worry gnawed at him. In their tent early that morning, had he been right to advise Yates against sharing the divergent views of the weather centrals? He knew full well that he was pushing Dunstable's glum predictions over Widewing's brighter prognostications. If dissent continued, how long should he preserve the illusion of unanimity?

"Was it fair to the Supreme Commander to withhold the cleavage of opinion from him? 'Yes,' I argued with myself: 'General Eisenhower has big enough problems of his own. He would not thank us for explaining (and he probably wouldn't understand) why the centers can't agree. We have no brief to make his task more arduous than it manifestly is.' And at the back of all this self-justification," he wrote after the war, "was the thought, even the hope, that my gloomy view might yet turn out to be wrong. There was still an outside chance of that."

Just as Dunstable and Widewing, and particularly Petterssen and Krick, were engaged in an increasingly strident conflict, Stagg believed for certain that a furious battle was erupting between the bitterly cold and increasingly powerful Arctic high and its warm, moist, and sunny cousin over the Azores. Where would the front line stretch between the two on Sunday night and Monday morning, the days of 4/5 June slated for D-day? Though many of the warships of the invasion fleet were already at sea, troopships would not leave port until Saturday or Sunday morning. Was that time enough to sort out an agreed upon forecast? Was any such forecast even possible?

Stagg arranged a mid-afternoon conference call in an attempt to find common ground. Rather than forging consensus on the details of the weather for D-day, he thought it might be helpful if each center discussed the broad rationale that underlay its predictions. This might, he felt, smooth the way for the call at 2000 DBST, where the forecast to be presented to Ike and his supreme commanders, an hour and a half later at 2130 DBST, would be forged.

Alas, Widewing and Dunstable were as far apart as ever, though the team at the Admiralty was beginning to side with the USSTAF weathermen. Royal Navy meteorologists felt the ridge from the Azores High would extend not so much over Ireland, but more northeastward over the Channel bringing with it a little cloudiness but negligible wind. Dunstable believed that three depressions, one a few hundred miles east of Newfoundland, another over the mid-Atlantic, and the closest about a third of the way between the tip of Greenland and the British Isles and their related fronts, would continue to move eastward. They were likely to strengthen over Scotland and winds, rotating counterclockwise, were likely to blow up the Channel from the west. If low-pressure troughs developed behind the fronts, sheets of low stratus cloud could mask Normandy.

Not only were Dunstable and Widewing in sharp disagreement, but a new voice had entered the fray in the morning's conference call. Reginald Cockcroft Sutcliffe, PhD, of the Met Office, was the senior meteorological advisor to Leigh-Mallory, commander-in-chief of air operations for Overlord. His role was similar to Fleming's in that he was responsible for interpreting weather discussions for his boss. Earlier in the day he, noting rising pressures from the Azores High, wondered if a ridge of it might push into southwest Ireland. On the phone in the afternoon, he asked if a lobe of the high might break off, drift northward, and produce little wind and cloud just as Widewing was predicting.

Now four views lay on the table. The Admiralty and now the RAF leaned toward the Americans' opinion that the weather on the night of 4 June and the morning of the 5th would be close to or above the minimums planners had set. Dunstable strongly disagreed and Stagg was inclined to side with his Met Office colleagues. Yates had been silent as a sphinx regarding his opinion, yet Stagg felt that he surely agreed with Widewing. After all he was their commanding officer. It was three against one. Though deeply concerned by the afternoon's discussion, Stagg held his ground, siding with Dunstable that worsening weather was but a day or two away. A wrong forecast could swamp the invasion.

His attempt at reaching agreement among the centrals prior to the scheduled call at 2000 DBST had failed utterly. Rather than clearing the air, he'd confused it as badly as if a fog from the Channel had rolled into Southwick's met hut. The evening call held no resolution. Widewing was increasingly obstinate in asserting that its forecast would prevail. Dunstable was diametrically opposed. The Admiralty felt stability was building over the Channel and that there'd be little change until 7 June. Sutcliffe continued to chime in, arguing against Douglas who insisted the lows coming from the northwest would cause any developing zones of high pressure to weaken. Stagg felt the same as the veteran Dunstable forecaster.

The hour and a half allotted for the call passed in heated discussion. The supreme commanders were convening in the library, and Stagg had to hustle to make the meeting. The commanders were now gathering twice a day for the primary purpose of hearing the latest forecast and discussing its implication. As much as he'd have wished, there was simply no time to go over the situation with Yates. Instead, they along with Fleming rose hastily from the burning phones, threw open the door, and dashed around the corner into the mansion's great hall where they waited to be summoned.[210]

2130 DBST—Supreme Commanders Meeting, Southwick House

Standing before Eisenhower and the gathered top brass, Stagg reported that the morning's forecast had not changed significantly and that weather patterns were developing sluggishly. He noted that winds for the most part would not exceed Force 4. However the "outlook for cloudiness was very uncertain; considerable periods of 10/10 cloud cover with base about 1,000 feet must be expected. The times of the periods cannot be forecast accurately," he concluded.

Ike questioned conditions for Tuesday and Wednesday. Stagg responded that little change was expected. When Maj. Gen. Hoyt Vandenberg, deputy commander-in-chief for air, asked about the weather for landing airborne troops, he was told that the ceiling for transports would probably be a little better than one thousand feet but in places, particularly after 0200 DBST on 5 June, the clouds would be lowering.[211]

Saturday—3 June—The Forecast—
Meteorological Office, Air Ministry

General Inference—*An anticyclone southwest of the British Isles is almost stationary and shallow secondary depressions are moving east-south-east across Scotland with associated troughs crossing the country. It will be cloudy in most districts with some rain or drizzle in the North and local rain in the South. It will be mainly rather warm and close.*

Further Outlook—*Little change.*

Saturday dawned mostly cloudy, cool, damp, and with a light wind out of the northwest. At sea already were the battleships, cruisers, and lighter warships that would bombard Normandy's beaches two days later on 5 June. Those troop transports and landing ships, crammed with tanks, artillery, trucks, and jeeps, that were not now underway, were getting up steam in English harbors all along the Channel.

Long before sunrise, Stagg and Yates were well at work in Fleming's little weather hut. On the 0500 conference call, Holzman, briefing for Widewing, reported that its forecast was not significantly changed. Air pressure was rising over the British Isles and over the Azores. Passage of a weak warm front had caused falling pressure over Blacksod Point as well as at the other stations in Ireland, but the following cold front was also weak. A high would fill in behind it after a trailing warm trough had passed. Except for cloud over the western Channel, weather for the next few days would be favorable for invasion. The Admiralty agreed completely with Widewing.

Dunstable was unyielding in its opposition to Widewing's and the Admiralty's view that the weather on the night of 4/5 June would be satisfactory for D-day. To make its case, Petterssen then began to lecture his colleagues as if they were his meteorology students at MIT. Laboriously, he delved into the entire weather picture from Manitoba to the Baltic Sea. Arctic air from above Hudson Bay would invigorate the low east of Newfoundland, which would begin to move rapidly toward the British Isles. The forecast depended on when and where this system would strike the Channel. He told the other centrals that Blacksod had just reported winds just shy of a near gale at Force 6 (22–27 knots) and plunging barometric pressure, data that had not yet come over Fleming's teleprinter. Had Dunstable's and Stagg's long anticipated breakthrough of the Arctic high begun?[212]

Just as Stagg had begun to consider this likelihood and to try to develop a consensus, he was summoned by Gen. Bull to give him a quick briefing for Eisenhower. Even though the Admiralty had thrown its lot in with Widewing's, Stagg wasn't buying their optimism. To Bull, Stagg reported that the forecast had not improved since the previous evening. To the contrary, it appeared that winds up to 20 knots would cover much of the Channel beginning on Sunday afternoon and continue into Monday. Low clouds would persist as well. He was just concluding when Gen. Vandenberg and Adm. George Creasy, Ramsay's chief of staff, entered the room and demanded to know the details. Stagg repeated the briefing he'd just given Bull while "trying hard to convey the impression that the outlook was still knife-edge marginal. It could still go either way by evening."

Returning to the weather hut, he discovered Yates on the phone with Holzman and Krick urging them to call Dunstable before the next centrals' conference and resolve their differences. The pair, evidently, was not enthralled with this idea. They'd base their evening forecast on the charts and would be willing to accept Stagg's opinion even if it conflicted with theirs. Stagg then telephoned his assistant, Squadron Leader George Robinson, who'd remained behind at Bushy Park, only to find that, like Sutcliffe and the Admiralty, he too tended to side with Widewing's positive perspective.[213]

With the exception of Dunstable, the centrals seemed allied against Stagg, which put Yates in an untenable position. Yates was his deputy, but only by default. His currency among American senior commanders was extremely high. Had he chosen to do so, he could have gone to Bull and reported that the feeling among all the other meteorologists, with the possible exception of Fleming, ran against Dunstable and Stagg. If he had done so, it is likely that Bull would have taken that news immediately to Eisenhower.

Eisenhower would have found himself faced with a terrible dilemma. He respected Stagg. Yet had he learned that all the other weather centrals disagreed with SHAEF's chief meteorologist, he would be likely to remember that Bull had demoted Stagg and replaced him with Yates. That thought might have further eroded Eisenhower's confidence in Stagg. Would there have been time to place Yates in charge?

It was the weather that worried the Supreme Commander most. A bad forecast would jeopardize the entire operation. If he gave the word to "go," and the weather turned sour, the lives of thousands of men and massive amounts of equipment and supplies would be lost. Worse yet the Germans would have learned beyond any doubt where the Allies planned to invade. If he did not go and the weather was good, Germans might have spied the massive build-up in Southern England and the elements of the invasion fleet headed for Normandy. The odds that the Allies' plans would have been discovered would increase exponentially.

To his credit, Yates kept mum. Instead of going to see Bull, he and Stagg took a walk around the long narrow pond at the base of the hill on which the manor sat. As they talked, they came around to the feeling that though the forecast they'd presented accurately presented the possible deterioration of the weather for D-day, they'd offered as well the prospect that the weather might not be unfavorable and that the senior commanders had been adequately prepared for either outcome.

In his diary, Stagg recalls 3 June as a day of "extreme strain." And in his book he reports that the day before, when he was about to depart SHAEF headquarters for the final journey down to Southwick, Gen. Morgan had said: "Good luck, Stagg; may all your depressions be nice little ones: but remember, we'll string you up from the nearest lamp post if you don't read the omens right."

As soon as Stagg and Yates reviewed Fleming's new weather chart at 1700 DBST, the weather patterns became clearer. Indeed, the lows were becoming more intense and the ridge from the Azores

High, which had extended toward Ireland, seemed to be drifting south. In a late afternoon conference, Widewing stuck to its position that the ridge would protect Normandy with some cloud and light winds. On the evening conference call three hours later, the Admiralty forecaster was the first to speak. The voice from the Citadel said their view had changed and now aligned more closely with Dunstable's. All but Widewing seemed to agree that the Azores High was no longer a factor. Rather the question was now, as Stagg had believed all along, how fast, how intense, and in what direction the string of lows crossing the North Atlantic would move.[214]

2130 DBST—Supreme Commanders Meeting, Southwick House

As Stagg and Yates waited in the great hall as the last of the commanders filed into the library, Air Chief Marshal Arthur Tedder, Ike's deputy supreme commander, approached.

"Serious, yet with a barely concealed twinkle, he threw at me, 'What the devil has been going on behind the scenes in recent days, Stagg? Will you please tell me?'" Tedder then explained that he and the deputy chief of staff for air, Vice Air-Marshal James Robb, had just arrived from Bushy Park after meeting with Gen. Carl Spaatz, commander of US Army Air Forces in England.

They and Spaatz had walked over to Widewing's weather central where Holzman and Krick had shown them their optimistic charts. "Tedder repeated, not unkindly, 'Now tell me, Stagg, just what has been going on around you?'

"I said, 'I'm afraid the weather centers haven't quite been seeing eye to eye in recent days. Widewing's techniques have led them to be more consistently optimistic than I have thought to be warranted, and I have taken the responsibility of toning down their contributions to the forecasts which I have been bringing you in there. I'm sorry if the Widewing people feel that I have not given their views the consideration they deserve; but I can assure you that nothing would have made me happier than if I could have accepted their forecast of weather for the week-end and Monday.'...Tedder then looked at Yates who had not spoken. He now nodded assent, and Tedder said, 'For everybody's sake let's hope it will turn out alright.'"

As Leigh-Mallory and Tedder were entering the library, Adm. Creasy approached. "'Well, you chaps, I hope you have some reassuring news for us tonight? When you (looking at me) went out from yesterday evening's meeting I remarked to the company— There goes six foot two of Stagg and six feet one of gloom. Is that how you really felt or was I misjudging you?'

"I smiled and said, 'I'm sorry, Sir; I didn't intend that my face should be used as the hall barometer. But you were right and I'm afraid I don't feel much happier now.'"[215]

Before Eisenhower and his assembled commanders, Stagg said that during 4/5 June, the depressions would cause "disturbed conditions in the Channel and assault area." He forecast west-southwest winds of Force 5 along the English Coast and of Force 3 to 4 on the invasion beaches. Cloud would likely be low and thick with visibility limited to three or four miles. These conditions would persist until early Wednesday 8 June, when a new low, situated south of Canada's Maritimes would probably blow through.

Air commander Leigh-Mallory wanted to know what weather his heavy bombers would face and the same for German fighters. A two-thousand-foot-thick layer of stratus cloud would obscure the ground above an altitude of five hundred to one thousand feet, Stagg reported. Another layer of cloud, though not continuous, would be encountered at around ten thousand feet. For the navy, Ramsay wondered whether the high winds would bluster Monday and Tuesday and whether cloudiness would abound on Tuesday. He was answered in the affirmative. Pressed for a prediction for weather beyond Wednesday, Stagg said no useful forecast could be given.[216]

Throughout Stagg's briefing, Ike sat still with his chin resting on his hand staring at his weatherman. When questions began, his gaze shifted to each commander as if to read their thoughts about Stagg's responses.

"He turned to me as for a final question: 'Now let me put this one to you. Last night you left us, or at least you left me, with a gleam of hope. Isn't there just a chance that you might be a bit more optimistic again tomorrow?'

"'No Sir. As I had hoped you would realize yesterday, I was most unhappy about the prospects for Monday and Tuesday.'" Stagg explained that the weather systems were evolving slowly, that the previous night it appeared to be improving slightly but now it had deteriorated again. Ike reassured Stagg that he hadn't been led astray, and Stagg was relieved that his briefing had not been misinterpreted.

As he was about to head for the door, Tedder tossed him one final question: "'Before you go, Stagg, will you tell us whether all the forecasting centres are agreed on the forecast you have just given us?'" Thanks to that long and pointed call from Yates to Widewing all but ordering them to get in line, with great relief, Stagg was able to answer, "Yes, Sir: they are."

The weathermen returned to the hall and waited for the ensuing discussion among the commanders to conclude. After several minutes, Bull emerged and informed them that Eisenhower had made the decision to hold up the invasion on a day-to-day basis pending improvement of the weather.[217]

Ike was vexed by this turn of events. Every contingency had been addressed: all the men, all the ships, all the vehicles, all the materiel, all the aircraft, every element of the grand assault was ready. Could the invasion be halted without compromising the secrecy so vital to its success? How could the return of loaded ships to port result in anything less than unimaginable logistical chaos? And what if the weather in the next favorable period of low tide and moonlight in mid-June proved unfavorable. What then? The Supreme Commander's greatest fear, that inclement weather would foil SHAEF's plans and worse yet at the very last minute, now stared him in the face.[218]

Stagg had just stepped onto the mansion's portico when Tedder came by lighting his pipe. "He turned to me and, smiling, said, 'Pleasant dreams, Stagg.' He knew there could not even be sleep for the next commanders meeting had been called for 0415 DBST well before sun-up. Through the trees we could see that the sky was almost clear and everything around was calm and quiet."[219]

CHAPTER TEN

The Horns of D-day

Out of the night that covers me,
Black as the pit from pole to pole,
I thank whatever gods may be,
For my unconquerable soul.
—William Ernest Henley, *Invictus*

Sunday—4 June—The Forecast—
Meteorological Office, Air Ministry

General Inference—*A depression northwest of Ireland is moving eastnortheast and associated troughs are crossing the country. There will be strong to gale force southwest to west winds in the North and fresh to strong in the South. It will be cloudy in most areas with some rain in the north and west and during the afternoon in the Southeast. Some break in the cloud will occur during today in the Southeast. Later conditions will become showery in the North and fair with broken cloud in the South. Mainly rather cold, but rather warm in the Southeast at first.*

Further Outlook—*Showers in the North, fair with broken cloud in the South. Gale warning in operation for districts 7, 8,*

12, 13a, 13b, 17 & 18 at time of issue 0800 4th June, 1944.
(The districts include western Scotland, Isle of Man, Manches-
ter, and Blacksod Point.)

0100 DBST—Blacksod Point Station, Meteorological Service,
Republic of Ireland

When Maureen Flavin rose to take weather readings from the instruments in the corner of the post office, she found that the barometer showed a slight drop in air pressure. Wind was out of the west southwest at 7 mph. Drizzle was intermittent. The readings were telegraphed to Dublin where they were compared with readings from other Irish weather stations at Malin Head, Alder Grove, Castle Archdale, Birr Castle, Collinstown, Foynes, Valentia, and Roches Point. Flavin, and the postmistress's son Ted Sweeney, noted that pressure continued to fall all morning, with drizzle growing into periods of rain and winds steadily blowing in from the south-southwest at 7 mph.

The drop in pressure reported at 0100 DBST by Irish stations was reasonably consistent with that recorded by most other Met Office stations throughout the British Isles. But from 0200 DBST through 0700 DBST, the pressure decline sharpened.[220]

0300 DBST—SHAEF Advanced Headquarters, Southwick

Rather than retiring to his tent and tossing in tortured slumber for an hour or two pondering the myriad possibilities presented by the rapidly changing weather systems, Stagg returned to the weather hut to set down in detailed notes the specifics of and rationale for each forecast. While Adm. Creasy's threat to string up Stagg had been made mostly in jest, it contained a huge element of truth. Stagg knew without a doubt that the weather centrals were all but united in condemning his selection as SHAEF's chief meteorologist. If he flubbed the forecast for D-day, it was his neck that would enter the noose.

Even Eisenhower had an out. Publicly, he would accept responsibility if a bad weather forecast caused the invasion to fail, but he would know and his subordinate commanders would know that Stagg had been the one who let them down. That prospect was almost too ghastly to contemplate, yet Stagg understood that his only defense lay in the written record, which he set about preparing as Fleming's Wrens and ratings plotted synoptic data on a new weather chart while the teleprinter clattered incessantly in the background.

The Admiralty opened the 0300 DBST call with a firm pronouncement that the weather would continue to deteriorate. The Azores High was fading and drifting westward. The ridge that had offered the prospect of protecting the Channel was melting away to the south. The gradient between high- and low-pressure zones over the British Isles was steepening and could generate winds of Force 6. Petterssen for the Met Office agreed and predicted that the low spotted near Newfoundland the previous afternoon would sweep through on 6 or 7 June.

As Stagg had come to expect, Holzman and Krick objected strongly to the pessimistic forecast. They had examined every weather map for the past fifty years. Every day like the one depicted by this morning's chart was followed by a day where the high-pressure ridge had strengthened and moved back to the north. That would save the Channel from the rapidly approaching low with its wind and cloud. Krick later recalled that the weather map for 12 May 1934 matched the 5 June invasion date.[221] Krick then went into a detailed analysis of synoptic data that supported his view. The Admiralty and Dunstable refused to accept it. And Krick, having felt the heat from Yates the day before to get on board with the others, agreed not to dispute the forecast Stagg and Yates would present at the 0415 DBST commanders meeting.[222]

Stagg once again stood before Eisenhower with Yates and Fleming behind him. He reported that the details of the previous night's forecast were essentially unchanged. The Channel would experience strong wind and heavy cloud. The only difference in the new set of predictions was that the cold front was moving faster than anticipated and could swing through Monday or Tuesday.

"Yates and I remained in the room. It was Admiral Ramsay who broke the silence.

"'The sky outside here at the moment is practically clear and there is no wind: when do you expect the cloud and wind of your forecast to appear here?'

"'In another four or five hours, Sir.'"

Ramsay said he didn't like the weather as forecast but was prepared to go. Gen. Montgomery, in charge of ground forces, was dead set against any delay. But Leigh-Mallory said that his bombers could not operate under the predicted conditions and Tedder agreed.

That turned the trick for Eisenhower. He was a ferocious bridge player and expert at calculating the odds. Once the Germans realized that the invasion to liberate France was coming ashore, Rommel would move his Panzer Corps into the bridgehead, ripping to shreds the first waves of soldiers holding the beach. The Germans vastly outnumbered the Allies on the ground, but in the air the positions were dramatically reversed. Bombers could blast Rommel's tank parks and assembly areas. Fighters armed with cannon could shoot up troop trains and strafe columns of trucks and tanks. Virtually unchallenged along the French coast, Allied bombers and fighters were Ike's trumps. If he couldn't play them, he'd have to hold them for a better day. With no dissent from any of the commanders, Ike postponed the invasion for twenty-four hours.

Aboard Landing Craft Control #70

Stagg and Yates returned to Fleming's weather hut as Ramsay sent word to halt the fleet. Though Stagg wanted to wait to see the next set of charts, Yates convinced them to return to their tent in the woods, and they set off just as a lovely rosy dawn was brightening the sky.[223]

Lt. Stephen L. Freeland commanded one of the scores of landing craft steaming out of Weymouth harbor on the afternoon of 3 June. A pair of ten-mile-long columns of LCTs was followed by ninety LCMs arranged in four shorter strings. Freeland's LCC flanked the rear of the procession to starboard. The flotilla had been ordered to make 5 knots, straining the LCTs against muscular Channel tides that at times reached 6 knots. Mechanical failures slowed many, and those immediately astern had to maneuver wildly to avoid collision. Thumps and bangs of ships brushing each other echoed over the water.

Shortly after dusk, overcast blackened the sky. Winds picked up, and the already troubled sea grew more turbulent. The fourth dawned glowery. Blustery gusts buffeted the ship. Says Freeland in *Nothing Less than Victory—An Oral History of D-Day,* "We were getting thoroughly wet and well slammed about by the steep chop building up on our starboard quarter. . . . an LCC in a sea has a snappy roll with a kind of walloping wriggle tied on to it that can jar the fillings out of your teeth. . . . (Emerging from the welter of men trying to rest below decks), one green-faced gunner's mate hoisted himself wearily topside explaining, 'Sleeping down there is damned rugged duty.'"

At roughly 0900 DBST, with waves breaking over the bow, the LCC received the signal that D-day had been postponed for twenty-four hours. The convoy was ordered to return to Weymouth to refuel and take on fresh water. For seven hours Freeland's fleet fought wind and tide before reaching the calm water of its home port.[224]

ZENTRAL WETTERDIENST GRUPPE AND LUFTFLOTTE III

Like the Met Office, the Zentral Wetterdienst Gruppe (ZWG) was composed of civilians. Though ZWG issued all forecasts for the Luftwaffe, assigned to each of the German Air Force's regions—*Luftflotte*—was a civilian meteorologist. Dr. Walther Stöbe was *Oberstmeteorologue* for Luftflotte III, which covered France from headquarters in Paris.[225]

Monthly weather predictions were the province of Franz Baur and his Institute for Long-Range Weather Forecasting at Bad Homburg, with whom Krick had spent time in 1934. The Germans did not consider Baur's predictions accurate enough for operations. However, a system similar to Krick's weather types provided a point of departure for making five- and ten-day forecasts. The Kriegsmarine had its own weather service, which coordinated little with the Luftwaffe. The Germans lacked the chain of communication that existed among SHAEF's weather centrals.

From reports from air reconnaissance flights, their automatic weather stations in the Arctic, and U-boats; from intercepted transmissions from Allied weather ships, airbases in England sending the barometric pressure readings needed by returning bombers to reset their altimeters; and from cancellations picked up from English radio stations of British football and soccer matches, the Germans were able to formulate a reasonably accurate idea of the weather over the North Atlantic. Not unlike the forecasts received at Widewing from the Pentagon, Luftflotte III would receive by teletype synoptic analysis from ZWG. It would then modify the predictions based on current local data and forward it to local commanders.

On 2 June ZWG identified the eastward drift of a weak low-pressure cell from the Irish Sea into the southern portion of the North Sea, which produced rain. Their forecast predicted that a high and then a new low moving in out of the Atlantic would follow the front. They would pick up the intensification of the pressure gradient over the eastern North Atlantic on 4 June and the worsening weather conditions over northwestern France, the Channel, and the North Sea.[226]

German commanders were relieved. Their forces had been on high alert throughout May, and many wondered why in the world the Allies had not taken advantage of the benign weather to invade.

1300 DBST—SHAEF Advanced Headquarters, Southwick

When Stagg arose later that morning, he was appalled to find the sky still clear and no sign of much wind. Yet when he and Yates made it up the hill to the manor house, the wind was approaching Force 4, tree boughs were bending, cloud was thickening, and the ceiling was lowering. Their relief was palpable. The much anticipated front moving at about 40 mph had passed the weather ship HMS *Hoste* between 0000 and 0400DBST, had swung across Ireland later that morning and was now driving across southern England and the Channel.[227]

The imminent passage of the front was borne out by the first sketches of the weather chart for 1300 DBST. The chart also suggested that the low in the mid-Atlantic was growing larger, more intense, and thus would likely move more slowly than they'd thought at the 0415 DBST commanders' meeting. If this were the case, a period of clearing skies with strong but moderating winds might follow the passage of the front that was now approaching Southwick. With nothing demanding his attention, Stagg set off on a rambling walk toward Ports Down to clear his head. It didn't help. All he could think about were troops in the transports and how far some had sailed before receiving the order to hove to.

He returned to the weather hut just in time to study the 1300 DBST weather chart before the conference with the centrals began. The chart seemed to support his opinion that a period of relatively moderate weather would build in behind the front. He imagined that the pending discussion would have little heat compared to last evening's. How wrong he was. Petterssen began the call stating that weather was developing just as they'd anticipated. He had no sooner finished his prediction when Krick jumped him with great fervor. Dunstable had most certainly not forecast the current situation, he argued, it had been Widewing's call. And so it began, the endless argument and still unresolved, now nearly three-quarters of a century later, over which of the centers had made the right forecast for D-day.

The salient question was whether the zone of high pressure trailing the front would be strong enough to protect the beaches during 6 and 7 June. It wasn't enough to put men ashore. Air power was the only reliable means of repulsing the German counterattack when it came and, to do that, pilots needed to see targets on the ground unobscured by cloud. Reinforcements needed to land to replace casualties and to expand the lodgment. That would require new landings of artillery, armor, and tanks, and the fuel, ammunition, and supplies to feed the fledgling foothold.

Widewing predicted that the lows would spin rapidly to the northeast allowing a strong ridge of high pressure to establish itself over the Channel. Dunstable thought the paths of the depressions would be more eastward and that any succeeding ridge would not be strong enough to dispel cloud from the area. This time, the Admiralty tended to side with Widewing, as did Stagg to a large degree.

Though not scheduled to brief Eisenhower and his commanders until 2100 DBST, Stagg was confident enough of these developments to prepare a short summary for Bull, who if it seemed worthwhile to him, would pass it along to Ike.[228] At 1745 DBST, he informed Bull that the situation had changed significantly since the 0415 DBST commanders meeting. He told the general that, starting about midnight, winds would die down and cloudiness would abate. He added though that the weather would begin again to become less favorable by the evening of 6 June.[229] Bull wondered if news of the probable break had come too late for the Allies to take advantage of it. Stagg thought that his commanding officer might also be thinking that if the forecast could change so diametrically and so quickly, could it not do so again in the next twenty-four hours?

1300 DBST—Blacksod Point Station, Meteorological Service, Republic of Ireland

In taking this hour's readings, Flavin noted that the barometer had ceased to fall. In the next few hours would pressure begin to climb? Wind was becoming more westerly.

1930 DBST—SHAEF Advanced Headquarters, Southwick

After the morning's highly charged arguments, Stagg was relieved that the centers seemed to have vented their earlier spleen when the conference call opened an hour and a half before the next scheduled commanders briefing. The centers generally agreed that the lows would pass to the northeast of the British Isles and that the weather late on the night of 5 June and through most of the 6th would be suitable for the landings and the skies clear enough for air support.[230] Bates and Crowell at the Admiralty forecast that swell off the beaches would drop from eight to ten feet to three to four feet and to two to three feet off Utah Beach, protected from westerlies by the Cotentin Peninsula.[231]

One key question remained: What would the weather be like on 7 and 8 June? Most agreed that winds would moderate, seldom rising above Force 4 and often less. Cloud cover was another question. Nobody was certain of that. And none of the centrals was willing to risk a longer-range prediction.

2130 DBST—SHAEF Advanced Headquarters, Southwick

Force 5 winds from the southwest and heavy intermittent squalls buffeted the blacked-out French doors of the library where the commanders were meeting. Stagg, Yates, and Fleming were asked into the meeting, and as Stagg remembers, he delivered this forecast:

"Gentlemen, since I presented the forecast last evening some rapid and unexpected developments have occurred over the north Atlantic. In particular a vigorous front—a cold front —from one of the depressions has pushed more quickly and much farther south than could have been foreseen. This front is approaching Portsmouth now and will pass through all Channel areas tonight or early tomorrow. After the strong winds and low cloud associated with that front have moved through there will be a brief period of improved weather from Monday afternoon. For most of the time the sky will not be more than half covered with cloud and its base should not often be below 2,000–3,000 feet. Winds will decrease substantially from what they are now. Those conditions will last over Monday night and into Tuesday. Behind that fair interlude cloud will probably increase again later on Tuesday with amounts up to 8/10ths to 10/10ths overnight Tuesday-Wednesday. From early Wednesday until at least Friday weather will continue unsettled — variable skies with cloud 10/10ths and base down to 1,000 feet for periods of not more than 4 to 6 hours at a time but intersperced with considerable fair intervals. Winds will be westerly throughout, force 4 to 5 along English coasts, force 3 to 4 on French coasts and probably less, force 2 to 3, along sheltered stretches on that side of the Channel."[232]

The morning after the meeting, Air Vice Marshal Robb recollected the conversation that followed Stagg's forecast:

"Admiral Ramsay: 'Admiral Kirk (commander of the naval task forces) must be told within the next half hour if "OVERLORD" is to take place on TUESDAY. If he is told it is on and his forces sail and are then recalled, they will not be ready again for Wednesday morning: therefore a further postponement would be for 48 hours.'

"General Eisenhower: 'Conditions are almost ideal up to a point, even if the operations of the heavy air may be held up later. Suppose you (to Ramsay) give orders tonight that TUESDAY is on; should we meet again in the morning?'

"General Montgomery: 'The only decision the weather experts could give at 0400 hours tomorrow would be the position of the next depression.'

"General Bedell-Smith: 'Looks to me like we've gotten a break that we could hardly hope for.'

"Air Chief Marshal Leigh-Mallory said he thought it would be likely to be only a moderate night and that Bomber Command would have great difficulty getting their markers down and in doing useful bombing. This brought a response from several members present that 'You are referring to another day, in fact you are a day out.' Leigh-Mallory's statement brought the following response from the Supreme Commander—'Don't be that pessimistic.'

"General Bedell-Smith: 'Our apprehension now concerns spotting for Naval gunfire and the second mission for the heavies. It's a helluva gamble this (the decision to go ahead) is the best possible gamble.'

"Air Chief Marshal Tedder mentioned that it would be a question of making the best use of gaps between the trailing fronts brought along by the series of 'lows.' 'Agree with Leigh-Mallory the operations of heavies and mediums are going to be chancey.'

"General Eisenhower: 'We have a great force of fighter-bombers. (turns to General Montgomery) Do you see any reason for not going on TUESDAY.'

"General Montgomery: 'I would say—Go!'

"General Eisenhower: 'The alternatives are too chancey. The question, just how long can you hang this operation on the end of a limb and let it hang there. The air will certainly be handicapped.'

"Air Chief Marshal Leigh-Mallory: 'Hell of a situation if German night bombers can operate and our night fighters cannot get off. At DIEPPE. . . .'

"General Eisenhower: 'If you don't give the instructions now, you cannot do it on Tuesday.'

"Air Chief Marshal Tedder to Leigh-Mallory: 'If the later forecast shows a deterioration earlier (i.e. during Tuesday night) putting on the night bombers at an earlier hour might be considered.'

"General Eisenhower: 'Well, I'm quite positive we must give the order; the only question is whether we should meet again in the morning.

"Well, I don't like it, but there it is.

"Well boys, there it is. I don't see how we can possibly do anything else.'"

The discussion had taken only fifteen minutes.[233] Provisional orders were issued for launching the D-day assault. It would begin at 0630 DBST on 6 June. A few moments after his meteorologists had been dismissed, Eisenhower came out and headed for the door to the portico. On the way he paused and said to his chief meteorologist, "Well, Stagg, we're putting it on again: for heaven's sake hold the weather to what you've told us and don't bring any more bad news." Gen. Bull then emerged and said the commanders would expect another briefing at 0415 DBST in the morning. Through driving rain, Stagg and Yates ran across the drive into the weather hut where they looked at the latest chart, called the centrals to alert them to the need for a conference at 0300 DBST, and then caught a ride down to their tent where they lay on their cots, dozed, and contemplated the decision and their role in it.[234]

5 June, 0800 DBST, The Forecast, Meteorological Office, Air Ministry

General Inference—*A depression centered over the Shetlands is drifting northeast and beginning to fill up. There will be strong to gale force west to northwest winds in Scotland at first, moderating steadily. It will be mainly cloudy throughout the British Isles with showers in Scotland, N. England and N. Ireland and scattered showers further south at first; later showers are expected to die out in England, Ireland, and S. Scotland. It will be rather cool in the South, and cool in the North.*

Further Outlook—*Rain spreading into W. Ireland and W. Scotland later tomorrow afternoon moving east. Gale warning in operation in districts 13a, 13b (the Hebrides) at time of issue 0800 DBST 4.6.44 (sic) and in districts 11, 15, and 16 (Scotland) at 1355 DBST 4.6.44.*

0100 DBST—Blacksod Point Station, Meteorological Service,
Republic of Ireland

At 1500 DBST on 4 June, Flavin recorded the first slight uptick
in pressure since the barometer had begun to fall the day before. It
would continue to build throughout the night as winds came around
to the west and then northwest, though they did not exceed 7 mph.

0300 DBST—SHAEF Advanced Headquarters, Southwick

Though Fleming's staff was still drawing isobars onto the new
chart when Stagg and Yates arrived, little had changed, and for that
both were mightily grateful. On the call, the three centers generally agreed, though Widewing believed that the weather on D-day
would be much better than that forecast by Dunstable and the
Admiralty. Wind and wave along the French coast might present
difficulty in landing men and materiel later on D-day and into the
morning of 7 June.

0415 DBST—SHAEF Advanced Headquarters, Supreme
Commanders Meeting, Southwick

With the exception of Montgomery, who was attired in a fawn
pullover and corduroys, all the assembled commanders were wearing battle dress as the meteorologists entered the room.

Stagg presented his briefing. The fair weather that had come
to Southwick in the past few hours would extend over Normandy
until at least midday and probably late on 6 June. Generally speaking about 3/10ths cloud cover could be expected. Though bursts of
wind up to Force 6 should be anticipated, most of the time it would
be about Force 3. Wind and cloud were expected to increase from
7 June through Friday, 9 June, but the extended forecast included
intervals of fair weather as well.

The tension that had filled the library during previous command-ers meetings had been swept away as if by passage of the night's front. Ike flashed his famous grin. "Well, Stagg, if this forecast comes off, I promise you we'll have a celebration when the time comes."[235]

Stagg did add that any future storm system to transit the North Atlantic would probably take a more northeasterly track and pass over Iceland rather than western Scotland, which could provide the Chan-nel with several good days. He noted, though, that all the centrals con-curred that the weather over the North Atlantic was quite unsettled.[236]

In the hall, Stagg and Yates joined the bevy of senior aides who awaited their commanders. Out they soon came with the final irre-vocable decision that D-day was on for the night of 5/6 June. Bull, Stagg's former nemesis, pressed through the crowd to offer him and Yates congratulations and ordered him to report to him at 0900 DBST any change in the weather. With that they walked down the hill to their tent under an increasingly fair sky. What they wanted was rest, but sleep would not visit them. Instead they lay tranquilly on their cots and listened to songbirds waking in the woods.

A few hours later Stagg, after examining the morning's new charts, reported to Bull that fair weather predicted for 6 June could well extend into the 7th. Later that morning as they returned from the war room with its wall-sized map showing the disposition of Allied forces headed for Normandy, Stagg and Yates were dismayed to see the sky filling with lowering cloud and to feel the wind pick-ing up. Stagg called Dunstable, and Douglas assured him that this lens of unpleasantness would dissipate by evening. Bombers should be able to spot most of their targets that night. Eisenhower and Creasy, concerned about the sudden cloudiness, entered the hut and were reassured that the weather was going to hold.

The 2100 DBST conference among the centrals reflected none of the bonhomie Stagg expected. Krick and Petterssen immediately began arguing about who had said what about this or that and who had been right or wrong. Widewing with its perpetual optimism predicted fair to fine weather from the 6th on while Dunstable and the Admiralty, to a lesser degree, were dubious. After reporting the fragile consensus of the centrals to Bull in the war room and hearing reports of diminishing wind and cloud over the invasion area, they once more headed down the hill to their tent, only this time to the endless drone of bombers and paratroop transports headed for Normandy.[237]

Jean Farren recalled the endless "drone, drone, drone" of unrelenting waves of big airplanes carpeting the night sky on 5 June as she and Harold Checketts returned from the birthday party for the daughter of the WREN captain with whom she shared quarters in the back half of the weather hut. The party was held in a pub in Cosham on the east end of Portsdown Hill. While the party had been quite gay, Jean had a very sobering thought as she walked up Southwick hill from the party. She worried that she and others involved in preparing the weather charts had made a huge mistake.

"I remember thinking it's going to be absolute hell tomorrow," she said weeping during a 1997 interview with Chris Bailey of the National Museum of the Royal Navy. "We thought everyone was going to get drowned . . . it was going to be a holocaust. . . . It was a tremendous decision. They were relying on knowing about this clearance. Of course the Germans never cottoned on to it. But that kind of decision is a bit heavy and we felt under the strain a bit because if we hadn't gotten our plotting right . . . it sounds rather silly now . . . if we hadn't gotten it right . . . and they did get wrong signals from ships . . . it would have put the whole thing out. Where the center of the low pressure was could be miles out if you got the wrong code coming through."[238]

CHAPTER ELEVEN

Worst Blow in Forty Years

O, what a man might know
The end of this day's business ere it comes!
But it sufficeth that the day will end
And then the end be known.

—WILLIAM SHAKESPEARE, FROM
BRUTUS'S SPEECH AT PHILIPPI IN *JULIUS CAESAR*

For 4 June, German forecasters at ZWG saw weather patterns similar to those predicted by Allied meteorologists for northwestern France.[239] At 06.00 hr Rommel motored from his headquarters in the castle at La Roche-Guyon on the Seine, which is about thirty miles downstream from Paris. He was off to Germany to celebrate his wife's birthday. He'd bought her a new pair of shoes as a present.

Later he'd continue on to plead with Hitler for permission to transfer two more Panzer divisions, an antiaircraft corps, and a mortar brigade to Normandy. He planned to remain away from 5 June to 8 June. As he left he said, "There were all the less doubts that an invasion might happen in the meantime as the tides are very unfavorable in the following days and no air reconnaissance of any kind had given any hints of an imminent landing."[240] This time the famed Desert Fox, who had led his armor with such brilliance in the sweep across France in 1940 and in North Africa, was himself outfoxed. The basic German defensive strategy was fatally flawed, for it held that the Allies would only invade at high tide. Precisely the opposite was true.

05.00 hr, 5 June—Luftflotte III Headquarters, Paris

Dr. Hans Müller, senior meteorologist on Von Rundstedt's staff, was watching the development of frontal systems coming in from the Atlantic and, early in the morning, passed along the following report to Walther Stöbe, the Luftwaffe's chief meteorologist in Luftflotte III headquarters in Paris:

> General Weather Situation—*The strong primary low-pressure system centered between Iceland and Scotland has caused, as expected, the high-pressure ridge over Western Europe to weaken. As a result, the track has been opened up for the movement of frontal systems into Western Europe. The first bad weather system, appearing as a cold front, is expected to cross the Command West area today (5 June). After its passage, clouds with isolated showers will disperse during the course of the day. It is expected that further secondary disturbances develop on the western and southern sides of the primary low-pressure system.*
>
> Outlook for tomorrow, 6 June 1944—*Moderate to fresh W. to NW winds; skies clearing locally during the night (5-6 June); variable cloud during the day with occasional showers particularly in the afternoon. Overnight temperature, 10° C, daytime temperature, 15 to 20° C. Visibility mostly good except in any showers and local morning mist patches.*

17.30 hr, 5 June—Luftflotte III Headquarters, Paris

For Allied activity on the night of 5–6 June, Müller sent the following predictions to Von Rundstedt's headquarters:

> Air Force—*Takeoffs from English airfields generally unimpeded; only occasional local increases in cloud cover. Enemy air force activities over Command West area generally without hindrance due to progressive dispersing clouds causing local clearances. Bad weather only prevails in S. and SW France; thick overcast persists only over Holland.*
>
> Navy—*In den Hoofden (Netherlands) and the Channel, fresh W and SW winds, force 3–5, locally 6, decreasing slightly toward morning. Waves 3–4 (moderate to rough) and occasionally 5 (very rough), also decreasing towards morning. Mostly good visibility.*
>
> Tides—*High in La Havre 22.30 hr, Ijmuiden 04.15 hr. Moonlight all night; one day before full moon; twilight on 6 June at 05.21 hr.*[241]

Little did the Germans know of the other front—a rolling and overpowering force, dispatched like a massive fist with tons of bombs and shells and legions of soldiers—would storm ashore as 5 June became the 6th.

Gory, Gory What a Helluva Way to Die

At 0030 DBST on 6 June, the first of the invasion force, troopers of reinforced D Company of the 2nd Ox and Bucks battalion of the British 6th Airborne Division, landed in six Horsa gliders next to their objectives, bridges over the Orne River north of Caen and just inland from Sword, the easternmost of the invasion beaches. In the next thirty minutes, forty-two hundred men of the division would jump from 264 transports to join them. They would be supported at 0330 DBST by sixty-eight more gliders filled with jeeps, light artillery, engineers with mines, and ammunition.

About midnight, the American airborne 82nd Division in 917 transports, ninety-six towing gliders, flew southwest from England, crossed the Channel, turned east over the Gulf of St. Malo, and proceeded to drop zones behind Utah Beach. They came in at fifteen hundred feet, dropped down to the prescribed jumping altitude of six hundred feet, and slowed to a safe speed to deliver their sticks of paratroopers. Instantly they ploughed into a thick mat of cloud. Bursts of flak flared orange-red. Streams of tracers from machine guns laced the sky. Pilots of the overladen C-47s, many of them inexperienced in night operations, took wild evasive action to avoid flak and collision with other aircraft. For safety, they increased speed and altitude.

Though evasive tactics badly scattered the 82nd, it nonetheless accomplished several of its objectives, among them seizing the crossroads at Ste. Mère-Église. The 101st Division, jumping north of Carentan, suffered similar dispersion. Many landed in marshes flooded by the Germans and were drowned. Still the will of enlisted men and officers of the 82nd and 101st overcame every defense the Germans could muster.[242]

The 82nd in a few hours would be reinforced by the US 4th Division's 8th Infantry Regiment, which landed more than a mile south of its objectives. This turned out to be a bit of good fortune on a day not known for much, because it came ashore in a sector lightly defended and protected to some degree from the westerly wind and wave. Soldiers, most of them seasick, their woolen uniforms soaked with spray and reeking of anti-gas agent and vomit, were only too glad to charge into whatever blazing Wehrmacht machine-gun fire might greet them. The 29th and 1st Divisions landing on the far more exposed Omaha Beach had a much rougher go of it. The Canadians and English at Gold, Juno, and Sword fared a little better.[243]

IF D-DAY HAD BEEN POSTPONED UNTIL MID-JUNE

Had Stagg and the disparate meteorologists at the Admiralty, Dunstable, and Widewing not foreseen the break in the weather for the night of June 5/6, the invasion fleet would have had to return to port to refuel and reorganize. D-day would have been postponed to June 19, the next period of low Normandy tide at dawn.

A decisive forecast for that date would have had to be made no later than early morning on June 18. On the 17th, the weather had looked ideal. A ridge of high pressure was sprawling across all of England. But the picture turned on a dime. A cold front passing through Iceland broke southeastward and began speeding through the British Isles. A steep ridge of high pressure followed it. At the same time, a low was spreading over France from the Mediterranean. Between the two systems the pressure gradient would be very sharp. Near gale force winds would howl down the Channel from the northeast toward the invasion beaches. Low scudding cloud would blanket Normandy.[244]

Immediately after D-day, the Mulberry artificial harbors off the fishing village of Arromanches on Gold Beach and a second one at Omaha Beach were installed. By June 18, 197,444 troops, 27,340 vehicles, and 68,799 long tons (a British long ton equals 2,240 pounds) of supplies had crossed the causeways from newly emplaced docks onto dry land at Omaha.

However, at midnight June 18–19, the weather turned violent. For the next four days winds gusting up to 37 mph pushed waves of eight feet or more, which tore at the pieced-together harbor. LCTs and LCVPs without enough power to turn and ride out the storm slammed into the docks. On June 20 and 21, the cacophony of screaming wind and the roar of driving rain was punctuated by the thunder of surf and the crash of grounding landing craft, DUKS, and their cargoes and by the grinding wreckage of disintegrating Mulberry harbors.

According to Bates, meteorologists had seen the storm coming and had warned the navy. But Adm. Ramsay, Adm. (John L.) Hall, and Army Engineers' reports agree that all weather forecasts received by them were for that period favorable.[245]

Imagine if this storm had happened on D-day. No wonder Eisenhower penciled on the corner of his commendation letter to Stagg: "I thank the gods of war we went when we did."[246]

Epilogue

Getting the forecast right was undoubtedly the professional wartime apogee for the meteorologists who made it. To his last breath, Krick asserted that he was the man who told Eisenhower when to launch the invasion of northwestern Europe. Hogben was more modest in claiming that role for himself and his colleagues in the Admiralty. All the others were justifiably very proud of their accomplishment but insisted that the forecast was a collective effort for which no one group bore complete responsibility. Implicit in the position that all had a role in the forecast is the notion that had it gone wrong, no one service, not the Met Office, not the Admiralty, not the USSTAF, would be blamed. Indeed, success has many fathers, failure is an orphan.

After finalizing his *Report on the Meteorological Implications in the Selection of the Day for the Allied Invasion of France* in late June 1944, Stagg became something of a supernumerary at SHAEF. The greatest Allied combined air, land, and sea operation had achieved success. Armies, with tactical air support, were driving toward Germany. The Allied bomber command continued to pummel strategic and military targets in Occupied Europe. There was no longer a perceived need to coordinate weather centrals. Stagg was, in effect, out of a real job. Demobilized in September 1946, he became principal deputy director, then director of services for the Met Office, a position he held until 1960. In addition he served as the general secretary of the International Union of Geodesy and Geophysics and as president of the Royal Meteorological Society, Having received the Officer of the Order of the British Empire for his leadership of the 1932 British Polar Year expedition, he clearly achieved the social respectability his mother had so desperately sought for him.

Krick returned from Europe, assumed chairmanship of the meteorology department at Caltech, and immediately became mired in controversy. Moonlighting on the side, he created a private consulting firm that provided forecasts to movie studios and California's burgeoning agriculture industry. His claims of being able to forecast weather weeks in advance were widely debunked by other meteorologists including those at the US Weather Bureau. Learning of these concerns, the university president, Lee A. DuBridge, ordered a committee of professors to assess Krick's work. Their report was damning: "He claims to do things that he can't do. He claims to have done things he didn't do." Krick's tenure at Caltech came to a bitter close when it was revealed that he was using the teletype and weather data that the Bureau provided the university for free to run his commercial business. DuBridge allowed Krick to resign and terminated Caltech's meteorology department in 1947.

Not one to be daunted, Krick's consulting became very lucrative. Along with business and agriculture, his seemingly miraculous ability to forecast weather for major events long in advance won him clients among the rich and powerful. He accurately predicted light morning snow followed by afternoon flurries for January 21, 1957, the date President Eisenhower was publically sworn in for his second term. He would continue to provide forecasts for social events to Presidents Lyndon Johnson and Jimmy Carter.[247]

Krick and the Weather Bureau remained at war until he retired in 1990. During the late 1940s, he barnstormed across the West claiming that by seeding clouds with silver iodide crystals he could make rain. Instead of deploying airplanes, which had been used in successful small-scale cloud seeding with dry ice, Krick invented a little oven that burned coke impregnated with the chemical.

Powered by a car battery, the ovens were fired up when Krick called ranchers and told them that a cloud formation suitably laden with moisture was on its way. Into the atmosphere, smoke from the ovens carried tiny particles of silver iodide around which droplets of water coalesced allegedly producing rain or snow. The Weather Bureau was incensed. Rain making could short-stop moisture as rain in Arizona that nature meant to fall as snow in Colorado. Threats of expensive lawsuits stemming from too much precipitation or too little forced him to desist after a few years.[248]

Mainstream meteorologists held that Krick was a charlatan, and the issue came to a head in the late 1950s when the American Meteorological Society questioned statements about long-range forecasting in an article carrying Krick's byline that seemed to violate the society's code of ethics. His differences with the conventional meteorologists who made up the society proved irreconcilable, and he resigned rather than face censure.[249]

Two of the American forecasters would earn flag rank in the US Air Force. Yates would become a lieutenant general and deputy director of defense research and engineering in the Office of the Secretary of Defense. Previously he had commanded the Air Force Missile Test Center at Patrick Air Force Base and served as president of the American Meteorological Society. Wearing the single star of a brigadier general, Holzman commanded the Air Force Cambridge Research Laboratories before retiring in 1964. He then worked as a special advisor to the National Space and Atmospheric Administration and then director of the National Oceanographic and Atmospheric Administration's environmental science data service before his second retirement in 1971.

Bates, one of the pair of Army Air Force lieutenants assigned to the Admiralty to forecast surf and swell, would retire from the service as a lieutenant colonel in 1964 after establishing a worldwide network of 120 seismic stations in thirty-eight countries to monitor nuclear tests. He continued his service as technical director of the US Naval Oceanographic Office and later as science advisor to the Commandant, US Coast Guard. Crowell, his partner, returned to academe, eventually chairing the department of earth sciences at the University of California, Santa Barbara, and winning the Penrose Medal, the top award presented by the Geological Society of America.

And what of the meteorologists who fell in love as D-day approached? Jean Farren and Harold Checketts married and were living in Eckington, England, when I interviewed them in 2011. Jean passed away in 2013. Out on Blacksod Point, Ted Sweeney married Maureen Flavin, and they lived in the lighthouse where he was its keeper. He passed away in 2001. After I finished my interview with Maureen a decade later, she poured me a stout tot of Irish whiskey, and we toasted their good fortune to be in the right place at the right time.

GLOSSARY

Admiralty—Headquarters of the Royal Navy in London.

Air Ministry—Headquarters for the Royal Air Force in London. The Meteorological Office was an agency of the Air Ministry.

AK—Armia Krojowa (Polish Home Army), a resistance group.

Allies—The countries that were united in efforts to defeat Germany and Japan.

ANCXF—Allied Naval Commander Expeditionary Force.

Army Air Corps—The flying combat arm, like infantry and armor, of the US Army.

Army Air Forces Weather Central—The weather bureau of the US Army Air Force housed in four different rings of the Pentagon.

Avro Lancaster—British four-engine heavy bomber built by Avro.

Azores High—Persistent atmospheric high pressure area in the mid-latitudes, i.e., 30–35 degrees north, often extending westward into the Bermuda area.

B-17—Flying Fortress, Boeing four-engine heavy bomber used extensively by the Army Air Forces for daylight bombing of Germany.

B-24—Liberator, Consolidated-Vultee four-engine heavy bomber replacement for B-17.

Beagle—Code name of Belgian resistance transmitting weather data to England.

Bergen school—Pioneering school of meteorological thought founded by Professor Vilhelm Bjerknes utilizing hydrodynamic principles to predict weather.

BIGOT—Code name (British Invasion of German Occupied Territory) for individuals cleared to know specifications for D-day.

Bletchley Park—Manor house where intercepted German radio messages were deciphered.

Blitzkrieg—Lightning War, German term for rapid coordinated attack by air, armor, and infantry.

Bushy Park—Eleven-hundred-acre deer park twelve miles southwest of London, headquarters of SHAEF and USSTAF.

C-47—Military version of Douglas DC-3, the primary aircraft used by paratroopers.

Caltech—California Institute of Technology, Pasadena, California.

Citadel—Massive concrete bunker butting the Admiralty offices in London.

cold front—Often stormy zone between advancing cool dry air associated with a high and warmer moist air drawn in by a low.

Copenhagen Code—International pre-war code for transmitting weather data.

COSSAC—Initial British/American planning group for D-day. Became SHAEF with Eisenhower's appointment.

DBST—Double British Summer Time, i.e., two hours before true local time, used to extend work hours in daylight.

depression—Area of low atmospheric pressure featuring unsettled weather often including cloud and rain.

Dieppe—French coastal town near the Pas de Calais raided by Allied Forces on August 19, 1942, with disastrous results.

Dornier 17—German medium bomber often called the "flying pencil."

DSC—Distinguished Service Cross, British military decoration.

DUKW—Amphibious truck with dual drive to both wheels and propeller.

Dunstable—English village north of London, location of the Met Office's Central Forecasting Office code-named ETA.

Enigma—German code machine.

Fort Southwick—Fortress erected during 1853 on the ridge just north of Portsmouth with a mile of tunnels housing the British Underground Combined Headquarters manned by 450 Royal Navy, 125 British Army, and 125 Royal Air Force communications personnel, primarily female. Two miles southeast of Southwick House.

front—Meteorological term introduced in 1919 by Jacob Bjerknes to define the interface between conflicting warm and cool air masses.

Groep Packard—Dutch resistance group providing weather data to Allies active 1942–1944.

Halifax—British four-engine heavy bomber built by Handley Page.

Hampden—British twin-engine medium bomber built by Handley Page also used for weather reconnaissance.

Higgins boat—Assault craft that evolved into the popular LCVP craft of the US Navy in World War II.

high—Zone of high barometric pressure featuring outflowing air and typically fair weather.

HMS—His Majesty's Ship, designation for a Royal Navy ship or shore stations.

Hudson—Twin-engine light bomber and reconnaissance aircraft built by Lockheed.

Husky—Code name for Allied invasion of Sicily.

IDA—Code name for Met Office unit specializing in decrypting radio weather transmissions from Germany and occupied countries.

isobars—Contour lines linking areas of equal atmospheric pressure used to map zones of high and low pressure.

jet stream—Bands of sub-polar air flowing at speeds up to 300 mph at altitudes between twenty-three thousand and thirty-nine thousand feet that markedly affect surface weather.

Ju 88—German twin-engine medium bomber by Junkers.

Kew—Location of Royal Observatory south of London built for King George III in 1769 and operated by the Met Office to take weather observations since 1910.

Kriegsmarine—German Navy.

low—Area of low barometric atmospheric pressure rotating counterclockwise featuring inflowing air and often poor weather.

Luftflotte III—Luftwaffe defense command for northwest Europe located in Paris.

Luftwaffe—German Air Force.

Meteorological Office (Met Office)—Civilian agency of the Air Ministry responsible for providing weather services to the RAF and the British Army as well as providing forecasts for the general public like the US Weather Bureau.

millibar (mb)—a unit of atmospheric pressure. Decreases with altitude (i.e., 700 mb occurs at approximately ten thousand feet, and 500 mb at approximately eighteen thousand feet).

MIT—Massachusetts Institute of Technology, Cambridge, Massachusetts.

Mosquito—Fast wooden Canadian twin-engine light bomber and reconnaissance aircraft.

Mulberry—Code name for concrete artificial harbors floated across the Channel to provide docks at D-day beaches where vehicles and supplies could easily be unloaded.

Nazis—Abbreviation for Nationalsozialistsche Arbeiterpartie (i.e., the National Socialist German Workers Party).

Neptune—Code name for naval phase of Operation Overlord.

Norfolk House—Headquarters of COSSAC in London that became SHAEF HQ in early 1944.

OKW—Oberkommando der Wehrmacht, Supreme Command, German Armed Forces coordinating German Army, Air Force, and Navy operations.

Overlord—Code name for Allied invasion of northwestern France.

P-38 Lightning—Fast twin-engine, single-seat fighter by Lockheed used for long-range bomber escort and low-level photo reconnaissance.

Panzer—Shortened form for Panzerkampfwagen, meaning armored vehicle.

Pas de Calais—French coastal province roughly twenty-five miles across the English Channel from Dover.

RAF—Royal Air Force.

ratings—Male enlisted personnel of the Royal Navy.

Reichwetterdienst—German national weather service.

RFC—Royal Flying Corps, the World War I predecessor to the Royal Air Force.

ridge—Meteorological term for a linear area of high atmospheric pressure.

RN—Royal Navy.

Rossby waves—Atmospheric variations influencing the path of the jet stream.

runnels—Troughs between offshore sand bars.

Sea Lion—In German, Unternehmen Seelowe (Operation Sea Lion), aborted German invasion of southern England planned for mid-September. 1940.

SHAEF—Supreme Headquarters, Allied Expeditionary Force.

Southwick House—Country manor house three miles north of Portsmouth and surrounded by Southwick Park which became SHAEF's advanced headquarters for D-day.

Spitfire—Famed single-seat British fighter built by Supermarine Aviation Works.

Steere Surf Code—Numerical code for denoting surf height and frequency for Operation Torch, the invasion of North Africa, by Lt. Commander Richard Steere, USN.

stratus—Continuous flat layer of cloud normally below 5,000 feet in altitude.

synoptic—Process for gathering weather data from a fixed location several times a day over the course of many weeks and months.

Torch—Code name for Allied invasion of North Africa, 8 November, 1942.

trough—Meteorological term designating a linear area of low atmospheric pressure.

Twenty-first (21st) Weather Squadron—Unit of the US Ninth Air Force performing meteorological duties.

U-boat—Short for German Unterseeboot, a submarine.

UCLA—University of California, Los Angeles

Ultra—Code name for closely held German messages decrypted at Bletchley Park.

USAAF—United States Army Air Forces, name of the administrative unit of the Army Air Corps which remained an Army combat arm until 1947.

USSTAF—United States Strategic and Tactical Air Forces in Europe.

Wehrmacht—Collective term for German Armed Forces.

Wekusta—Abbreviation for Wetter-Erkundcorps Staffeln, the weather reconnaissance units of the Luftwaffe.

Whitley—British twin-engine medium bomber built by Whitley Aircraft and favored for parachuting agents into occupied Europe.

Widewing—Code name for Camp Griffiss, Supreme Headquarters, Allied Expeditionary Force and the US Eighth Air Force, Bushy Park, Teddington.

WRNS—Women's Royal Naval Service, whose members were typically known as "Wrens."

Zenit Schüssel—Weather code used by Luftwaffe.

Zentrale Wetterdienst Gruppe (ZWG)—German weather central located in Wildpark near Potsdam, Germany.

Sources

A NOTE ABOUT SOURCES

Memoirs written decades after great events with uneven documentation of details often appear at odds with analyses of data by a new generation of experts. Conflicts between recollection and fact are rampant in Stagg's *The Forecast for Overlord* published in 1971, Petterssen's 2001 book *Weathering the Storm*, and to a far lesser degree in presentations at the Fort Ord symposium, *Some Meteorological Aspects of the D-Day Invasion of Europe 6 June 1944* held on May 19, 1984, nearly forty years after the event.

How much is to be gained by attempting to resolve these differences and debunk tales told by participants in making the forecast is as uncertain as the make-up of the weather over the North Atlantic was in the first week of June 1944. The D-day weathermen were there and they remember what they remember, colored as it may be by personal jealousy, ambition, or the vagaries of time. In the end, their stories take us into what they were likely to have been thinking and make this a yarn more about the men and women who worked under extreme pressure to get the forecast right than about an indisputable historical record.

PRIMARY SOURCES

Personal Interviews
Charles C. Bates: Surf and swell forecaster, US Air Corps
Brian Booth: Retired Met Office meteorologist
Robert Bundgaard: Upper air forecaster, US Air Corps
Jean and Harold Checketts: Weather map plotters, Royal Navy

John C. Crowell: Surf and swell forecaster, US Air Corps

Lawrence Hogben: Admiralty meteorologist, Royal Navy New Zealand

Heinz Lettau: Luftwaffe meteorologist

Elizabeth Smith: Widow of James Martin Stagg

Alexander and Bridget Stagg: Son and daughter-in-law of James Martin Stagg

Maureen Flavin Sweeney: Weather observer, Met Éireann

Geoffrey Wolfe: Admiralty meteorologist, Royal Navy

Published Books

America's Weather Warriors 1814–1985, Charles C. Bates and John F. Fuller, Texas A&M University Press, 1986.

Forecast for Overlord, J. M. Stagg, W. W. Norton, 1971.

Some Meteorological Aspects of the D-Day Invasion of Europe 6 Jun, 1944, Proceedings of a Symposium, 19 May 1984, American Meteorological Society.

Storm, Irving Krick vs. the U.S. Weather Bureau, Victor Boesen, G. P. Putnam's Sons, 1978.

Thor's Legions, Weather Support for the U.S. Air Force and Army, 1937–1987, John F. Fuller, American Meteorological Society, 1990.

Weathering the Storm: Sverre Petterssen, the D-day Forecast, and the Rise of Modern Meteorology, Sverre Petterssen, James Rodger Fleming Editor, American Meteorological Society, 2001.

Wekust: Luftwaffe Meteorological Reconnaissance Units and Operations, John A. Kington and Franz Selinger, Flight Recorder Publications, 2006.

With Wind and Sword: The story of meteorology and D-Day 6 June, 1944, by Stan Cornford, Meteorological Office, 1994.

ENDNOTES

Prologue: Whether the Weather

1   Eisenhower, Dwight D., *Crusade in Europe*, The Johns Hopkins University Press, Baltimore and London, paperback edition, 1997, 240.

2   Cox, John D., *Storm Watchers: The Turbulent History of Weather Prediction from Franklin's Kite to El Niño*, John Wiley & Sons, Hoboken, N.J., 2002, 56.

3   Halford, Pauline, *Storm Warning—The Origins of the Weather Forecast*, Sutton Publishing, Phoenix Mill, England, 2004, 93–94.

4   Cox, 91.

5   Halford, 223.

Chapter One: The Front

6   Butcher, Harry C., *My Three Years with Eisenhower*, Simon and Schuster, N.Y., 1946, 610.

7   Hammond, William M., *Normandy*, U. S. Army Center for Military History, Washington, D.C., 1994, CMH pub 72-18, 14.

8   Schofield, B. B., *Operation Neptune: The Inside Story of Naval Operations for the Normandy Landings 1944*, Pen & Sword Military, Barnsley, Great Britain, 2008, 134–36.

9   Love, Robert W. and John Major, eds., *The Year of D-Day: the 1944 Diary of Sir Bertram Ramsay*, University of Hull Press, Hull, England, 1994, 79.

10   Eisenhower, 239–40.

11   Stagg, James Martin, *Report on the Meteorological Implications in the Selection of the Day for the Allied Invasion of France, June 1944*, Meteorological Section, SHAEF, June 22, 1944, 1–3.

12   http://en.wikipedia.org/wiki Battle_of_Monte_Cassino #Battle_2.

13   Weber, Mark, "An Unsettled Legacy," review of *Churchill's War: Triumph in Adversity, Journal for Historical Review*, vol. 20, no. 4, 43.

14   http://en.wikipedia.org/wiki/Vergeltungswaffe.

15   Wieviorka, Olivier, *Normandy: The Landings to the Liberation of Paris*, Belknap–Harvard, Cambridge, Mass., 2008, 15.

16   Blair, Clair, *The Forgotten War: America in Korea 1950–1953*, Time Books, New York, 1987, 671.

17   Showalter, Dennis E., and Harold C. Deutsch, *If the Allies Had Fallen*, Fontaine Books, Yorkshire, England, 2010, 165.

18   *Weather Service Bulletin*, vol. 3, no. 1, March 1945.

19   Obituary, Rear Adm. Sir John Fleming, *The London Times*, November, 1994.

20   Memorandum, British Embassy Dublin, January 1953.

21   http://en.wikipedia.org/wiki/Exercise_Tiger.

Chapter Two: Polar Extremes

22   Petterssen, Sverre, *Weathering the Storm*, American Meteorological Society, Boston, Mass., 2001, 192.

23   Petterssen, 222.

24   Computers in WWII meteorology—www.airweaassn.org/Library/afwa/history.html.

25   *Weather Service Bulletin*, vol. 3, no. 5, March 1945.

26   Boesen, Victor, *Storm: Irving Krick vs. the U.S. Weather Bureaucracy*, G.P. Putnam's Sons, 1978, 36.

27   Stagg, J. M. (James Martin), *Forecast for Overlord*, W. W. Norton, New York, N.Y., 1971, 46.

28   AIR 73/8 CA451995.

29   http://en.wikipedia.org/wiki/RAF_Halton.

30 http://earlyradiohistory.us/1963hw14.htm.
31 E-mail from Sally Pagan, University of Edinburgh Special
    Collections Library.
32 AIR 73/8 CA451995.
33 http://en.wikipedia.org/wiki/List_of_recessions_in_the
    _United_Kingdom.
34 AIR 73/8.
35 AIR 73/8.
36 AIR 73/8.
37 AIR 73/8.
38 www.arctic.noaa.gov/aro/ipy-1/History.htm.
39 http://en.wikipedia.org/wiki/SS_Athenia#Sinking.
40 Stagg, James M., *Report of the British Polar Year Expedition*,
    Fort Rae, vol. 1, 4–12.
41 http://en.wikipedia.org/wiki/1936%E2%80%931939_
    Arab_revolt_in_Palestine#The_role_of_the_Royal_Air_
    Force.
42 Ratcliffe, R. A. S., "Pen Portraits of Presidents—Dr. J. M.
    Stagg, CBE, OBE, FRSE," *Weather*, vol. 49, no. 5, 1994, 187.
43 Stagg, *Report on the Meteorological Implications*, 8.
44 Yates, Donald Norton, (Hasdorff, James C. interviewer),
    United States Air Force Oral History Program, Tavernier,
    Fla, June 1980, transcript, 67.
45 Boesen, 16–19.
46 http://en.wikipedia.org/wiki/Horace_R._Byers.
47 www.agu.org/about/honors/bowie_lectures/gutenberg.shtml.
48 Boesen, 22.
49 http://en.wikipedia.org/wiki/USS_Akron_%28ZRS-
    4%29#Fourth_accident_and_loss_of_USS_
    Akron_.28April.2C_1933.29.

50   Boesen, 23.

51   Harper, Kristine C., "Weather and Climate," *Facts on File*, New York, N.Y., 2007, 69.

52   Boesen, 24.

53   Fuller, John F., *Thor's Legions—Weather Support for the U. S. Air Force and Army 1937–1987*, American Meteorological Society, Boston, Mass., 1990, 32.

54   Boesen, 23.

55   Personal interview with John C. Crowell, 2004, Santa Barbara, Calif.

56   Boesen, 25.

57   Boesen, 26.

58   Hasdorff, James C., Interview of Lt. Gen. Donald N. Yates, United States Oral History Project, June 10–12, 1980, Tavernier, Fla., 38–39.

59   Fuller, 41.

60   Fuller, 42.

61   Fuller, 81.

62   Yates, 69.

63   Fuller, 82.

Chapter Three: Bitter Maritimes

64   Richardson, Lewis Fry, *Weather Prediction by Numerical Process*, The University Press, Cambridge, England, 1922, 26.

65   Kington, John A., and Franz Selinger, *Wekusta: Luftwaffe Meteorological Reconnaissance Units & Operations 1938–1945*, Flight Recorder Publications Ltd., Ottringham, England, 2006, 192–93.

66   Schuster, Carl O. *The Weather War*, Aberdeen Test Center, Aberdeen. Md. (no date).

67   Syrett, David, "German Meteorological Intelligence from the Arctic and North Atlantic," *Mariner's Mirror*, vol. 71, no. 3, 1985, 325.

68   Kahn, David, *Seizing the Enigma*, Houghton Mifflin, Boston, 1991, 150.

69   Kahn, 135.

70   Kahn, 149–59.

71   Dege, Wilhelm, and William Barr (ed. and transl.), *War North of 80: The Last Arctic Weather Station of World War II (Wettertrupp Haudegen. Eine deutsche Arkktiesexpedition 1944/45*, F.A Brockhaus, Wiesbaden, Germany, 1954), University of Calgary Press, Alberta, Canada, 2003, xvi.

72   Olson, Roger H., *Strange Things Done in the Midnight Sun*, Monograph prepared for the Air Force Weather Office Historical Office, Offutt Air Force Base, ch. 2, 4–5.

73   Dege, xvii.

74   Olson, ch. 2, 7.

75   Dege, xix–xx.

76   Kingston and Selinger, 172.

77   Dege, xxvii–xxviii.

78   Dege, xv–xvi.

79   Smith, Edward H., *The U. S. Coast Guard in the Arctic and Sub Arctic*, U. S. Coast Guard, Washington, D.C., 1949, 1.

80   Obituary of Rear Adm. Edward H. "Iceberg" Smith, U. S. Coast Guard, (RET), U.S. Coast Guard Public Information Office, Washington, D.C., 1961.

81   Tilley, John A., *The Coast Guard & The Greenland Patrol*, U. S. Coast Guard, Washington, D.C., 2–16.

Chapter Four: Unseen Allies

82   www.halcyon-class.co.uk/skipjack/hms_skipjack.htm.

83   www.tempsford-squadrons.info.

84   Ogden, R. J., "Meteorology in Belgium 1940–1944," *Weather,* vol. 48, no. 8, Royal Meteorological Society, Reading, England, 265–67; Malengreau, Roger, "Clandestine Courage," in Lucas, Laddie, ed., *Wings of War: Airmen of All Nations Tell Their Stories 1939–1945,* 314–15; and *The Opposition in WO 2—Intelligence Beagle,* www.praats.be/beagle.htm.

85   Carrozza, Philippe, "She Was a Secret Agent at Age 16," *L'Avenir du Luxembourg,* October 20, 2004.

86   Carrozza.

87   Memorandum from Macfie to Stagg, Feb. 26, 1944.

88   Bartkowski, Z., "Polish Meteorology in the Second World War: A War without Weapons," *Weather,* Royal Meteorological Society, vol. 47, no. 4, April 1992, 124.

89   Bartkowski, 123–26.

90   http://nl.wikipedia.org/wiki/Groep_Packard; http://nl.wikipedia.org/wiki/Pierre_Louis_d%27Aulnis_de_Bourouill; http://nl.wikipedia.org/wiki/Marinus_Vader.

91   Yates, Oral History, 60.

92   Fuller, 36–37.

93   De Cogan, Donard, and John A. Kington, "Ireland, the Irish Meteorological Service and 'The Emergency,'" *Weather,* vol. 56, no. 11, Royal Meteorological Society, Reading, England, 2001, 387.

94   Author interview with Maureen Sweeney, July 10, 2011.

95   Kahn, 80–81.

96   Kahn, 189.

97   Interview of George C. McVittie by David DeVorkin on March 21, 1978, Niels Bohr Library & Archives, American Institute of Physics, College Park, Md., www.aip.org/history/ohilist/4774.html.

98   Kahn, 189–90.

99   en.wikipedia.org/wiki/Bombe.

100 Audric, Brian, *The Meteorological Office Dunstable and the IDA Unit in World War II,* The Royal Meteorological Society, Reading, England, 2000, 7–11.

101 Lewis, R. P. W., "The Use by the Meteorological Office of Deciphered German Meteorological Data during the Second World War," *Meteorological Magazine,* vol. 114, Bracknell, England, 1985, 113–18.

Chapter Five: Fractious Fellowship

102 Bates, Charles C., and John F. Fuller, *America's Weather Warriors,* Texas A&M University Press, College Station, Texas, 1986, 31.

103 Narins, Brigham and Carl-Gustav Rossby, *Notable Scientists: From 1900 to the Present,* The Gale Group, Farmington Hills, Mich., 2001.

104 Bates and Fuller, 34.

105 Namias, Jerome, *Francis W. Reichelderfer: A Biographical Memoir,* National Academy of Science, Washington, D.C., 1991.

106 Bates and Fuller, 46–51; also Fuller, 40.

107 Bundgaard, Robert, "Sverre Petterssen, Weather Forecaster," *Bulletin,* American Meteorological Society, vol. 60, no. 3, March 1979, 188–89.

108 Fuller, 32.

109 Bates and Fuller, 46–51; also Fuller, 40.

110 Fuller, 41.

111 Bundgaard, e-mail July 5, 2013.

112 Bundgaard, Robert C., personal letter to George P. Cressman, December 5, 1994.

113 http://en.wikipedia.org/wiki/Peace_for_our_time.

114 Walker, Malcolm, *History of the Meteorological Office,* Cambridge University Press, Cambridge, England, 2012, 272–73.

115 Roucoux, Omer, "The Meteorological Office in Dunstable during World War II," *Weather,* January, 2001, vol. 56, Royal Meteorological Society, Reading, England, 28–31.

116 Petterssen, Sverre with John Rodger Fleming (ed.), *Weathering the Storm: Sverre Petterssen, the D-Day Forecast, and the Rise of Modern Meteorology,* American Meteorological Society, Boston, 2001, 95–115.

117 Audric, 8.

118 Dickson, R. K, from a speech broadcast on Sept. 5, 6, 7, 1945, www.bbc.co.uk/history/ww2peopleswar/stories/29/a5760029.shtml.

119 Charles, Gill, *Part Two: How Meteorology Became Part of the Royal Navy,* www.weathershop.co.uk/magazine-top/general-interest26/194-meteorologyroyalnavyparttwo.

120 Boyden, J. C., "Meteorological Office Training Scheme: the First Ten Years," *Meteorological Magazine,* Meteorological Office, Bracknell, England, 1986, no. 115, 190–92.

121 Obituary, "Rear Admiral Sir John Fleming," *The Times,* London, England, November 11, 1994, 20.

122 Fairfax, Dennis, "One Schoolie's War: Instructor Lieutenant Commander George Lawrence Hogben, DSC, US Bronze Star, RNZN, 1939 –1945," *Headmark,* Australian Naval Institute, Canberra, Australia, no. 133, July 2009, 16–17.

Chapter Six: From the Sea They Will Come
123 Furlough, Ellen, "Making Mass Vacations: Tourism and Consumer Culture in France, 1930s to 1970s," *Comparative*

Studies in Society and History, vol. 40, no. 2, Cambridge University Press, Cambridge, England, April 1998, 252.

124 Commander Task Force 122, *Neptune Monograph,* 13.

125 Bates and Fuller, 70–71.

126 Bates and Fuller, 74–76.

127 Hlebica, Joel, *The Call to War,* Scripps Institution of Oceanography, 100th anniversary publication, 23.

128 Crowell, John C., *Surf Forecasting for Invasions During World War II,* Marty Magic Books, Santa Clara, Calif., 2010, 32–36.

129 Bates, Charles C., e-mail July 29, 2013.

130 Crowell, 37–39.

131 Crowell, 41–60.

132 https://en.wikipedia.org/wiki/Lockheed_P-38_Lightning.

133 www.militaryhistoryonline.com/wwii/dday/omaha.aspx.

134 www.bbc.co.uk/history/worldwars/wwtwo/dieppe_raid_01.shtml.

135 www.combiedops.com/COPPs.htm.

136 Trenowden, Mark, *Stealthily By Night: Clandestine Beach Reconnaissance and Operations in World War II,* Crecy Books Limited, 1995, 63–133.

Chapter Seven: Nothing Can Stop the Army Air Corps

137 Williams, Clifford, *Supreme HQs for D-day, After the Battle,* no. 84, 1994, 14–21.

138 Revised telephone directory, Widewing, Bushy Park, March 1944, Eisenhower Library.

139 Williams, 14–21.

140 Stagg, *Forecast,* 10.

141 Stagg, *Forecast,* 56.

142 Simon, Richard L., "Eisenhower's Meteorological Support for D-day, in Some Meteorological Aspects of the D-Day Invasion of Europe, 6 June 1944," *Proceedings of the Fort Ord Symposium*, American Meteorological Society, Boston, Mass., May 1984, 9.

143 Author interview, Robert C. Bundgaard, June, 2003.

144 Petterssen, 211–12.

145 Bundgaard, Robert C., "Operation Overlord's Chief Weatherman," *18th Weather Squadron Newsletter*, no. 35, February 2005, 2.

146 Britten, C. E., Stagg mobilization order, November 30, 1943, AIR 73/8 – C451995 –.

147 Meade, P. J., presentation at *Meteorology & the Second World War*, Royal Meteorological Society, University of Birmingham, 1986.

148 Cornford, Stan, *With Wind and Sword: The Story of Meteorology and D-day 6 June 1944*, Met Office, Bracknell, 1994.

149 Stagg, *Forecast*, 33–38.

150 Author interview with Robert Bundgaard, May 6–7, 2003, Colorado Springs, Colo.

151 Bundgaard interview.

152 Eisenhower, 239.

153 Stagg, *Forecast*, 13.

154 Stagg, *Forecast*, 14.

155 www.canadiansoldiers.com/organization/fieldforces/casf/3rdivision.htm.

156 Stagg, J. M., *Report on the Meteorological Implications in the Selection of the Day for the Invasion of France June 1944*, November 1944.

157 Petterssen, 216.

158 Stagg, *Forecast*, 21.

159 Stagg, *Forecast*, 30.

160 Stagg, *Forecast*, 32.

Chapter Eight: Ridge of High Pressure

161 http://en.wikipedia.org/wiki/%28There%27ll_Be_
Bluebirds_Over%29_The_White_Cliffs_of_Dover.

162 O'Connell, Geoffrey, *Southwick, the D-Day Village That Went
to War*, Ashford, Buchan & Enright, Leatherhead, England,
77.

163 Miller, Russell, *Nothing Less Than Victory: The Oral History of
D-day*, Quill/William Morrow, New York, 1993, 141.

164 www.skylighters.org/sausage/, 3.

165 Suzanne Arsenault, personal interview, May 2003.

166 www.portsdown-tunnels.org.uk/palmerston_forts/
fort_southwick/1_overview_p1.html.

167 Williams, 28–31.

168 Petterssen, 234.

169 Author interview, Harold Checketts, July, 2011.

170 www.britishtelephones.com/t394.htm.

171 Stagg, *Forecast*, 63.

172 Stagg, *Report on the Meteorological Implications*, 5.

173 Stagg, *Forecast*, 63–64.

174 Stagg, *Forecast*, 64–65.

175 Petterssen, 223–24.

176 *Coast Guard at War—Weather Patrol VII*, Historical
Section, Office of Public Information, U.S. Coast Guard,
Washington, D.C., 1949, 1.

177 http://en.wikipedia.org/wiki/USS_Monomoy_%28AG
-40%29.

178 http://en.wikipedia.org/wiki/USCGC_Conifer_%28WLB -301%29.

179 www.uscg.mil/history/webcutters/conifer1943.asp.

180 www.usmm.org/sunk39-41.html#anchor325668.

181 http://en.wikipedia.org/wiki/USS_Zircon.

182 http://en.wikipedia.org/wiki/Sea_Cloud.

183 http://en.wikipedia.org/wiki/Marjorie_Merriweather_Post.

184 www.uscg.mil/history/webcutters/sea_cloud_ix99.asp.

185 www.navy-net.co.uk/history/55248-hms-grindall-hms-hoste-d-day-weather-ships.html.

186 Curry, Henry T., unpublished memoir.

187 Kington, John A., and Peter G. Rackliff, *Even the Birds Were Walking—The Story of Wartime Meteorological Reconnaissance,* Tempus, Charleston, S.C., 2000, 63–67.

188 Bundgaard, Robert C. "Forecasts Leading to the Postponement of D-Day," *Proceedings of the Fort Ord Symposium*, American Meteorological Society, Boston, Mass., May, 1984, 15.

189 Kington and Rackliff, 85–86.

190 www.google.com/url?sa=t&rct=j&q=&esrc=s&source=web &cd=1&ved=0CCsQFjAA&url=http%3A%2F%2Fwww. csn.ul.ie%2F~dan%2Fwar%2FHalifax_LL145.pdf&ei=JaE kUqrgMdStsQTW2IAw&usg=AFQjCNGQWEnUmQ2-RyAM-1xmozhqmLsDhQ&bvm=bv.51495398,d.cWc.

191 http://en.wikipedia.org/wiki/25th_Tactical_Reconnaissance _Wing.

192 Sesler, George, *Air Force 50,* Turner Publishing, Nashville, Tenn., 1998, 51.

193 http://voices.yahoo.com/the-first-stealth-fighter-de-havilland-mosquito-486295.html.

194 Kington and Selinger, 12.

195 Kington and Selinger, 160.

196 Kington and Selinger, 37–39.

197 Kington and Selinger, 40.

198 Kington and Selinger, 41.

199 Checketts, Jean, *Interview with Jean Checketts*, National Museum of the Royal Navy, Accession #1997.37.

200 Checketts, Harold J., *The War Service of a Naval Rating 1940–1945*, unpublished memoir, 1994.

Chapter Nine: Earthquake in the Sky

201 Bundgaard, Fort Ord Symposium, 17.

202 Petterssen, 225.

203 Stagg, *Report on the Meteorological Implications*, 6.

204 Stagg, *Forecast*, 64–65.

205 Ramsay, Adm. Sir Bertram, *The Year of D-Day*, University of Hull Press, Hull, England, 1994, 79.

206 Stagg, *Report on the Meteorological Implications*, 6.

207 Stagg, *Forecast*, 66–79.

208 Stagg, *Forecast*, 89.

209 Stagg, *Report on the Meteorological Implications*, 6.

210 Stagg, *Forecast*, 80–87.

211 Stagg, *Report on the Meteorological Implications*, 7.

212 Stagg, *Forecast*, 89–90.

213 Stagg, *Forecast*, 91.

214 Stagg, *Forecast*, 91–94.

215 Stagg, *Forecast*, 95–97.

216 Stagg, *Report on the Meteorological Implications*, 8.

217 Stagg, *Forecast*, 98.

218 Cornford, 6.2.

219 Stagg, *Forecast*, 99.

Chapter Ten: The Horns of D-day

220 Station Weather Record for Blacksod Point, Meteorological Service, Department of Industry and Commerce, June 4, 1944.

221 Allen, Robert M. Jr. "The Weather Intelligence for D-Day and 40 Years Since," Fort Ord Symposium, 6.

222 Stagg, *Forecast*, 100–101.

223 Stagg, *Forecast*, 102–4.

224 Miller, 180–81.

225 Kington and Selinger, 217.

226 Monteverdi, John P. (translator), "Weather Maps and Weather Summaries by the German Weather Service Group 2 June 1944 Through 6 June 1944," Fort Ord Symposium, 112–20.

227 Stagg, *Report on the Meteorological Implications*, 21.

228 Stagg, *Forecast*, 107–10.

229 Stagg, *Report on the Meteorological Implications*, 9.

230 Stagg, *Forecast*, 110–11.

231 Bates, Charles C., "Sea, Swell, and Surf Forecasting for Operation Overlord," Fort Ord Symposium, 30–38.

232 Stagg, *Forecast*, 112–13.

233 Robb, Vice Air Chief Marshal James, *Operation Overlord— The Decision to Launch the Operation*, June 5, 1944, National Archives AIR/37 – 1124 A, Kew, England.

234 Stagg, *Forecast*, 114–15.

235 Stagg, *Forecast*, 117–18.

236 Stagg, *Report on the Meteorological Implications*, 11.

237 Stagg, *Forecast*, 119–22.

238 Interview with Jean Checketts, National Museum of the Royal Navy, accession #1997.37.

Chapter Eleven: Worst Blow in Forty Years

239 Monteverdi, Fort Ord Symposium, 120.

240 Ruge, Friedrich, *Rommel in Normandy,* Macdonald and Jane's, London, 1979, 169.

241 Kington and Selinger, 224.

242 Penrose, Jane, ed., *The D-Day Companion,* Osprey Publishing, Oxford, England, 2004, 177–91.

243 Beevor, Anthony, *D-Day—The Battle for Normandy,* Penguin, New York, 2009, 117–51.

244 Stagg, *Forecast,* 126.

245 Morrison, Samuel E., "The Invasion of France and Germany," *History of United States Naval Operations in World War II,* vol. XI, Castle Books, Edison, N.J, 1957, 166–77.

246 Stagg, *Forecast,* 126.

Epilogue

247 Cerveny, Randy, and Ron Holle, "Irving P. Krick: Weather Fraud or Weather Genius," *Weatherwise,* July/August 2008, 21–25.

248 Williams, Verne O., "Can Rain Makers Really Make Rain?" *Saturday Evening Post,* vol. 224, no. 22, December 1, 1951, 26–27, 123–24.

249 Cerveny and Holle, 25–26.

INDEX

Air Corps (US), 88–89
  Weather Section, 89–92
Akron (Navy airship), xix, 40–41
Allies
  Arcadia Conference, xv–xvi
  and Channel weather, 129
  Command Operations Assault
    Pilotage Parties, 110–17
  and Enigma codes, 54
  invasion of Italy, 4–5
  Operation Husky, 104–5
  Operation Torch, 102–4, 105
  Sledge Patrol, 56–57, 60, 64
  See also United States; Great
    Britain; D-day invasion
America's Weather Warriors (Bates &
  Fuller), 84
Anglo-Irish Treaty, 78
Armia Krajowa (AK), 74, 75, 76
Arnold, Henry H., 26, 41
  and Krick, 38, 45, 46
  long-range weather forecasts,
    90, 91
  on Russian weather
    observation, 77
  and Yates, 45, 47, 48
Arromanches, France, 100
Arsenault, Alphonse, 136
Atlantic Weather Patrol, 140–46
aviation, growth of, 83–84
Azores High, xiii, 140, 145–46, 155,
  159, 166

Bailey, Chris, 191
Barkla, C. S., 32
Barthram, John A., 149

Bartkowski, Z., 75
Bassett, Hunt, 91–92
Bates, Charles C., 42, 84, 101,
    103, 107
  at Scripps, 106
  and wave height, 110
Baur, Franz, 90, 181
Belgium
  German invasion of, 66–68
  weather observers in (Beagle),
    69, 70–72
Bergeron, Tor, 86
Bermuda-Azores High, 13
Bertholf, E. P., 62
Bjerknes, Jacob, 84–85, 87, 88, 106
Bjerknes, Vilhelm, 25, 84–85
Blacksod Point, Ireland, 19, 79, 163,
    169, 177, 184, 189, 201
Bletchley Park. *See* Met Office
    (British)
Boesen, Victor, 39, 40
Bounds, Rufus G., 121
Bradley, Follett, 77
Brichet, Madame Edmond, 70, 71
Brichet, Robert, 70, 71
Brichet, Thérése, 71, 72
Brooke, Alan, 124
Bull, Harold, 18, 123, 125, 136
  D-day forecasts, 130, 131, 133,
    138, 161, 169, 170
  postponing D-day, 184, 188,
    190, 191
Bundgaard, Robert C., 121, 122,
    123, 147
  and Stagg, 127–28
Burgess, C. R. Dick, 109

Burton, Nat, 134
Bushy Park. *See* Widewing
Byers, Horace R., 39, 86

Carroza, Phillipe, 72
Cauthery, Harold, 101
centrals (military weather bureaus).
      See Met Office (British);
      SHAEF; United States Strategic
      Air Force (USSTAF)
Chamberlain, Neville, 66, 92
Checketts, Harold, 152–53,
      154, 191
Chree, Charles, 33
Churchill, Winston S., 96
      "Europe first" strategy, xi, xv–xvi
      and post-war Europe, 5, 6
      and invasion date, 91
Cline, Isaac, xix
Comanche (cutter), 61–62
Command Operations Assault
      Pilotage Parties (COPP),
      110–17
Cosmological Theory (Whittaker), 80
COSSAC. *See* SHAEF
Cosyns, Max, 70, 71
Courtney, Roger, 112–13
Creasy, George, 170, 173, 190
Crimean War, xvii
Crowell, John C., 42, 101, 107–8
      and wave height, 108–9, 110
Crusade in Europe (Eisenhower), 2
Curry, Henry, 144–45

d'Aulnis de Bourouill, Louis, 76–77
Davies, Joseph E., 143
D-day invasion, ix–x, xvi–xvii, 194–97

Combined Assault Operations
      Pilotage Parties, 110–17
      consequences of failure, 6–9
      forecasts for, 3–4, 13–14, 19–22,
      138–40, 155–75, 176–79
      landing craft, 107–8, 180
      optimum forecast for, 128–29,
      130–31
      postponing of, 179–81, 182–91
      predicting tide height, 100,
      101–2
      preparations for, 1–2, 135–37
      proposed landing beaches,
      100–102, 103
      wave and swell observations, 110
      weather charts for, 152–54
de Backer, Simon, 68
de Dorlodot, Albert, 67, 72
Dege, Wilhelm, 58
Deinum, Henk, 76
de Roode, Aad, 76
Deutsch, Harold C., 9
DeVorkin, David, 80
Dewey, Thomas, 7
Dickson, R. K., 96
Diesing, Kurt, 151
Dobrzański, Wiktor, 74
Dönitz, Karl, 80
Douglas, C. K. M., 24–25, 48, 93,
      121, 131
      5-day forecasts, 132, 133
      D-day forecasts, 139, 167
      opinion of Stagg, 26
Dunstable. *See* Met Office (British)

Eisenhower, Dwight D., ix,
      xiii–xiv, 1

D-day forecasts, 17–18, 139, 168, 170–71, 174–75, 179
D-day's date, xvi–xvii, 1, 2–3
headquarters of, 136–37
and Operation Torch, 103
opinion of Stagg, 27
optimum forecast for D-day, 128–29
postponing D-day, xi–xii, 186–88, 190, 197
England. *See* Great Britain
Enigma codes, xiii, 15, 50, 53, 54, 80, 81–82
Europe
sharing weather data in, 50, 146–48
war in, 4–6
weather and high-pressure systems in, xiii
See also specific countries in

Farren, Jean, 152–53, 191
Federov, Yevginiy K., 77
Fisher, Fred J., 142–43
FitzRoy, Robert, xvii–xviii
Flavin, Maureen, 79, 177, 184, 189
Fleming, John, 14, 16, 19, 20, 98, 102
D-day forecasts, 137, 138, 152, 167
passage of front, 185
and Stagg, 35
Fleming, Richard H., 106
Forecast for Overlord (Stagg), xii, 157
Fort Southwick (England), 136
Freeland, Stephen L., 180–81
Frye, Maine, 10
Fulford, J. H. C., 101, 110

Fuller, John F., 46, 84, 89, 103

Gadomski, Jan, 74
Garbett, Leonard G., 97
George, Joseph J., 42, 155
Germany
and Channel forecasts, 181–82, 192, 193–94
Enigma codes, xi, 15, 80, 81–82
invasion of Belgium, 66–68
plan to invade England, 95
and Spanish Civil War, 88
war prior to D-day, 4–5, 89
weather observations by, 50, 51–54, 55–56, 58–60
weather reconnaissance sorties, 150–52
Goering, Hermann, 89
Grant, President Ulysses, xviii
Great Britain
after World War I, 30
first weather service in, xvii–xviii
meteorological organizations in, 97
obtains Enigma machine, 80–82
predicting weather in, 24
preparations for D-day, xi, 1–2, 135–37
weather observations with Ireland, 78–79
See also Met Office (British); Royal Naval Meteorological Service
Greenland
German weather stations on, 52–60
protection of, 51, 61
Groep Kees, 77

Groep Packard, 76
Guminski, Romuald, 74
Gurney, Robert J., 148
Gutenberg, Beno, 39–40, 42

Habermehl, Richard, 89
Henry, Joseph, xvii
Hewitt, Henry K., 103, 104
Hinsley, Henry, 53, 54
History of the Meteorological Office
  (Walker), 92
Hitler, Adolf, 89, 92, 96
  See also Germany
HMS *Grindall,* 143–44, 145
HMS *Hoste,* 143–44, 147
HMS *Skipjack,* 68
Hoare, Peter James Hill, 146
Hogben, Lawrence, 98, 132
Holzman, Benjamin, 26, 48, 121, 132
  D-day forecasts, 156, 159, 169,
  170, 178
Howgate, Henry W., xviii

If the Allies had Fallen? (Deutsch &
  Showalter), 9
International Ice Patrol, 62, 63
International Meteorological
  Organization, 146–47
Ireland, weather observations in,
  78–79, 177
Italy, 4–5, 88

James, Jimmy, 40
Japan, 88
Jaumotte, Jules-M. Ch., 67, 72
Jensen, Marius, 56–58, 60
jet stream, xiii, 49–50
Johnson, Martin W., 106

Johnson, Nelson, 94, 125, 126, 131
Jooris, Pierre, 69–70

Karman, Theodore von, 42
Kauffmann, Henrik, 51, 52
Kennedy, Joseph P., 66
Kerkhofs en Luc, Frans, 70
Kington, John A., 51, 151
Knudsen, Eli, 58
Köhler, Otto, 61
Krick, Irving P., xii, xiii, 26, 45–48,
  121, 181
  background of, 38–42
  and 5-day forecasts, 132–33
  D-day forecasts, 138, 156, 158,
  159, 170, 178–79, 183
  influence of, 86, 87, 88
  long-range forecasting, 90, 91, 92
  and Operation Torch, 46–47, 103
  postponing D-day, 190–91
  and Yates, 43

Lachner, Ernest, 102, 108–9, 109–10
landing craft, xi, 3, 107–8
Leigh-Mallory, Trafford, 4, 15, 17
  D-day forecasts, 166, 173, 179,
  186, 187
  and SHAEF headquarters, 120
Lewis, R. P. W., 82
Lorenz, Edward, xx

MacArthur, Douglas, 8
Maris, H. B., 35
Marshall, George C., x, 45
Martin, Everett, 13
Marvin, Charles F., 86
McCluskey, Leroy, 65
McVittie, George C., 80–81

Meade, Patrick J., 123–24
Merewether, Arthur, 44, 89, 90
meteorology, xiv
  and air reconnaissance, 148–50
  analog forecasting, 26
  Bjerknes' ideas, 84–85
  Coriolis effect, 122–23
  development of, xvii–xix
  and earth's atmosphere, xv
  five-day forecasting, 128
  and growth of aviation, 83–84, 85
  high-pressure systems, xiii
  importance of long-range
    forecasts, 91
  International Meteorological
    Organization, 146–47
  jet stream, 49–50
  and magnetic poles, 29–30
  major variables of systems, xix–xx
  military's attitude towards, xvii,
    xix, 43
  swell and surf forecasting, 102,
    105, 106
Meteorology (Milham), 87
Met Office (British), xii–xiii, 23–24,
  37, 97–99
  D-day forecasts, 132–33, 138,
    160, 162, 163, 166, 167, 169
  and Enigma machine, 80, 81–82
  headquarters of, 93–94
  and IDA group, 94–95
  and long-range forecasts, 131
  passage of front, 183–84
  postponing D-day, 191
Milham, Willis I., 87
Millikan, Robert A., 41, 42, 87
Mitchell, A. Crichton, 31
Montgomery, Bernard, 4, 15, 17, 124

  D-day forecasts, 179, 186
Morgan, Frederick, 118
Morris, C., 135
Mountbatten, Louis, 112
Mulberry harbors, 100, 196–97
Müller, Hans, 193, 194
Munk, Walter, 103, 105, 106
  on swell and surf, 108–9, 110

Narins, Brigham, 86
Naujocks, Alfred, 73
Netherlands, weather observations
  from, 76–77
Nielsen, Peter, 58
Northland (cutter), 64, 65
*Nothing Less than Victory—An Oral
  History of D-Day* (Freeland), 180

*The Oceans, Their Physics, Chemistry,
  and General Biology* (Sverdrup,
  Johnson, Fleming), 106
Ogden-Smith, Bruce, 114–15, 116
On the Structure of Moving Cyclones
  (Bjerknes), 87
Operation Barbarossa, 51
Operation Beagle, 67–72
Operation Husky, 104–5
Operation Neptune, xvi, 102
Operation Overlord, x, xvi
  See also D-day Invasion
Operation Sea Lion, 51, 95
Operation Torch, 46–47, 102–4, 105

Państwowy Instytut Meteorologiczny
  (PIM), 73–74
Patton, George S., 46, 102, 103
Penfield, James K., 61

Petterssen, Sverre, 25, 26, 48, 88, 121, 130
  D-day forecasts, 138, 139–40, 156, 169, 178, 183
  and long-range forecasting, 131, 132
  meeting with Habermehl, 89
  in Met Office, 93–95
  postponing D-day, 190–91
Piccard, Auguste, 70
Pinks, Pamela, 152
Poland
  and Enigma machines, 80
  weather observations from, 73–76
Polar High, xiii, 13
Polish Meteorology in the Second World War: A War without Weapons (Bartkowski), 75
Post, Marjorie Merriweather, 143
Poulsen, Ib, 56, 57

Ramsay, Bertram, 2, 15, 17, 136
  D-day forecasts, 159, 173, 179, 180
Reichelderfer, Francis W., 87
Revenue Cutter Service. *See* US Coast Guard
Richardson, Lewis Fry, 49
Riiser-Larsen, Hjalmar, 93
Ritter, Hermann, 55–56, 57, 58
Robb, James, 172, 186
Robinson, George D., 121, 170
Roblain, Augustin, 69–70
Rommel, Erwin, 192–93
Roosevelt, Franklin D.
  "Europe first" strategy, x–xi, xv–xvi
  ferrying fighters to Russia, 77

  and post-war Europe, 5, 6
  protecting Greenland, 51
  sets invasion date, 91
Rossby, Carl-Gustav, 48, 85–87, 88
Royal Naval Meteorological Service, 97–99, 101
  charting for D-day, 152–54
  Swell Forecast Section, 102
Russia, weather observations from, 77, 95

Sashen (German ship), 52, 55
Schwerdtfeger, Werner, 151–52
Scott, Robert F., 28
Scott-Bowden, Logan, 114–15, 116–17
Seilkopf, Heinrich, 49
Selinger, Franz, 51, 151
Shackleton, Ernest, 28
SHAEF (Supreme Commander Allied Expeditionary Force), xvi, 2, 118–20, 128
  D-day forecasts, 131, 132, 159–60, 162, 163, 166, 167, 169, 172
  move to Widewing, 123
  passage of front, 183–84
  postponing D-day, 191
Showalter, Dennis E., 9
Signal Corps, 88, 89
Simpson, G. C., 33–34, 36
Sledge Patrol, 56–57, 60, 64
Smith, Edward H., 62–65, 136, 140
Smith, Walter Bedell, 17, 186–87
  and SHAEF headquarters, 118–19, 120
Smithsonian Institution, xvii

Southwick House (SHAEF
Advanced HQ), xvi, 2, 9, 14,
19, 27, 121, 136–39, 152–53,
157–77, 182–91
Spaatz, Carl A., 47–48, 172
Spanish Civil War, 88
Spitsbergen, 61
SS *Athenia*, 34
Stagg, James Martin, xii, xiv, 14, 16,
23, 48, 63
background and early career,
26–38
and Bundgaard, 127–28
5-day forecasts, 128, 131–32, 133
D-day forecasts, 17–22, 129–30,
137, 138–39, 156–75, 178, 179
family of, 126–27
forecasting trip of, 123–24
lack of staff for, 120–21
postponing D-day, 182–83, 184,
185, 188, 189–91
reputation of, 26–27
at SHAEF, 120, 124–26
and Toussaint's plan, 72
Stalin, Joseph, 5, 6, 77
Steere, Richard C., 103, 104
Stöbe, Walther, 181, 193
*Storm—Irving Krick vs. the
U.S. Weather Bureaucracy*
(Boesen), 38–39
Stratemeyer, George, 91
Strong, George V., 45
Summersby, Kay, 137
*Surf Forecasting for Invasions During
World War II* (Crowell), 107
Sutcliffe, Reginald Cockcroft,
166, 167

Sverdrup, Harald, 105, 106, 108, 110
Sweeney, Ted, 177

Tedder, Arthur, 17, 126, 187
D-day forecasts, 172, 173, 174,
175, 179
Thomas, Taffy, 152, 153
Thorpe, John, 98
*Thor's Legions—Weather Support for the
U.S. Air Force and Army 1937-
1987* (Fuller), 46
Toussaint, Albert, 66, 68–72
Truman, Harry, 7, 8
Turing, Alan, 81

United Kingdom. *See* Great Britain
United States
Air Corps, 88–90, 89–92
early weather service in, xvii,
xviii–xx
growth of aviation in, 83–84, 85
isolationist policy in, 88, 89
military meteorology in, 90–92
preparations for D-day in, xi
See also US Weather Bureau;
United States Strategic Air
Force (USSTAF)
United States Strategic Air Force
(USSTAF), xii–xiii, 23–24,
120, 121
D-day forecast, 155–56
meteorologists in, 25–26
US Coast Guard, 61–62
USS *Conifer*, 141–42
USS *Sea Cloud*, 143
USS *Zircon*, 142–43
US Weather Bureau, xviii, xix, 85–88

and *Akron* accident, 40–41
forecasting upper-air weather,
    121–22
gathering data for D-day, 140–46
and Reichelderfer, 87
and Rossby, 86
Weather Directorate, 90–91, 140

Vader, Marinus, 76, 77
Vandenberg, Hoyt, 168, 170
van der Stok, Paul Johan, 76

Walker, Malcolm, 92
Warmington, George Clitheroe,
    52–53, 54
War North of 80 (Dege), 58
Warren, Emaline A., 13
Weather Bureau. *See* US Weather
    Bureau
Weather Directorate, 90–91, 140
weather systems. *See* meteorology
Weickmann, Ludwig F., 42
Wekusta (Kington & Selinger), 51
Welchman, Gordon, 81
West, George L., 61
Weyprecht, Carl, 34
Whilmot, Chester, 153
Whittaker, E. T., 31, 80

Widewing, 119–20, 121
    See also SHAEF
Willmott, Nigel Clogstoun, 112–13,
    114, 116
Wilson, Woodrow, 88
Wolfe, Geoffrey, 98–99, 132
    D-day forecasts, 138, 156
Wouters, Louis, 68

Yates, Donald N., xi, 14, 16, 43–45,
    47, 48, 121
    5-day forecasts, 132, 133
    D-day forecasts, 19–22, 137–39,
        156, 159, 161–63, 167,
        169–71, 173
    importance of air pressure at
        altitudes, 122
    passage of front, 185
    postponing D-day, 189, 190
    and Russian weather
        observations, 77–78
    status of, 125, 126

Zacher, Gerhard, 60
Zentral Wetterdienst Gruppe
    (ZWG), 181–82, 192, 193–94
Zimmerman, Don, 46, 90–91

ABOUT THE AUTHOR

From the day when a professor of geology demonstrated how massive beds of limestone could bend under intense pressure, **John E. Ross** has been fascinated by the forces that shape the earth's environment. Neither a scientist nor an historian, Ross's schooling in journalism led him to believe that the most important of a reporter's core questions—what, who, when, where, how, and why—*how* and *why* are by far the most interesting.

After decades of writing articles for sporting magazines and books on trout fishing—the first edition of the *Trout Unlimited Guide to America's 100 Best Trout Streams* (Falcon Press, 1999) earned him a National Outdoor Book Award—he began to focus more on the story behind the story in the vein of *Isaac's Storm* and *The Map That Changed the World*.

Son of a World War II Air Corps pilot instructor, he was weaned on a diet of US military history. Ross knew well that Eisenhower postponed the D-day invasion of Normandy for 24 hours because of the weather. Given the state of meteorology in the 1940s, he wondered: How did Ike know? Over the last decade, he interviewed several men and women who participated in making the all important weather forecast and scoured archives in England and the United States for its historic documentation.

Ross is at work on a book about the history of one of the world's oldest watersheds that has traveled some 5,500 miles over the past 325 million years and been inhabited for more than 12,000 years. He lives in Asheville, North Carolina, with his wife, a psychologist who not only knows what he is thinking before he does, but why.